BETWEEN CAPITALISM
AND DEMOCRACY

CRITICAL STUDIES IN EDUCATION SERIES

Broken Promises
Reading Instruction in Twentieth-Century America
Patrick Shannon

Critical Pedagogy & Cultural Power
David Livingstone & Contributors

Education & the American Dream
Conservatives, Liberals & Radicals Debate the Future of Education
Harvey Holtz & Associates

Education Under Siege
The Conservative, Liberal & Radical Debate over Schooling
Stanley Aronowitz & Henry A. Giroux

Literacy
Reading the Word & the World
Paulo Freire & Donaldo Macedo

The Moral & Spiritual Crisis in Education
A Curriculum for Justice & Compassion
David Purpel

The Politics of Education
Culture, Power & Liberation
Paulo Freire

Popular Culture, Schooling & the Language of Everyday Life
Henry A. Giroux & Roger I. Simon

Teachers as Intellectuals
Toward a Critical Pedagogy of Learning
Henry A. Giroux

Women Teaching for Change
Gender, Class & Power
Kathleen Weiler

BETWEEN CAPITALISM AND DEMOCRACY

Educational Policy and the Crisis of the Welfare State

Svi Shapiro

Introduction by Henry A. Giroux and Paulo Freire

CRITICAL STUDIES IN EDUCATION SERIES

BERGIN & GARVEY PUBLISHERS
NEW YORK • WESTPORT, CONNECTICUT • LONDON

Library of Congress Cataloging-in-Publication Data

Shapiro, Svi.
    Between capitalism and democracy: educational policy and the crisis of the welfare state / Svi Shapiro: introduction by Henry A. Giroux and Paulo Freire.
      p.   cm.—(Critical studies in education series)
    Includes bibliographical references.
    ISBN 0-89789-150-3 (alk. paper)
    ISBN 0-89789-149-X (pbk.: alk. paper)
    1. Education and state—United States. I. Title. II. Series.
LC89.S485   1989
379.73—dc20   89-37674

Copyright © 1990 by Bergin & Garvey Publishers

All rights reserved. No portion of this book may be reproduced, by any process or technique, without the express written consent of the publisher.

Library of Congress Catalog Card Number: 89-37674
ISBN: 0-89789-150-3
ISBN: 0-89789-149-X (pbk.)

First published in 1990

Bergin & Garvey Publishers, One Madison Avenue, New York, NY 10010
A division of Greenwood Press, Inc.

Printed in the United States of America

The paper used in this book complies with the Permanent Paper Standard issued by the National Information Standards Organization (Z39.48-1984).

Copyright Acknowledgments

The author is grateful to the following journals for allowing his material to be reprinted:

H. Svi Shapiro, "Ideology, Class, and the Autonomy of the Capitalist State: The Petty Bourgeois 'World-View' and Schooling," *Philosophy and Social Criticism* 10, no. 1 (1984): pp. 39-57; "Choosing Our Educational Legacy: Disempowerment or Emancipation," *Issues in Education* 2, no. 1 (1984): pp. 11-22; "Ideology, Hegemony, and the Individualizing of Instruction: The Incorporation of 'Progressive Education'," *Journal of Curriculum Studies* 16, no. 45 (1984): pp. 367-378; "Schools, Work and Consumption: Education and the Cultural Contradictions of Capitalism," *Journal of Educational Thought* 17, no. 3 (1983): pp. 209-220; "Education and the Crisis of the Welfare State: The Extension of Citizenship and the Roots of Politics in the 80's," *Education and Society* 3, no. 1 (1985): pp. 21-34; "Education in Capitalist Society: Towards a Reconsideration of the State in Educational Policy," *Teachers College Record* 83, no. 4 (1982): pp. 515-527; "Educational Theory and Recent Political Discourse: A New Agenda for the Left," *Teachers College Record* 89, no. 2 (1987): pp. 171-200; "The Making of Conservative Educational Policy: Middle Class Anxieties and Corporate Profitability in the 1980's," *Urban Education* 17, no. 2 (1982): pp. 233-252; "Education, the Welfare State, and Reaganomics: The Limits of Conservative Reform," *Urban Education* 20, no. 4 (1986): pp. 443-471; "Class, Ideology, and the Basic Skills Movement: A Study in the Sociology of Educational Reform," *Interchange* 14, no. 2 (1983): pp. 14-24; "School, Society, and the Crisis of Legitimation: The Sociology of the Declining Faith in Education," *Interchange* 15, no. 4 (1984): pp. 26-39; "Education and the State in Capitalist Society: Aspects of the Sociology of Nicos Poulantzas," *Harvard Educational Review*, 50: 3, pp. 321-331. Copyright © 1980 by the President and Fellows of Harvard College. All rights reserved; "Beyond the Sociology of Education: Culture, Politics and the Power of Educational Change," *Educational Theory* 38, no. 4 (Fall 1988): pp. 415-430; "Capitalism at Risk: The Political Economy of the Educational Reports of 1983," *Educational Theory* 35, no. 1 (Winter 1985): pp. 57-72; "Habermas, O'Connor, and Wolfe, and the Crisis of the Welfare-Capitalist State," *Educational Theory* 33, no. 4 (Fall 1983): pp. 135-147; "Shaping the Educational Imagination: Class, Culture, and the Contradictions of the Dominant Ideology," *The Journal of Curriculum Theorizing* 4, no. 2 (1982): pp. 153-165; "Education and the Language of Politics: Towards an Agenda for Radical Change," *Educational Policy* 2, no. 3 (1988): pp. 251-263; "Education and the Crisis of the Welfare State," *New Education* 3, nos. 1, 2 (1985).

The author is also grateful to the following for granting permission to use material:

Portions of material reprinted from *The New Class War*, by Frances Fox Piven and Richard A. Cloward. Copyright © 1982 by Frances Fox Piven and Richard A. Cloward. Reprinted by permission of Pantheon Books, a division of Random House, Inc.

From *Legitimation Crisis* by Jürgen Habermas, English Translation. Copyright © 1975 by Beacon Press. Reprinted by permission of Beacon Press.

For Sarah
Whose education does not yet oppose her life

Contents

	Introduction: Education and the Politics of Democratic Struggle by Henry A. Giroux and Paulo Freire	*xi*
	Preface	*xv*
	Acknowledgments	*xix*
1	From Critical Theory to the Politics of Educational Change	1
2	Education and the Cultural Contradictions of Capitalism	29
3	Education as a "Complex Unity"	57
4	Educational Reform and Liberal Democracy	79
5	Crisis of the State and Educational Politics in the '80s	103
6	The Making of Conservative Educational Policy	119
7	The Dialectic of the Welfare-Educational State, I	139
8	Crisis and Hope: The Dialectic of the Welfare-Educational State, II	154
	Notes	*169*
	Selected Bibliography	*183*
	Index	*187*

Introduction: Education and the Politics of Democratic Struggle

Radical educational criticism over the course of the last two decades has increasingly served to question the role and purpose of public schooling in the United States. Broadly construed, radical critics have heightened the discourse of social criticism by exposing the role that schools play in reproducing the economic imperatives of the state and the legitimating ideologies of the dominant social order. In its initial stages, much of this type of criticism was narrowly conceived and overly functional. Schools were viewed either as appendages of the economic order or seen as overly determined sites of domination. Within this perspective, the language of critique was so pronounced that it failed to even consider how schools might be theorized as sites of struggle and transformation. As such, the language of radical reform verged on collapsing into cynicism while radical critics effectively removed themselves from the wider debate on the theory and practice of American education.

Educational criticism has changed with the times. Radical educators now view the schools in more complex terms and are less inclined to overly stress their functional relationship to the wider economic and political order. But if functionalist criticisms are on the wane, new forms of reductionism appear to be structuring current forms of radical educational criticism. More specifically, functionalism has now been replaced with the discourse of practicality and experience, on the one hand, and the language of particularized interests on the other. In the first instance, a number of educators have argued that those who teach and work directly in the schools represent the most progressive voices to articulate a language of educational reform. Social position, in this case, mandates one's ability to develop a language of critique and hope. But there is more at stake here than a reductionistic view of the relationship between social position and political agency. In addition, a growing number of radical educators use this position to eschew the political importance of developing demanding theoretical discourses on the grounds that practice derived from the classroom itself is now the most important context from which to develop a politics and reform of schooling. In reality, this is a thinly veiled form of anti-intellectualism that dissolves theory into practice under the vote-catching call for the importance of relevance and a politics of specificity. Moreover, in its various versions, this form of populist discourse either ignores the larger political project that drives it, or simply subordinates questions of purpose and policy to instrumental and methodological considerations. In this context, the voice of practice endlessly repeats itself in exhortations to develop concrete methods that resemble recipes out of a Julia Child cookbook.

Another emerging version of radical criticism has embraced what we call the politics of separatism and assertion. In this discourse, radical educational critics organize around a notion of difference that celebrates rigidly-defined interests as the basis for mobilizing educational reform. Hegemony in this discourse, like the process of reform itself, is tied to waging particular battles over specific race, class, and gender concerns. Difference, in this view, becomes a political and cultural marker for asserting antagonistic relations, while eschewing the possibility of uniting such differences around a shared notion of social justice and political community. Difference in this discourse has no place for creating unity without denying specificity and consequently has no language for relating educational reform to broader notions of democratic community, citizenship, and social justice. Particularity in this case, is stripped of its progressive possibilities and becomes an obstacle rather than a basis for entering into dialogue with other groups or interests as part of a wider construction of a democratic public sphere where struggle, conflict, and difference constitute the beginning rather than the end of a dialogue and the forging of a democratic political project.

Svi Shapiro is fully aware of the history of left educational reform and goes out of his way to detail both its strengths and weaknesses. But if that is all he did there would be nothing unique about his discussion. What is exemplary about Shapiro's analysis is that he recognizes the contributions that radical educational critics have made over the years, but he begins with a very different question. Rather than focusing on merely the strengths and weaknesses of their theoretical approaches, he raises the question as to why these critics have had so little effect in shaping educational policy and practice in the United States. Such a starting point allows him to situate the discourse of radical educational reform within a broader historical, political, and cultural context and examine the crisis of educational reform as part of an ongoing hegemonic struggle among a number of competing political and ideological factions.

Shapiro makes it very clear that educational criticism is not merely the terrain of the left and progressive critics. As he points out in this important book, it is precisely the various factions on the right that have been able to use the language of educational criticism and reform to mobilize popular considerations and desires regarding the broader relationship between citizenship, education, and power. In fact, educational reform has been inserted into the popular sphere as a mobilizing language, not because of liberal and centrist approaches to education which have been primarily positivistic and instrumentalist in nature, but because of the new right's success at linking questions of schooling to a language which embraces the problems of everyday life, which resonates with a populist morality, and engages questions of civic life. In effect, what this means for Shapiro is not that educators should take up the doctrinal ideologies proffered by the right wing and neo-conservatives but, instead, take seriously the ideological and political necessity to connect issues of schooling to broader structures, problems, and considerations at work in the politics, practices, and workings of the welfare state. In effect, Shapiro argues brilliantly that progressive and left educators need to popularize their approach to schooling by inserting it into the broader politics of the state and everyday life.

Worked out through a variety of contexts, Shapiro illustrates the need for progressive and left educators to develop a discourse of schooling as part of a broader concern with questions that focus on democracy, power, citizenship, and social justice. If the language of educational reform is to move out of the academy and into the streets, Shapiro rightly argues that educational issues must serve to illuminate the larger crises that plague the capitalist welfare state. For Shapiro, the politics of schooling must be deepened so as to address a series of critical issues that structure American life. In this case, educational criticism must become a form of social criticism that addresses the domination of commodity relations, the destruction of the environment, the rise of bureaucracy, the crisis of the state, unemployment, and the increasing mass uniformity that reaches into everyday life. As Shapiro cogently points out, for example, the attack on student loans must be seen as part of a wider assault on the idea of economic justice. The reduction of cutbacks in school resources must be analyzed as part of a broader attack on democratic aspirations that have sustained, at least in utopian terms, the very purpose of American schooling, and the argument for school vouchers must be seen as part of a broader assault on the very idea of public education.

One of the major contributions that this book makes is to redefine the concept of hegemony as a political and educational category. Shapiro keenly understands the roles that ideology and culture play in the formation of knowledge, subjectivities, social practices, and institutional policies. Culture is not an innocent conceptualization for Shapiro. He recognizes that it not only designates areas where experiences are named, social subjects constituted, and material and symbolic economies are constructed, but that all forms of power are constituted by cultural questions and practices. This does not suggest avoiding the materiality of power, particularly as it works in both the state and civil society, but a way of reconceptualizing its constitution and effects in ideological and cultural terms. For Shapiro, the sphere of politics is broader than both the school and the economy; moreover, all spheres on which ideologies are constructed are seen as sites of contestation and struggle. Shapiro wants to connect hegemony not only to forms of domination, but also to forms of collective leadership that are rooted in the empowerment of democratic communities. He is concerned with how subject positions are taken up, how identities are shaped and fought over, and how alliances can be formed at the level of the popular to fight forms of ideological and institutional oppression. Like Gramsci, Shapiro recognizes that every crisis offers a moment of reconstruction; that repression offers the possibility for transformation, and that education represents a central terrain on which new forms of power and human agency can be developed.

If educators and others are to take Shapiro seriously, and we strongly believe that educators need to read him carefully, then educators will have to move away from the mechanical, one-dimensional, interest-ridden politics that have dominated their thinking in the past and construct forms of social authority that enable them to take a leading position in relating pedagogical concerns to those spheres of everyday life that have traditionally existed outside the realm of radical educational discourse. This means developing a theory of articulation that links the struggle over schools to struggles that are ongoing in a number of different spheres. Or, as Stuart Hall puts it, "Hegemony implies: the struggle to contest and dis-organize an existing political formation; the taking of the 'leading position' over a number of different spheres of society at once—economy, civil society, intellectual and moral life, culture; the conduct of a wide and differentiated type of struggle; the winning of a strategic measure of popular consent; and, thus, the securing of a social authority sufficiently deep to conform society into a new historic project" (*Thatcherism and the Crisis of the Left* [London: Verso Press, 1988], p. 7). For Shapiro, this project is one that links schooling to the creation of a democratic society that takes seriously what it means to educate students to live in a future free from suffering, domination, and subjugation. It is a vision of schooling that broadens and deepens not merely the democratic principles that inform it, but also speaks to a language of possibility and hope that engages rather than represses the meaning of political and pedagogical struggle. Shapiro has provided an important theoretical and political service in helping us to both understand this struggle and to work toward implementing its best visions.

Henry A. Giroux
Paulo Freire

Preface

The chapters in this book were written between 1979 and 1985. They draw on, elaborate, and extend arguments and themes developed by radical educators and educational theorists within the past two decades. Like theirs, my work uses the categories of critical analysis in which education is ultimately connected to structures of social domination and forms of human oppression and alienation. While the work is not "Marxist," I am not as ready as some critical intellectuals to abandon what I believe are the essential insights of Marxist sociology and political economy. The chapters reflect many of the prevailing political concerns of the 1980s: the disintegration of the welfare state and the fiscal crisis of the state, resurgent conservatism, the "deindustrialization" of America, the cultural and moral crisis, and the "new class war" waged against social spending. Although the book provides commentary on these issues and their effects on education, my deeper concern has been to explore the interconnections between educational policy and the structures of economic, political, and cultural life in the United States and, to a lesser extent, in other developed capitalist states.

Far from there being a univocal chain of causality, educational policy, I argue, is the effect of continuing and contradictory political and ideological struggles centered on the capitalist state. Such struggles brim with competing visions of social relations, moral norms, and "solutions" to the problems of economic and cultural life. Resolution of these struggles frequently embodies a complex crystallization of social or class interests rather than a simple, one-sided settlement. Throughout this book I have attempted to convey the dialectical process through which educational policy and practices emerge. Liberal capitalism forms an inescapable contradiction: no sooner does the state's intervention solve one set of economic problems than it generates others; liberal and conservative political reforms set off as many new demands as they satisfy old ones; democratic values and the imperatives of capital dance an uneasy tango. And, in all of this, educational policies mirror, indeed focus, the competing moments of social, ideological, and political struggle. Notions of "basic skills," "minimum competence," "special education reform," "individualized instruction," "alternative research paradigms," and "academic excellence" are terms deeply encoded with all of the complexity of these struggles. I have attempted in this book to amplify recent critical analysis's rejection of education's epiphenomenal role, seeing it, instead, as the eye of recent social, ideological, and political storms.

Although they antedate the "Bush Years," the chapters do, I believe, foreshadow the themes and likely turns of this administration. Indeed it seems reasonable to assume that the emphases and concerns of the Reagan years will persist on into the nineties. Despite the apparent dissipation of the right-wing ideological crusade, we may expect that the reemergent, "centrist" Republicanism will continue the familiar pattern of procorporate, promilitary, racist, and sexist policies. The social tensions and contradictions that form the backdrop to the development of educational policies will continue to work their disruptive effects on the cultural, economic, and political life of the country. Efforts to produce a "kinder, gentler nation," for example, must surely confront that alignment of forces that oppose any significant renewal of the federal government's involvement in liberal reformist politics. Notwithstanding election demagoguery about patriotism, "American values," and law and order, there is less reason to believe now than in 1980 that there will be a politics that seriously attempts to address the cultural disarray and moral disintegration that pervade life in America. The looming global environmental catastrophe as well as the runaway speculative dealings of big business heighten the dilemma around free market or *dirigiste* state policies. It seems likely that tensions checked in recent years through the pressures of intensified cold war, the deficit-financed economic boom, and the peculiar persona of the president will become far more visible, even explosive. Their effects on education are, to an extent, anticipated here.

My concerns are with more than purely exegesis. Indeed, perhaps the most significant value of this book is the contribution it may make to our understanding of the possibilities of educational change. For this reason the first chapter examines the present openings to a political agenda of educational reform. It does seem to me that future work in critical educational analysis will need to be far more oriented to this practical task. Throughout the book I have sought to represent the dialectic of educational reforms, practices, and policies—one that makes evident, in all of these, the continuing presence of those moments of social conformity and reproduction, as well as the moments of resistance and even transformation, imprinted by the struggles of collective action and social movements. In subsequent chapters, I examine the dialectic at work in the erosion and reconstitution of culture, the duality of political and civil society, the spread of social rights and entitlements, and the state's role as both guarantor of the capital accumulation process and embodiment of ideological legitimacy.

In all of this I want not only to understand better the way in which educational policies and practices are structured and defined by the social world in which they are embedded, but also the way in which they express the concerns, anxieties, needs, and travails of those who are subordinate or suffer discrimination or exclusion in our society. Such expressions, whether in education or elsewhere, bear all the distorted meanings of the hegemonic ideology. Nonetheless, it is among them, I am convinced, that we will find pointers to the formulation of an effective agenda for social and educational change. In the growing injustice and callous inhumanity of our national life and the exploitation and destructiveness of the world social order, efforts toward such an agenda are the inescapable responsibility of intellectual critique.

Greensboro, N.C.
May 1989

Acknowledgments

I am indebted to the editors of the following journals for allowing me to include materials previously published in them:

Philosophy and Social Criticism, Issues in Education, Journal of Curriculum Studies, Journal of Educational Thought, Education and Society, Teachers College Record, Urban Education, Interchange, Harvard Educational Review, Educational Theory, Journal of Curriculum Theorizing, New Education, and *Educational Policy.*

I would like to acknowledge the care and support over the past ten years of my colleague, David Purpel. His work in establishing what Sharon Welch has termed a community of solidarity and resistance has helped nourish and sustain an educational discoursse that is both prophetic and critical. He has constantly urged me to join critique to an affirmative vision of the kind of world for which we yearn. I wish also to acknowledge the support and friendship of my colleague Fritz Mengert. My graduate students at this university have constantly challenged me to clarify and make accessible the sometimes abstruse language of critical social theory. Jeannette Dean handled my typing demands with patience and good humor. Of course, I am indebted to the larger community of critical scholars of education. Among these I would like to especially acknowledge the support and interest of Henry A. Giroux and Michael Apple. To my wife Karen goes gratitude for her love and concern. And to my daughter Sarah appreciation (not always obvious at the time) for reminding me of the precious quality of human life and of our responsibilities towards it.

BETWEEN CAPITALISM AND DEMOCRACY

1
From Critical Theory to the Politics of Educational Change

Taking Stock: The Agony of the Educational Left

ON THE FACE of it these are dismal times indeed to be writing an introductory chapter to a volume of radical studies in the sociology and politics of education. Certainly, for the Left in the United States, the early and mid '80s has been a period of considerable anguish—added suffering to what, in Christopher Lasch's words, was its already agonized condition.[1] Whatever promises of progressive change might be heralded by left seers in the long run, for the present a measure of despair is not without some justification. (Indeed, under the Reagan administration, Keynes's famous dictum, "In the long run we're all dead!" has assumed a far more menacing relevance.) At this historical juncture the democratic and egalitarian hopes of a generation have been profoundly set back. For a generation that grew up eagerly, if naively, anticipating a far more free, rational, and humane world, the twilight of capitalism has shown itself possessed of unexpected staying power; the impending night might be casting its shadows, but the period of transition is excruciatingly long and uncertain.

We are not the first generation in this century, in this country, to grow up with fervent hopes of impending radical change only to see those hopes crushed before the world could, in any fundamental sense, be turned upside down. To be aware at all of the history of the Left in the United States is to be cognizant, for example, of the period of the '20s and the violent dissolution of an indigenous mass socialist movement: a movement in which, James Weinstein tells us, socialists held 12,000 public offices in 340 municipalities; in which the 1912

Socialist Party presidential candidate polled about 6 percent of the vote (847,000); and in which socialist ideas exerted a wide impact on the political, social, and intellectual life of the country.[2] Or of the '50s and the cold war hysteria which took vengeful reprisal against the leftist upsurge of preceding decades. And in this generation the grinding resistance of the '70s to the social, political, and cultural challenges of the short but turbulent radical era that preceded it has turned into the far-reaching movement of reaction of the '80s. Whatever intellectual lessons history might have taught us, the wrenching emotional and existential traumas must still be lived through. The flesh-and-blood hopes, dreams, and struggles of our time provide a human resonance quite distinct from the abstractions of historical analysis, and so it must be. For those generations bound up in the process of remaking a world, it is no mere rehearsal of a schematic sociological formula or the spinning of wheels in some predetermined mechanical process.

It is not only the personal phenomenology of the historical moment that marks the time off as distinct and irreducible, though the Left's eagerness for intellectual formulations too frequently leaves only what appears as the dry husks of human agency in its description of social change. The incomparable phenomenology of human experience is matched by the specific qualities of time and place. The circumstantial or the structured moments of social change must indeed be seen as following their own distinct trajectory and imperatives. But while social analysis (or Marxist analysis) provides us with a set of categories, schemata, and concepts by which to order and organize our evidence, the purpose is not to subsume the particular or lose the specifics or to elbow out the idiosyncratic from our analysis. Too often our analysis, in its pursuit of the lofty heights of abstraction and universalization, becomes far removed from the particular and singular historical moment in which our struggles for a better world occur.

In both its existential as well as its structured moments our recent history can, in no simple way, be reduced to prior situations or predetermined configuration of elements. For the Left the social upsurge of the '60s was certainly an incomparable event (or set of events), not the least parts of which were its generally unexpected emergence, its short-lived but luminous presence, and its rapid disappearance from the historical stage. On the face of it, it is precisely such historical events that might be expected to augur the despair or trauma I have referred to. Certainly there can be no denying the momentary presence of an anti-imperialist, antiauthoritarian mass movement in the United States that has gone, leaving no small remnant of souls stranded in the icy waters of resurgent reaction (of such situations are popular Hollywood movies constructed). The disappearance of a vibrant movement of the radical Left in the United States has meant a return to politics as usual—only more so. On any explicit level of unified, mass political action there is, once again, no real challenge to corporate power whether at home or abroad. The buckling of liberalism has meant that the center of politics has moved to the right. The voices advocating a return to an unbridled capitalism have been, for several years now, in full cry. While at the center of American politics liberals and conservatives may disagree on strategies, there is little real disagreement that the real business of America is business.

Recent Political Discourse and the Educational Consensus

The ideological poverty of contemporary political debate is made clear when one looks at the 1984 and 1988 primary campaigns for the Democratic Party presidential nomination. Analysis of the language of those campaigns is stark testimony to the fundamental consensus. The results of my own inquiry into the discourse on education serve as a vivid example of the wider failure of the Left to reframe the issues and concerns that constitute public debate, or become part of the political agenda. For the educational Left, in particular, the failure to reorient this debate or reset the agenda has been especially pronounced. As elsewhere in the domain of public and political discourse, but even more sharply around issues of education and schooling, there is the failure to find articulated arguments that depart in any important way from the fundamental moral, ideological, and social commitments of American capitalism. On the levels of politics the icy waters of the reactionary '80s run deep indeed.

The failure to reorient educational debate or the politics of the educational agenda, is made clear in reading the texts of the major candidates. Their remarks and proposals are (with one notable exception) unremittingly suffused by corporate priorities and capitalist values. Judged even by the modest reformist standards of these political contests, the failure to reframe educational issues or restate educational concerns in more critical terms was startling. In 1984, discussion of the economic implications of schooling—the foremost concern—was framed most often in terms of the connection between education and its effect on human capital formation. The "new ideas" Hart campaign reiterated time and time again the connection between investments in education and corporate rejuvenation. In his overwhelming emphasis on developing human capital, Gary Hart viewed educational policy as part of a larger industrial strategy.

> The truth is that we are undergoing a revolution in our economy as profound and transforming as the first Industrial Revolution that brought factories to an agrarian nation. In the new global economy what counts most is people—their knowledge and skills.[3]

There was little in the language of this campaign that spoke to education's relationship to issues of empowerment, justice, or human dignity. Most of the points concerned the modernization of industry, facilitating economic growth, and the education/training of workers for high technology. Investment in the skills and knowledge of our work force, he argued, was the challenge of the '80s. This message, consistently sounded throughout the campaign, was part of Gary Hart's clarion call to the Democratic National Convention:

> We must invest in the education and training of our workers and our young people, and in research that will guarantee America's leadership in trade and technology.[4]

Such goals lead to a preoccupation with education as an economic investment, evidenced in a particular kind of educational discourse: "the training of skilled minds," "new knowledge for improving productivity," "modernizing schools for the information age."

Hart's zealous advocacy of education as the means to enhance the nation's military and economic competitiveness was matched by other candidates. The same fundamental ideological, moral, and social commitments were embodied in John Glenn's statements on education. For Glenn the human capital message was couched in the language of aggressive patriotism—education was the instrument to beat other countries to regain our number one position in the world.

While John Glenn left no doubt as to the primary intent of all this—"What is at stake in the debate over education is nothing less than American economic and technological leadership"[5]—the language of Walter Mondale's primary campaign contained a somewhat more complex confluence of ideological concerns. It attempted to evoke and resolve disparate concerns that might be made to appear collapsible, one into the other. His educational arguments are more fully paradigmatic of liberal ideology in the 1980s, and, consequently, reveal even more sharply their failure as an agenda of the Left in the United States. The compromised (i.e., nonsocialist) leftism of this ideology means that it must concern itself, primarily, with the means through which capitalism in American may be successfully administered and reinvigorated. Of course, Mondale's agenda for education, no less than that of his competitors in the liberal pantheon, was glaring testimony to the educational Left's failure to reorient and reframe the educational debate—to redirect public discourse around alternative concerns and issues, and redefine for at least a significant segment of the polity, the vision of the nature and purpose of schooling.

Mondale's agenda for education concerned itself with moving the United States toward a more competitive level of technological, military, and economic performance. A Mondale press release stated the challenge to education in these terms:

> By the end of this decade, the quality of American education and research must be second to none. Unless we act boldly our nation's position in the world will decline. Unless we recommit our schools, colleges and research centers to excellence, no strategy to get America's competitive edge back has a chance to succeed.[6]

Mondale's dominant conception of education as an investment in future economic and technological capacity was made clearer still in the candidate's campaign speech:

> Another thing we have to do to get our competitive edge back is to invest in this next generation. We often say that a mind is a terrible thing to waste. We cannot afford to waste a single one. . . . But we also have to invest in these kids and give them the chance they need in this knowledge-intensive world. If we do our job we'll be number one; we'll out compete everybody; we'll be able to defend this nation and keep the peace. . . .[7]

No less than with the other candidates of the liberal and neoliberal Left, the language of the Mondale campaign was the language of human capital management, the instrumental, nonaesthetic use of human abilities and talents, and educational purposes predicated on the growth of the nation's economic product.

In looking at the liberal language affecting questions of equality and social justice, utilitarian considerations of "not wasting human talent" loomed large. Efficient utilization of relatively scarce human capacity forms one important leg in the discourse on education and social equality. At the same time as Democratic candidates employed an economic calculus in their concern for social justice, there were appeals to more straightforward ethical considerations. Such considerations carry all the ideological baggage (conflicts, contradictions) of liberal notions of individual freedom and justice in class structured, hierarchical societies. Mondale's position, for example, incorporates the complexities of ideological discourse that center on the issue of equality. The language of his campaign sought to wed utilitarian economic, technical, and national concerns with moral demands for social fairness, and the claim to fulfill and sustain meritocratic ideology. He synthesized, for example, his concern for social justice and equality with the notion of efficient management of human resources:

> In the coming years, disadvantaged and minority children will make up a larger percentage of the population than they do today. Our national economic health demands that they . . . no less than anyone else be able to compete and succeed. . . .[8]

In all probability, the 1988 Democratic campaign will see an intensification of the neoliberal turn in educational discourse; an increased emphasis on the educational changes that are needed to service the high tech and information-oriented American economy. Mike Davis has argued that Mondale's incontestable defeat has dramatically accelerated the succession process through which younger neoliberals with scant loyalty to labor and minorities are replacing the older New Dealers and Southern conservatives at all levels of the Democratic party.[9] Richard Gephardt, for example, who Davis says earned his seniority opposing programs for the poor, school busing, and women's rights, drafted the 1982 House Democratic caucus's economic blueprint that "shoved aside traditional Democratic welfare priorities to argue for a high tech industrial policy along lines that anticipated Hart's platform in 1984."[10] Davis also noted that a center for neoliberal succession has emerged among Democratic leaders in the sunbelt, particularly the Democratic governors. Among these Arizona Governor Bruce Babbitt is a principal ideologue—the functional counterpart of Gephardt in Congress:

> ... an exponent of "radical centrism"... he has connived to combine Gary Hart themes with consistent support for major Reagan programs like tax simplification (a superb proposal), merit pay, and anti-urban federalism. At San Francisco he was the leading proponent of Iaccoca for vice-president.[11]

Neoliberals Gephardt and Babbitt were joined by others emphasizing similar concerns. Michael Dukakis, three-time governor of Massachusetts, had an enviable economic record in no small way helped by the Reagan military build-up and the massive transfer of funds to his state's centers of high-tech research. Each emphasized the singular importance of education to the formation of a technically skilled and scientifically trained work force. In the battle for higher productivity and competitive trade advantage, education assumes its most critical role. Babbitt, who centered his educational proposals around "economic renewal," stated:

> As we debate public policies to stimulate economic growth and regain our economic strength we ought to remember that our public schools are a stronger economic weapon than any monetary theory, trade policy or book on Japanese management. Education generally—the public school in particular—is the most basic source of long term American productivity and economic well-being.[12]

He continued:

> Educational excellence is not an abstract issue.... Arizona has already cast its future with high technology... and that commitment accelerates each year. If we are to sustain the trend, we must invest more intensively in an entire new generation of human capital and technical skills.[13]

Not surprisingly, Babbitt's proposals focuses on the issue of achievement in mathematics and science. This included a doubling of math and science requirements for high school graduation, and partnerships between high technology firms and public schools. In addition there was the familiar advocacy of improvements in teaching through technocratic reforms—statewide achievement testing, career ladder and "performance-pay" programs for teachers, and the research and development of model programs "based upon concrete measures of student achievement."[14]

The same emphasis was found in Senator Joseph Biden's proposals.

Quoting from the 1983 National Commission on Excellence in Education he declared:

> Our nation is at risk. Our once unchallenged prominence in commerce, industry, science and technological innovation is being overtaken by competitors throughout the world. . . .[15]

In proposing solutions to the problem he first suggested that we increase the quantity of American education:

> Our children must go to school 30 or 40 more days a year, and several more hours a day. . . . America will not be able to compete with Japan, much less command the economy of tomorrow, if we give our children vastly less education than they give theirs.[16]

He also proposed that:

> Our school curriculums [sic] must be sufficient—not just to meet the challenge of foreign competition, but to win this competition! Our kids should be educated in the "new basics"—four years of English, three of math, science and social studies, and a semester of computer science.[17]

There was the usual call for more rigorous standards, achievement that is demonstrated in "objective measures," and technological partnership between schools and business. (Biden proposed something called "Star Schools"—lessons given by scientists and engineers that would be beamed via satellite to any school with a satellite dish.)

Besides the characteristically neoliberal emphasis on high technology, economic competitiveness, and human capital formation through public education, there was also, among these candidates, some common responses to the moral and social consequences of Reaganism. First they promised to redress the deepening problems of poverty and inequity in American society through remedial programs, federal support for local community expenditures, and expanded student loan programs. These concerns, as well as the economic ones, imply a renewed and expanded role for the federal government—a discourse that, as we will see later, at least partially rejects the standard conservative tirade against the ineffectiveness of big government. There were also some tentative attempts to respond to the monopolization of the moral issue by the right. Biden, for example, excoriated the injection of politics into the classroom and insisted that it was time for "ideological agendas to be set aside."[18] At the same time he argued that there was an urgent necessity for an education in "the values which define us as a people . . . honesty, tolerance, hard work and community."[19] Such an education, he argued, was the means to deal with the problems of drugs, teen pregnancies, and youth violence as well as solving the "biggest obstacle to improving our education—poor discipline in our schools."[20] Against the Reagan ethic of individual greed and self-aggrandizement, there was also the need to foster among young people an increased sense of social responsibility and a Kennedyesque ethic of service to the country.

Opposition and Hegemony in the Politics of Educational Discourse

I have taken this rather lengthy detour through the 1984 and 1988 Democratic Party primary campaigns in order to illustrate how little mainstream political discourse in the United States has been affected or transformed by leftist educational analysis. There was little in the statements and arguments I examined that marked the inroads of some alternative or oppositional set of meanings in regard to the place of schooling in this society. The campaigns in no way registered even a rhetorical awareness of a critical discourse on pedagogy and schools in the same way that mainstream liberal discourse must demonstrate obeisance to ecological, feminist, gay, minority, or peace concerns. There is an interesting comparison to be made here with the political Right. Whatever its real consequences in the reformulation of state policy, the Republican Party has indeed absorbed an alternative agenda for education in its political platform, an agenda that sharply departs from aspects of the postwar political consensus on education in the United States. Its demand, for example, that schools address the moral/cultural crisis of American society (through a new agenda of repression and authoritarianism) must be understood as a departure from the hitherto dominant ideology. (I shall return to this phenomenon in a later chapter.)

The reading I have given to recent political statements and assertions concerning education certainly indicates that the despair alluded to earlier is not without some justification. Yet, the failure to introduce critical educational themes into any major arena of public discourse is only a part of the story. Certainly my overall perspective is not one that sees history as an inexorable and uniform unfolding of forms of domination. Capitalism, as has been stated often enough, develops in an uneven manner. Successes or defeats in the struggle for greater human freedom, social justice, and collective empowerment are frequently regional matters. Stasis and regression in some areas can coexist with ferment and progress elsewhere. I have already noted liberalism's absorption (however selectively) of an emergent agenda of environmental concerns, feminist issues, gay rights, and peace demands. Nor would it be correct to interpret this as some kind of simple and functional co-optation of dissent (the simplistic and erroneous, though frequently held, understanding of hegemony). To do so is to ignore the continuing pressures required to maintain the presence of these issues in the face of those who argue that they are too radical and unsuited to the formulation of a national political agenda.

Within the complexity and disjunctions of the present society, ideological incursions are present even in areas that seemed impervious to change. Thus, in education, our assessment of the state of public discourse, and assertion of the absence of any reference to critical themes in mainstream political debate, is not entirely warranted. The educational region, whatever its practical and ideological autonomy, is not closed off from disruptions and dislocations found elsewhere in the society. Minority discrimination, urban decay, segmented labor markets, and the uneven results of the economic cycle have their effects elsewhere. Such conditions force new issues and questions onto the ideological and policy agenda. We are looking at the displacement into the areas of schools and education of a wider series of crises that confront the *lumpen* class in America—crises that are experienced as economic deprivation, political disempowerment, and cultural disintegration. The stasis of liberal ideology notwithstanding, such social, political, and economic crises are not to be denied. The brutalizing effects of the social system on some of its members create the conditions for a more radical political challenge, from the Left. And within that challenge at least some of the aspects of a more critical agenda for schooling find expression. The ideological wall that up until now seemed entirely impervious to the possibilities of an alternative agenda for education reveals some cracks. Our despair at the apparently unassailable nature of capitalist hegemony gives way to a more dialectical view in which the social formation is revealed as something other than a seamless and impenetrable structure. At the same time, and as we will see when we look at the Jesse Jackson campaign, it is clear how much in the discourse remains unchanged—how little has been absorbed of the theoretical labor in, for example, critical pedagogy or curriculum theory as the discourse on the relation between knowledge and power, school practices and cultural domination. While I want here to recognize the existence of a challenge from the Left in regard to educational politics, we must, ultimately, return to the limits and failures of this challenge as they exist in that region of the social formation called education.

The discourse of Jesse Jackson's 1983–84 Democratic Party primary campaign expressed some of these developments. His campaign statements concerning educational matters were rooted in concerns of a far wider nature. In looking at the language used by the major candidates it is clear that only Jackson's statements contain any significant departure from the usual logic of liberal educational discourse. Jackson engaged several issues in ways that are quite different—indeed radically different—from the other candidates. (It should be added that the noncandidate in the 1988 campaign, Governor Mario Cuomo of New York, had also forcefully and eloquently argued for the centrality of affirming ethical concerns in the process of public education. Among these Cuomo asserted the importance of schools teaching equality, individual rights and dignity, community, compassion, and love of country.) Jackson unequivocally related educational purposes to ethical concerns. Education must be connected to issues of justice, compassion, conscience, and the reshaping of society. As he stated in his address to the Democratic National Convention, the young should

> exercise the right to dream: You must face reality—that which is. But then dream of the reality that ought to be. Live beyond the pain of reality with the dreams of a bright tomorrow. Use hope and imagination as weapons of survival and progress. Use love to motivate you and obligate you to serve the human family.
>
> Young American, dream. Choose the human race over the nuclear race. Bury the weapons and don't bury the people. Dream of a new value system. Teachers who teach for life, not just a living, teach because they can't help it. Dream of lawyers more concerned with justice than a judgeship. Dream of doctors more concerned with public health than personal wealth. . . .[21]

Not only was the call to look to education as part of a morally concerned remaking of reality different, so too was the demand that education promote the critical use of imagination. Jesse Jackson, alone among all the candidates, viewed education in these terms. It is not issues of human capital and raising productivity that he spoke to in his discussion of schools but the schools' capacity to generate a sense of social responsibility and social concern. In his speech to the graduates of North Carolina A & T University he stated:

> Your generation must have a philosophy of the human family . . . . We're all precious in God's sight. Everybody is somebody. Feed the hungry. Give them more than butter and cheese . . . . Use your mind to solve problems and not engage in warfare.[22]

For Jackson, the nexus of educational/social responsibility is mediated by the question of power. Unlike other candidates (but certainly in the tradition of black education in the United States) the process of education was linked explicitly with the acquisition of power. Democratic empowerment is, in part at least, the purpose of increased education:

> You have the power to be more than you are. Three million high school seniors will graduate this May and June. You should come across that stage with a diploma in one hand symbolizing knowledge and wisdom, and a voter card in the other hand symbolizing power and responsibility. You can make a difference . . . . There are so many of us that want the same thing . . . the chance to use our minds and hearts to improve the world around us.[23]

In important ways Jackson seemed to advocate what some might call conservative schooling for radical purposes. He emphasized the need, on the part of teachers and parents, for more discipline and more determination, more attention and more monitoring of children's performance and actions. Such discipline and such attention have become critical because of the enormous and destructive effects of the mass media on the minds of the young:

> This is the first generation who by age 15 has watched 17,000 hours of T.V. and more radio than that. Which means that mass media quantitatively has more access to our children's minds than home, church and school combined, and qualitatively it penetrates deeply.[24]

Once again, in ways that represent a distinct departure from the discourse of other candidates, Jackson began to raise what he terms the "present gap of estrangement and alienation"; what he calls elsewhere the "crisis of effort" that is enfeebling the young. At the candidates' debate in Iowa he stated the issue this way:

> There's a dual dimension to this educational pursuit. One dimension is adequate opportunity, enough money to pay teachers, enough money for scholarships. No child in this society who wants to go to college, has a mind to learn and a will to work ought to be turned away just because of a lack of money ....
>
> But with all this talk about opportunity there is a flip side we don't talk about very much, the crisis in effort. Our children are watching five hours of T.V. a night, choosing entertainment over education and that's a crisis. The same kind of energy spent on developing our motor skills athletically is not spent on developing our cognitive skills intellectually ....[25]

In ways that were unique to his candidacy, Jackson raised a set of issues that are quite different from those we have seen discussed up till now. They dealt with questions of power, of social concern and responsibility, of the dominant culture and its debilitating effect on the young, and of the need to develop intellectual ability in order to address problems facing the community. In this context it is not surprising to find Jackson excoriating the disempowering and humanly invalidating aspects of schooling. He demands, for example, that "competency tests are used to make people competent"[26] rather than to eliminate students from school. And in contrast to the dominant human capital view of schooling Jackson noted that "the broader community, such as business and labor, is more interested in the end product (efficient and productive workers) than in children."[27]

Issues of community which figure prominently in the language concerning the goals of education are, not surprisingly, key issues in the process of education itself. Consistent with Jackson's general concern with a politics that seeks to empower the masses, that attempts to broaden the popular base of involvement, influence, and decision making, the candidate emphasized that education must become a community responsibility:

> Any national movement to save public education must have a grass roots, mass-oriented, motivational and mobilizational approach to education. It must be designed to challenge and involve the maximum number of persons and organizations ... to impact creatively and constructively on

> public education. I contend that our schools are too isolated from the rest of the community and the responsibility for educating students is too narrow. My goal, and my role as president, would be to broaden the community support base so that more people share the responsibility for public education ... As president I would take public education and put it in the center of our social-cultural matrix.[28]

The candidate's reference to saving the public schools implied a crisis in education of far greater intensity than was understood by other candidates. While Jackson spoke to the importance of addressing the nation's larger social ills by "attacking ... problems as they arise in public schools," he also made clear that issues of justice and equality require concern with factors—social, economic, political, and legal—external to schools. Jackson did assert that pragmatic responses do exist that can effectively address the problems of the public schools. He, too, dismissed the exaggerated intellectual discussions surrounding education:

> A president must move beyond the endless academic debate about what is wrong with public schools, the "paralysis of analysis," by focusing on what the nation's school children, their parents and the broader community can do to change and improve public education. [29]

What could be done amounts to a rather simple potpourri of traditional educational remedies, such as greater parent involvement in the school process, including coming to school on the first day, meeting children's teachers, exchanging home telephone numbers, not allowing homework to be interrupted by TV or stereo, and picking up report cards directly from the teacher. Of course, for Jackson such simplistic responses to the school crisis (especially the urban school crisis) are rooted in his populist politics, in particular the need for parents and the community to seize their rightful power over public education:

> Recognizing the critical role that parents play should not frighten them but rather should serve to make them aware of the real power and responsibility they have. ... The power of the school board is derived from and granted by parents. Even striking teachers are powerful not because of their union but ultimately because parents respect the picket line.[30]

He continued:

> We must place public education at the center of our socio-cultural matrix and recognize and consciously plan for the involvement of everyone who impacts on the minds of our children in proportion to the power they have to educate.[31]

Of course, as we have seen, the purpose of the community's usurpation of the power to control public education is for what appears as a curious mixture of conservative and progressive educational ends. They are summarized by Jackson in his speech in Newark, N.J.:

The major goals of a national educational effort are to: re-connect the critical links between school, home and community; restore high expectations for academic achievement and personal behavior in public schools; reduce significantly the incidence of conflict, disruption, violence, and vandalism in public schools; reverse the downward trend in the indicators of educational success—regular attendance, completion of high school, improved attitudes and qualification for higher education or advanced vocational training; influence moral and ethical value systems of students in ways consistent with democratic principles.[32]

However superficially, Jackson addressed himself to a concern that is distinct from the other candidates, and one that speaks to the political and ethical context of schooling. In this, the apparent total imperviousness of public discourse to the themes and concerns of critical school analysis needs to be modified into an alternative view. Such a view would recognize the pervasive, but by no means impenetrable, power of hegemonic domination. Within the apparently unbroken wall of ideological silence that seems to block all attempts at an alternative or oppositional discourse on educational matters, cracks or weaknesses appear which indicate vulnerabilities overlooked in our earlier, more dispirited moments. The Jackson campaign has indicated some, though certainly not all, of the places where social experience, political demands, and the redefinition of educational issues might be joined.

Educational Reform and the Language of Positivism

Such openings notwithstanding, it is clear from reading the texts of the Democratic candidates in the 1984 and 1988 primary campaign how much their discourse was saturated with values that affirmed the dominant positivist outlook. This outlook suffused discussion to such an extent that almost all talk of school reform was ideologically encircled before there was even the possibility of breaking out of the dominant form of educational discourse. Notions of quantifiable results, demonstrable competencies, the search for verifiable and empirical criteria for judging excellence (of students and teachers), an emphasis on performance and discrete skills—these permeated all of the candidates' statements. There was a strongly shared desire to assimilate the process of schooling to the forms and methods of technology. Their statements attempted to shape teaching and knowledge to a technical discourse in which these would become amenable to the manipulation of improved and expanded inputs (better resources, improved training of practitioners, better techniques, more time). There was the frequently enunciated conviction that harder work (in the form of longer hours and more days) would increase the output of the educational process. Learning, in this sense, was assumed to be a process of incremental additions, a process subject to the mechanism of a linear progressive rationality (more time on task equals more learning). It contained the same emphasis on the language of skills and skill training—whether in regard to students or upgrading the quality of teachers. Such discourse, with its implicit assumptions of discrete competencies, technical knowledge, and empirically verifiable abilities, discounts alternative visions of pedagogy—critical and reflexive, aesthetic and imaginative, democratic and empowering. The pervasive valorization of positivist values in the statements of these political leaders reifies this view of education, that is, makes it the natural and the only possible version of educational practice.

Consideration of curriculum is limited, as we have seen, to more directly technical and scientific preparation and to that ubiquitous rallying focus, the basics. The constricted, functional nature of this curriculum is quite remote from traditional academic, literary, aesthetic pursuits as well as from progressive citizenship goals. Few words are to be found concerning the liberal values of all-round development, humanistic concern for spiritual or aesthetic enrichment, or education as an instrument of social and ethical commitment. The emphasis on skills in the curriculum discourse of all the candidates, is the tip-off as to the instrumentally oriented, positivist rationality that undergirds the human purposes of education in contemporary America. The language of skills—basic or new—must be seen as closely associated (as it usually is) with the capacity to function (or as it is sometimes referred to, grimly, by educators, to "survive") in the world of bureaucratic and consumption-oriented advanced capitalism. Such skills, so strongly asserted as the fundamental goals of schooling, equip individuals with the ability to perform those tasks that are essential to fulfilling their roles as consumers and as producers. Basic skills, or Hart's and Biden's new skills, are the route to a successful coping with, and adaptation to, the institutions and practices that produce, exchange, and distribute commodities. The skills represent little more than a simplified inventory of technical knowledge functional to the administrative, work, and consumptive activities in contemporary society. Talk of education for the enhancement of human imaginative capabilities, development of critical intellectual faculties, social responsibilities, and ethical commitment is far removed from such circumscribed, prosaic, and adjustment-oriented concerns.

The restricted and narrow concerns of education and their impoverished view of human existence are further underlined by the paucity of attention given to the relationship between schooling and democratic values. With the exception of Jackson, there were few attempts to connect education to the commonly taken meanings of democratic ideology—choice, participation, self, and collective empowerment. The mainstream discourse on liberal education in the 1984 and 1988 campaigns carried little of the traditional rhetoric that historically linked mass schooling with an informed citizenry capable of exercising its democratic rights. Little in the candidates' language referred to the role of schooling in providing a democratic citizenry with the power of critical rationality, the capacity for informed choice, or the exercise of dissent. Little referred to the enhancement of the capability for self-determination or the empowerment of human beings with respect to their social and institutional environment— a striking omission in view of the increasingly penetrating capability of the mass media to manipulate information and knowledge and to mystify the issues that confront Americans in both their private and public lives. The texts of most of the candidates, to a large extent, ignored the connection between an educated population and one empowered by knowledge and experience to manage its social, political, and economic lives. In neither the restricted sense of democracy—concern with political-constitutional and civil rights—nor in the expanded sense of a concern with the social rights of citizens, workers, consumers, women, and minorities was there much evidence of a political or educational discourse that is predicated on such issues. It is well to remind ourselves that this omission is of enormous ideological and political significance. It represents a selective response to the problems or crises of the present era, a mobilization of bias around which issues or concerns ought to constitute the educational or political debate. It ignores or refutes the continuing accumulation of evidence that points to the authoritarian character of public education. Silence on this issue naturalizes the deepening obsession with social control in our schools: increasing regimentation, widespread paternalism, and rigidity of classrooms. It represents the continued and widespread failures of our public schools to cultivate questioning, thoughtful, and imaginative individuals.[33]

On the broader, social side, failure to speak to democratic values in the context of schooling represents a larger failure to address a series of critical issues in American public life—the pervasive and largely uncontrolled influence of television and the media, the alienation from the instruments of political democracy, and the absence of just about any form of economic democracy. Most important, there is an absence of any rhetoric that speaks to the erosion of those traditions concerned with community empowerment.

It is precisely here that the particular and distinct nature of the Jackson campaign was so marked. Jackson, alone among the candidates, made the question of democracy central to his campaign. Both his specific pronouncements on education, as well as his more general language, showed that questions of popular power—its concentration in a few hands and its absence among the masses—were principal concerns. Thus the most important purpose of education would be about the struggle for power by those who are socially and economically disenfranchised. Even so, his association of literacy and schooling with the increased capacity for collective determination were within the distinctively black view of public education which, as historians have made clear, has always specifically linked the opportunity for mass public schooling with the growth of social power.

The significance of community power in regard to the control of public schools raises another important issue. Jackson took up and embraced the cause of decentralized power and the need for popular control of bureaucratic structures.* This issue of schooling and power, raised by the candidate, marked an important departure from the mainstream of liberal democratic discourse in the 1984 primary campaign. Jackson attributed a distinctly social purpose to education. Unlike the other candidates, whose concerns are either individualistic or national (equal opportunity is, after all, preeminently concerned with the opportunity for individual improvement, an opportunity to get ahead), Jackson dealt with seldom raised questions of community and mutual responsibility. He was the only one who explicitly stated that they ought to be among the purposes of our curriculum. Indeed his statements were among the few by those on the Left that in any way considered questions of ethical and social values in the context of the classroom. Contrast this with the centrality of such concerns in the pronouncements and rhetoric of rightist politicians. By 1988 more Democrats had become aware of the silence on values and attempted to address it.

Finally Jackson confronted (if guardedly) one other issue in American life. Going beyond concerns with equal opportunity he raised what he called the crisis of effort in our schools—the complex and fundamental question of alienation. While his methods of redress for parents and teachers is nothing more than a simplistic formula which might help a few but would surely do little for the great majority, it represented a critical departure into a world that educational commentators on the Left have long described. This is the world of classroom boredom, apathy, and frustration resulting from the characteristic public school pedagogy. Such pedagogy, with its typical indifference and frequent hostility to the cultural experience and existential reality of students' lives, has been described by a legion of critical observers. In representing classroom experience in these terms such observers have argued that one must reverse the usual approach that blames the victim. Instead, what constitutes bad student behavior—anger, hostility, apathy—must be seen as resistance to the dehumanizing environment represented by schooling. It is a rational and comprehensible response to an institution that seeks to discount and subordinate that which is not already a part of the dominant culture embodied in the values, practices, and knowledge disseminated by the school.

What Jackson calls the crisis of effort might be seen as some kind of

---

* This is an issue that has remained largely within the ideological bailiwick of the Republican Party and the American Right, at least insofar as it concerns centralized and bureaucratic government.

a reference (albeit coded) to the phenomenon of school alienation. It speaks, if rather circumspectly, to the existence of a crisis in our public schools—especially urban schools—in regard to the estrangement, disaffiliation, and outright resistance of students to the realities of their school lives. While raising the issue of power, Jackson was unable or unwilling, however, to raise those questions pertaining to pedagogy and curriculum, as the other crucial elements. It is clear he is limited by his educational ideology to conventional notions of what constitutes the proper method, purpose, and concern of education. In no sense did he speak to what some call a pedagogy of liberation, that is, a process of education that seeks to empower those he calls his constituency, "the damned, disinherited, disrespected, and the despised," through critical reflection on the nature and condition of their lives. The goal for Jackson, it would appear, was still skewed strongly in the direction of acquiring those technical and interpersonal skills that facilitate entry into the business and corporate world of the American middle class. And yet, if nothing else, Jackson raised those issues of power, participation, social responsibility, the ideological effect of the media, and alienation, as well as, of course, the question of equality and justice, that will surely form key elements in any future agenda of a radical Left in America. For this, his contribution to the shape of political and educational debate in the United States might be far more significant than electoral numbers alone would indicate.

The Sociology of Radical Educational Theory

Whatever the openings created by the Jackson campaign into new areas of ideological and educational discourse, we are still compelled to confront the overall minimal gains of a critical pedagogical perspective in the larger domain of public debate. In ways that are too obvious to those of us who follow the educational news, the public fruits of twenty years of radical intellectual labor have been meager indeed. In the domain of educational ideas and practices, the orientation towards an instrumental, narrow, positivistic schooling not only continues but does so at an increasingly intensified pace. Indeed, at the level of local and state policy making, the plethora of educational reforms that have followed the 1983 reports on the status of education in the United States have demonstrated a sickeningly uniform tendency to resolve our educational crisis in ways that simply add new layers of technically motivated curriculum to the existing pedagogy. At work in this deteriorating situation is, however, a startling paradox: the widening dissonance between the prevailing forms of theory and practice as these are expressed in policies and reform strategies adopted by the authorities, and the, by now, massive and rapidly expanding critical literature on education emanating from what Bertel Ollman calls the "left academy."[34] The Left academy has undeniably burrowed deeply into the intellectual ramparts of the hegemonic fortress. Its intellectual critique of the institution of schooling, curriculum, pedagogy, and the hidden curriculum now constitutes a devastatingly powerful intellectual statement which denies, forcefully, the consensual version of school purposes, practices, and theories. Whatever goes on in the real world, in the academy the critical perspective on schooling appears as an increasingly influential and persuasive force. Though far from being the only intellectual show in town, the body of work that comprises its diverse categories provides, for an increasing movement of adherents, a rich and powerful intellectual perspective in which to confront the banalities of reactionary educational nostrums, or exhausted liberal prescriptions.

Yet, however creative, productive, and persuasive this critical tradition may be, it remains resolutely on the outside, far removed from the conventionally constituted discourse concerning the problems and issues of education in America today. The intellectual and common-sense categories that comprise this discourse serve as a powerfully resilient bulwark against change in this ideological war of position. Whatever reasons (and we will suggest some later) for the failure to breach these bulwarks, they are certainly not to be found in the inappropriateness or lack of incisiveness of the critique itself. Limited as this critique may be in some important ways, weakened by theoretical shortcomings and absences, and driven by theoretical disputes and disagreements, it is still difficult to deny its relevance, and relatedness, to our contemporary situation. The left critique of schooling, produced during the past decade or so, is an undeniably apposite response to the conditions, crises, and predicaments of our social, economic, cultural, and political world. Whatever might be said about its weaknesses, limitations, and contradictions as a body of theory, it must also be acknowledged that the work as a whole represents an ongoing series of statements that powerfully illuminate the realities of the social and educational crises we have witnessed during the last two decades.

Avoiding any kind of commentary or appreciation, it is worthwhile simply to pause for a moment in order to situate, as a social product, the body of intellectual work I have been referring to. In a complex variety of ways this work is a product of its time: a response to this particular social, cultural, economic, and political juncture. While in no way discounting the logic that is internal to, and impels, the development of theoretical knowledge, it is important to recognize just how much it is impelled by engagement with the critical social conditions of our time. Indeed, it is precisely this historical engagement that gives intellectual analysis its power and significance—influencing markedly those who are exposed to it.

It is little wonder that the earlier forays of those concerned with developing a critical view of schooling were concerned with issues of authority, hierarchy, and social control. The focus on such issues by what has been called the romantic critics of schooling, as well as by revisionist educational historians, arose in a context in which there was a crisis of legitimacy around the issue of authority. So their work may be read as a response to the social and political crisis which had eroded the taken-for-granted authority of institutions and social roles. It is not difficult to identify some of the predisposing conditions for this crisis: the credibility and ethical tribulations of the Vietnam war and of Watergate; the egalitarian surges of this period; and the student revolt against bureaucratic hierarchy in the institutions of higher education. This latter revolt was conjoined with the deep suspicion and questioning of the moral legitimacy of teachers, leaders, parents—the older generation. Of course, in addition to these eruptions there were the long-term effects of developments within capitalism (as well as within communist society). Thus, for example, the cultivation of an adolescent market had created the phenomenon of a youth culture with its attendant assault on adult sensibilities, values, and concerns. This youth culture, in all of its myriad forms, facilitated and nurtured the expression of the cultural, social, sexual, and economic grievances of young people and provided opportunities for a partial penetration of the dominant culture. The result of these developments has been the spectacular manifestations of youth protests against established authority. The phenomenon of youth culture can certainly be located in the wider erosion of traditional virtues and established authority under the continued impact of consumption-oriented capitalism. The motivations and need dispositions of such societies, with their incessant demand for novelty, innovation, spectacle, and youthful vitality, are antagonistic to any notion of traditional authority. There are also those tendencies described by Jürgen Habermas: the spread of bureaucratic and technical rationality which subjects increasing areas of cultural meaning to administrative criteria of validity, as well as public discussion.[35] The result of this is the undermining of those hitherto taken-for-granted normative assumptions which govern our social world. The combined effect of the spread of technical rationality and the commodity-dominated culture is the erosion of any authority rooted in some transcendent standards of ethical conduct or moral values. As part of this erosion of authority in advanced capitalist societies Habermas also points to the increasing dissonance between that ideological linchpin of bourgeois culture—the achievement ethic—and the realities of reward and failure. Declining ability to make good on the promises of this ethic brings into further disrepute the authority of these socialization agencies, such as schools, most strongly identified with the cultivation of an achievement orientation and strongly rooted in notions of impulse restraint and delayed gratification. The result is to intensify the influence of those sources of socialization that "democratize sensibilities," and that invalidate the authority of those who claim association with higher cultural values.

The relation between schooling and hierarchy, education and authority, was not the only place where critical analysis arose in response to social crisis. Such commentary attempted to provide intellectual insight into the movements, the crises, the dislocations, and the dysfunctions of the social formation as well. The work of critical scholars has been, and continues to be, a response to such conditions. The centrality of the state in studies of schooling in capitalist society is a key. At the core of this work has been a concern with what Nicos Poulantzas, among others, calls the "relative autonomy" of the state, a concern no doubt fomented by the perception of an increasingly chaotic or irrational relationship between elements of the state and civil society. Far from being the well ordered blueprint of those who sit at the commanding heights of the economy and government, advanced capitalism demonstrated, after the relative quiescence of the forties and fifties, its glaringly incoherent and fractious nature. Schools moved along a social and economic trajectory quite different from, and not infrequently at odds with, other parts of the system. Overproduction of trained and schooled manpower, curriculum rooted in nonutilitarian, traditional cultural values, among other things, evidenced the distinctive nature of schooling in capitalist society. A part of the state it might be, but education was, in no simple sense, the handmaiden of the corporate hierarchy. At the same time, the need to move from universal condemnation of the state as the tool of the capitalist class to the possibility of defending some aspects of the state's activities became increasingly demanded by the Left as conservative attacks on the state—in particular, that part of it concerned with social and human needs—mounted. Political realities impelled a recognition of the state as a complexly structured entity—itself a terrain of social conflict and the struggle for power—in which classes and social interests battle over the equilibrium point of hegemony. Defense of the state, or aspects of it, against rightist attacks, while recognizing the role of the state in maintaining capitalist hegemony, demands a far more nuanced appreciation of the functions and dynamic of political power.

Part of this more nuanced appreciation was impelled too by the successive fiscal crises of the state that characterized the '70s and '80s. Such crises, with their deleterious effects on education and social services, compelled attention towards the bifurcated role of the state—at once concerned with the profitability of big business and the accumulation of capital and also with legitimation of the social structure and the distribution of power. Radical scholars of education were forced to recognize that school (as an agency of the state) is not, as earlier critics had observed, merely an economic instrument to produce trained manpower and new technical knowledge; it contains, also, political functions. The school is indeed the very embodiment of the state's role as the illusory community.

The context of crisis and upheaval which surrounded the state in the 1960s and '70s, which disputed any view of it as inexorably powerful and effective in its process of domination, also engendered a revision of the theory of socialization. In this far from smoothly functioning, monolithically controlled world, human beings do not as readily become the agents or dupes of capitalism as a functionalist (albeit neo-Marxist) view of schooling would have us believe. The Marcusean emphasis on control and domination in advanced capitalist societies gave way to the realization of the constant and unresolved struggle for power that characterized all of the institutions of public life. Theories of *resistance* developed as a response to the widening recognition of the complex dialectic that really existed in industrial societies between forms of socialization that entirely incorporated individuals into the dominant culture and ideology and those subordinate cultures that expressed a nonacceptance of some part of this hegemonic structure. Such theories embodied a move from the resignation of the perspective of a "one-dimensional" civilization to a recognition of the enormous and varied currents of alternative and oppositional behavior found in societies such as the United States or Great Britain. Especially influential in this regard was the empirical work of the Center for Contemporary Cultural Studies at the University of Birmingham in England with its studies of the subcultures of resistance found among British youth.[36] This work, and other parallel studies, describes a world seething with the struggles of subordinate groups who, if not quite committed to a revolutionary overthrow of the system, are very far from acquiescing to their domination; such groups, from youth gangs to school troublemakers, from adolescent girls to industrial workers, and many others, were far from passive observers in the making and the ratification of social reality.

As we locate the critical scholarship about schooling, with its varying emphases, in its social and historical context, it becomes evident to what extent this work is a response to, and an interpretation of, the turbulence, the upheavals, and the social struggles of the last twenty years or so. It is a body of intellectual and theoretical work inseparable from contemporary human practices and social experience and from historical developments. Nowhere is this more apparent than in the centrality of theories of reproduction in studies of schooling. Such studies, with their attention to the reproduction of the division of labor and the inequalities of class, gender, and race have been the overarching focus of concern in almost all critical educational scholarship. Nor is the centrality of this focus so surprising. It is, for one thing, certainly coincident with the rediscovery of class as a central organizing category of human experience. This was surely the case in Britain when, after twenty years of apparent embourgeoisement, the late '60s saw the re-emergence of working-class militancy. Neither the welfare state nor social democracy in its various forms have eliminated the fundamental class nature and class contradictions of capitalist society. Far from melting away, class identities and conflicts continue to structure the cultural, economic, and political issues of our time. In the United States, while social class continues its more shadowy existence (as compared to Europe), struggles around race and gender assume spectacular forms. Revealing their complexly structured natures, these struggles move quite rapidly from an initial cultural focus to a concern with their political and economic embeddedness.

Henry Giroux is correct to distinguish among these theories of reproduction, between the "economic-reproduction" and the "cultural-reproduction" models.[37] Central to the former, says Giroux, is the relationship between schools and the "structural effects of the workplace." The thematic concerns of this approach are the social division of labor, capitalist relations of production, and the power of capital to construct, through the hidden curriculum, the subjectivity of labor. This concern with the relationship between school and the workplace is certainly grounded in the economic dislocations of the 1970s and 1980s, as one aspect of the economic crisis became the inability of the job market to satisfy the upwardly mobile aspirations of working-class and middle-class youth. Ironically, it was precisely the lack of congruency between schooling and available jobs that was the context for the landmark study of Samuel Bowles and Herbert Gintis and its theory of correspondence between school, work, and home. Schooling in the United States, and even more in Western Europe, is marked by its surplus production of overeducated individuals. Nor has the problematic nature of the relationship between schooling and work been one simply of the quantity of available opportunities. Although the credentialling process demands increasing numbers of years at school, there is a concomitant erosion of the need for any education other than the most highly circumscribed and technical. The ultrafragmentation of the workplace offers experiences that less and less meet the expectations of creative, responsible, and stimulating labor!

The cultural-reproductive theories of schooling have less to do with the problematic nature of jobs and the workplace than with the role of what Pierre Bourdieu calls "symbolic violence" in reproducing class domination. The emphasis of this perspective is, Giroux notes, "the mediating role of culture in reproducing class societies . . . over the study of related issues, such as the source and consequences of economic inequality."[38] Emphasizing culture rather than the workplace is a relatively new development in Marxist-influenced sociology. Perhaps the most important source of this change lies in the emergence of the sphere of consumption as an area of spectacular importance in the topography of advanced capitalist societies. In the delineation and self-definition of classes, consumption activities and patterns demand the kind of attention once reserved for the sphere of production: life-style and private life imply need-dispositions and motivations at least as powerful as those emanating from the workplace. Nor are they coterminous with one another. Demographic changes and changes in the nature of work and housing patterns, added to the socially inclusive effects of popular culture and advertising, separate the ideological effects of work and nonwork. The need to develop a sociology of schooling that links culture, class, and domination in a distinct way has been given added significance by the proliferation, in recent years, of forms of resistance or opposition that are centered, not in the workplace, but around street life, life-style, sexual identification, and age cultures. Indeed, it is apparent that the most virulent opposition to bourgeois society has been expressed in such forms of cultural or symbolic demonstrations. The real theoretical challenge has been to explicate the way in which these forms of cultural resistance are interpenetrated by forms of economic inequality—a task of special salience in the study of schooling and the reproduction of capitalist hegemony.

Toward an Educational Agenda of the Political Left

Thus we see the paradoxical threads that wind their way through our account of the recent politics of schooling and of the production of a critical theory of education in the United States. The latter represents a significant body of theoretical work arising from, and illuminating in important ways, the practices and structures of education in the societies of what have come to be called advanced capitalism. Theoretical work here implies not detached, disinterested theory, but analysis that is both a moral and a political indictment of the dehumanizing, alienating, and authoritarian structures of contemporary schooling. It is an indictment of such incisiveness and power that it goes, in many important ways, unanswered. At the same time, the theoretical work has borne little political fruit. Our inquiry into the discourse of a recent political campaign shows how little of the public discussion of educational matters has been affected by this theoretical work. In this somewhat reactionary political juncture we are speaking only to the making or remaking of a political agenda, the possibility of extending the scope of political debate. However badly treated by a conservative administration, environmental concerns insist on their place within the agenda of public debate; the positing of medical care as the production of use values, not merely exchange values, continues as an ineradicable component of public debate and political struggle. This is the real meaning of Gramsci's "war of position." It is the struggle to remake the hegemonic ideology so that it admits new problems, accommodates hitherto unstated questions, and acknowledges injustice where before it was invisible or exploitation where previously it was politically and morally assumed. Yet despite the acuity and scope of our theoretical production in recent years, we have failed to alter the boundaries of political debate and public discourse on issues of schooling. We have failed to incorporate new themes, moral concerns, and social visions into the general discourse on education. We have failed, in Gramsci's metaphor, to mark out a radically altered and expanded terrain on which to conduct our war of position and on which to struggle for a reshaping of the hegemonic ideology that affects schooling.

At the core of the failure has been the inability or reluctance to develop a political agenda for education resonant with the cultural concerns and social needs of subordinate and intermediary groups and rooted in the critical analysis of schooling briefly surveyed above. Why such an agenda remains largely unconstructed is a matter of speculation. We might look to the *totalistic* schema of much radical analysis that seems incompatible with the partial reform of any one institutional sector. The sometimes complex conceptual and linguistic formulations of left intellectual work do not lend themselves to the necessarily readily accessible language of political mobilization. (While intellectual snobbery is a not unjustified complaint here, a degree of intellectual withdrawal and linguistic separation have some justification in efforts to mark out a terrain of theoretical discourse fundamentally distinct from the assumptions of the hegemonic culture.) Whatever the reasons, the need is for a political agenda that speaks to the interrelatedness of the social crisis and the education crisis, an agenda that is able to mediate, through educational demands, resistance to the wider structures of social domination.

Such an agenda would take seriously those resonant themes of rightist politics—the disintegration of culture and the erosion of moral values. Concerns about moral renewal and cultural reinvigoration are not simply a swindle perpetrated by demagogic politicians. They do contain, at another level, a *cri de coeur* that is the expression of the social, economic, and cultural anxieties of middle-class existence in the 1970s and 1980s, a point made so well by Harvey Cox in his book *Religion in the Secular City*.[39] Rightist politicians both express and capitalize on a social illiteracy which fails to tie our moral crisis to the working of an economic system which, through its ideology of pervasive consumption and commodification, has wrought a society that, in the words of Karl Marx,

> cannot exist without constantly revolutionizing the instruments of production, and thereby the relations of production and with them the whole relations of society.... All fixed, fast, frozen relations ... are swept away, all newly formed ones become antiquated before they can ossify. All that is solid melts into air, all that is holy is profaned.[40]

Such a world knows less and less of human values that are not marketable, of meanings that do not express a cash value or an exchange relationship. A left political agenda for education must certainly address the ensuing crisis of values and meanings that consumption capitalism makes inevitable, especially in so far as they affect the young. (The consequences of this in drug and alcohol abuse, apathy, suicide, vandalism—the natural landscape of schooling—are not inherently conservative themes.) It will need to recognize the enormous salience of these issues to many people, while offering an alternative to the vacuities of prayer-in-school type remedies. Such a response must address the inseparability of education from moral and political commitments and the rootedness of the quest for personal meaning in the interrelatedness and solidarity of human community. It will need to reappropriate the language that has been utilized so effectively by conservatism, this time locating the moral crisis in the commodification of culture and the incessant consumerist message of our economic system with all of its material waste and spiritual emptiness. Such an agenda would thus link moral and cultural invigoration with an education that insists on the need to take sides—for social justice, human dignity and the compassionate community—and provides the critical cultural skills through which society's real embodiment of these values can be assessed.

A second theme for a left educational agenda must certainly be related to the question of empowerment or, more precisely, the overwhelming sense of disempowerment experienced by subordinate and intermediary groups in American society. Our agenda will draw on democratic citizenry traditions concerning public education (idealized and residual as these may be) in the same way that our first agenda item draws on traditions of ethical community in American life. Here, however, the interest is to link schools to a widening struggle for a radical democratic restructuring of American life—in the workplace, the community, the media, politics, the church, and in other basic social institutions. Every phase of school life—pedagogy, curriculum, institutional governance—can become a focus of demands connected to a reinvigoration of the notion of citizenship preparation. Nor should it be too difficult to incorporate into our educational agenda themes resonant of middle-class and working-class impotence and the resulting social resentments and anxieties; among these (as Jackson rightly asserted) is the demand for a critical literacy attuned to the manipulative and exploitative effects of the mass media, and the erosion of political legitimacy that is exhibited in low voter turnouts. The latter certainly offers possibilities of radical new ventures in social studies and citizenship education.* And the time is surely ripe for demands to reconceptualize all kinds of vocational preparation so that they address the themes of cooperative management of the workplace, worker participation in decision making, quality circles, and similar concerns. There will be a struggle to reappropriate language from its rightist meanings; notions of accountability, professionalism, local control, excellence, which have become vehicles for repressive forms of scrutiny and control, the centralization of power, and the assertion of

---

* Even from the perspective of bourgeois interests, the current abysmal level of voter participation poses a potential threat to the hegemonic role of the political culture. In this sense a space is created within the ideological functioning of schools for political education that transcends the bland vacuousness of traditional citizenship training.

parochial interests, can be transformed into their more generous, open, and participative meanings.

The latter struggle against centralized and bureaucratic control systems is certainly linked to a recognition of the structurally differentiated forms of disempowerment, that is, an appreciation that the forms of subordination in this society are differentiated with reference to ideological, cultural, political, and economic conditions. The demands that public schooling address democratic concerns implies a diverse set of political demands and priorities. Within this context, for example, it is possible to place black demands for adequate literacy training—a traditional concern in this group's struggle for power. (At the same time, however, there is a need to transform the concept of literacy from its circumscribed technical meaning to the kind of liberating pedagogy described by Paulo Freire.) It might also include integrated programs of women's (or minority group) studies, peace curricula that address the fatalism among young people associated with the threat of nuclear disaster, and instruction concerned with critical analysis of the popular culture.

The final element of a left political agenda for education is the issue of social justice. The choice of the word justice, as opposed to equality or equity, is significant. Unlike the latter terms (which have become fixed in too many minds with particular assumptions and associations—part of the liberal agenda), social justice is open and unformalized, requiring a more active and creative process of interpretation. It seems to transcend the political-legal domain and brings attention, instead, to civil society, to community and economic life. Rooting itself also in traditional meanings and concerns, it opens the way for exploring a series of questions that cannot but become an increasing focus of attention in the years to come. Among these are certain to be questions about hunger in the world as well as in our own society, the distribution of wealth and economic power, the inadequate supply of shelter and medical care, and problems of infant mortality. Such issues have a human and spiritual resonance that are not easily shunted aside as political questions. While capitalism in the United States is not on the agenda of mass political discourse, social justice issues, as they become an aspect of curriculum, open the way for a critical probing of taken-for-granted assumptions about our own social relations and social practices as they are structured around issues of national oppression, class domination, forms of gender and racial subordination, and discrimination as a function of age, sexuality, or mental or physical handicap. (One of the more significant recent examples of educational intervention concerning this issue is found in the Catholic schools' "Infusion" project. Such a curriculum stands as a harbinger not only of what is educationally possible, but also of the way in which a transformative consciousness can be generated and established in existing centers of cultural and ideological production.)

Obviously I have provided only a brief and schematic outline of directions and emphases for a political agenda of the educational Left. It is intended to be the beginning of an effort that would mediate the radical theoretical discourse of a decade or more with the moral, cognitive, and feeling structures that constitute the ideological dispositions of subordinate and intermediate groups in the United States at this historical juncture. In choosing three foci for the elaboration of such an agenda—moral and cultural crisis, empowerment, and justice—I have sought to form an ideological bridge that would connect those explicitly affirmed values and meanings of the official ideology (community, democracy, equality) with what Gramsci calls the consciousness that arises "in the practical transformation of reality." The former becomes more than merely false consciousness—a mechanism for mystifying what really exists in our social world. It provides, instead, the basis for moral affirmation as well as outrage—a set of transcendent values that have their roots in national mythology and in the vision of an idealized, if illusory, community. Such a vision is, as Marx noted in his discussion of religion, more than an opiate of the people; it is, too, the "sigh of the oppressed." It is our noble side, the side that yearns for a better world of more justice, freedom, and humanity that has been prefigured in the historical past. It offers itself to the present as a standard of critical judgment. In this sense such religious, national and popular mythologies become a potential source of real ideological weight in the ebb and flow of public debate and political discourse. While this provides the basis for the morally affirmative vision of our educational agenda, the latter—consciousness derived from the practical transformation of reality—is attuned to a critical awareness of the present reality. It incorporates into our agenda the deprivations and frustrations experienced by men and women in our culture and mediated through educational concerns and issues. One of these without the other will not do. Ethical admonitions and idealizations without critical apprehension of our real existing lives leads to an empty moralism; analytical insights, however penetrating, without the force of morally inspired demands leads to a sterile scientism. The effectiveness of the Right is its capacity to combine powerful moral exhortation with false, though seductive, depictions of reality. On the Left, on the other hand, one may locate brilliant forms of critical analysis in a landscape of moral aridity. Real human progress is inseparable from social movements that are impelled by the synthesis of consciousness and conscience (perhaps the more complete, if untranslatable, meaning of Freire's "consciencization"). It is the combination of self and social understanding linked to the force of moral outrage and assertion that is the indispensable condition for making possible greater freedom and justice and more democratic, cooperative, and compassionate forms of living. An educational agenda that seeks to do more than understand the world, that has the power to reshape at least a part of our reality, must effectively incorporate both forms of discourse. In the next chapter I will return to the part of this agenda concerned with the moral and cultural crisis, to explore the roots of what has been called "the politics of cultural despair."

2
Education and the Cultural Contradictions of Capitalism

AT THE CENTER of those attempts to revise critical descriptions of schooling is the rejection of the overly coherent or functionalist view of the social system, and the place of schools in it. There is a rejection of a social model in which the elements comprising it appear to be linked in an almost seamless fit.[1] Earlier attempts to employ Marxian categories in the analysis of schooling, whether in studies of the hidden curriculum, revisionist versions of educational history or, perhaps most notably, in the use of the "Correspondence Principle," talk overwhelmingly of the way in which school mirrors the industrial/ bureaucratic infrastructure. Education, as part of the ideological superstructure, does little more than reflect, correspond with, or provide a homologue to, the economic base. From this perspective, school becomes no more than a "transmission belt" for the delivery of capitalist ideology, and educational policies the unmediated product of dominant class interests. In the use of a simple or mechanical version of the Marxian categories of base and superstructure, school appears as part of a social system whose degree of functionality or integration excludes the possibilities of significant dissonance, opposition or contradictions. Not only do schools function to achieve a thorough accommodation of their students to the dominant ideology, but themselves fit into a broader process of socialization to produce an effect that is cohesive and mutually reinforcing.

In contrast, revised versions of radical school analysis recognize the extent to which opposition, disjunction and autonomy must be included in any description of the institutional and social structure. Drawing on both Gramscian and Althusserian theory, society, and especially capitalist society, is described as a precarious articulation of frequently disharmonious elements. In his study of schooling and the reproduction of labor, Paul Willis notes, "There are many breaks, lags, antagonisms, deep struggles and real subversive logics within and behind cultural processes of reproduction . . . ."[2] There is, says Willis, a tenuous and changing balance of ever-heightening contradictions at the heart of capitalism.

In the work that has emerged from this perspective, there is an awareness of schools being part of a social system in which an entirely coherent or integrated culture or ideology cannot be assumed. While some students develop a "counter school culture" to resist the imposition of dominant values and attitudes, schools themselves encourage beliefs and meanings which are, in no certain manner, congruous with all the demands of industrial capitalism. Neither in the internal processes of schools, or in the larger ideological arena of which schools are a part, can we expect the existence of a smoothly harmonious or seamless process of socialization.

Yet while such studies indicate a view of schooling that reflects the dissonant nature of our social experience, they still, in many ways, assume a functionalist standpoint. An adequate recognition of the conflicting and contradictory nature of the society is far from complete. Thus, even in the study by Willis, with its extraordinary sensitivity to the issue of disjunction and conflict, there is still a view of capitalist ideology as unitary and undivided. He argues that the "crucial divisions, distortions, and transferences which have been examined arise very often not so much from ideas and values mediated *downward* from the dominant social group but from internal cultural relationships."[3] It would appear in the argument that the ideology of capital itself is not the focus of significant divisions or contradictions. It is, of course, more typical of Marxist analysis to view cultural and ideological divisions occurring along a vertical rather than a horizontal axis: the cultural distinctions between groups that are hierarchically related form the usual focus of attention. In Willis's study of schooling (and his work is fairly typical in this regard) the actual focus of conflict is between the "official" and superordinate norms, values, and symbols of the institution, and the meanings, practices, typifications, attitudes of a subordinate group. Such a focus, not surprisingly, follows his concern to delineate the forms and modes of class antagonism in capitalist society. It is a product of the desire to demonstrate, above all other forms of division, the continued centrality of the struggle between dominant and subordinate classes. Such a concern carries a special urgency in the study of ideological transmission through schools. There is a critical need to reclaim the forms of social conflict, resistance and transformation from the dead hand of the Althusserian version of ideological dissemination, or the more simplistic versions of cultural hegemony.[4] While the first offers a lifeless and functional view of the process by which subjects are "interpellated" by the dominant ideology, the latter emphasizes the extent to which ideology, by so deeply saturating consciousness, prevents the emergence of counter interpretations of reality or experience. In contrast to this, school may be understood as not merely a place where society and consciousness are reproduced, but also as a place where these are *produced*—and done so with all the heat and sparks of a process in which the disempowered subvert, resist, and, sometimes, transform the power of those in control.

In attending to the process by which the social relations of capitalist society are reproduced (and the forms of vertical conflict that are a consequence of this) radical educational studies have usually ignored the separate and distinct issue of the reproduction of capital. While the former is concerned with the reproduction of the social structure focused around questions of hierarchy, and the division of the work force along sex, race, and class lines, the latter concerns the matter of ensuring the ideological conditions through which profit may be extracted from producers and realized through consumption. These conditions are fraught with tensions and conflicts that derive from the dual concerns of the capital accumulation process, that is, production *and* consumption. This duality necessitates ideological conditions structured in fundamentally contradictory ways. While emphasizing and demonstrating the cultural disjunctions and social conflicts within the hierarchical structures of schooling, critical scholars of education have paid scant attention to the dissonant nature of capital's own ideology. While this absence is notable among these scholars, other social commentators have not been so remiss. A major portion of this chapter attempts to draw together the work of those who have, in recent years, focused on the horizontal conflict in contemporary culture, and what has been called the "cultural contradictions of capitalism."[5] These writers describe in a variety of ways how the ruling ideology itself is fragmented and the source of serious discrepancies in the way the world may be understood and acted upon. Without seriously attending to this phenomenon, those concerned with schooling, ideological transmission and the formation of subjectivity are unable to develop an adequate theory of socialization in advanced capitalist societies.

The tendency to view the ruling ideology as monolithically structured must be sought in the predilection to see ideology as if it were (in Althusser's terms) a number worn on the back of a particular class. Ideology, in this sense, represents a badge of identity; a static configuration of values and beliefs that is possessed by a class and carried along by it, relatively unchanged as it makes its way through society. Whatever transformations this ideology undergoes as it encounters the dissonant subcultures of subordinate groups in no way alters the view of this ideology as a unitary entity, an ensemble of discursive elements defined by their coherence and consistency. In contrast to this is the belief—and underpinning the view presented in this chapter—that ideology is the correlate of human practices and social relationships. It is the representation at the level of language, imagery, and belief of the field of human activity and experience. It is, however, not merely a symbolic echo of the latter. Ideology provides the very medium that makes it possible to conduct these forms of human interaction, and to meaningfully anticipate our actions on, and in, the world. Such a view opens the possibility of far greater complexity in understanding the relations between capital and ideology. It is the foundation for grasping many of the conflicts, disjunctions and polarities found in the culture. Thus, for example, we must expect that as we move through the circuit of capital in contemporary society, from the phase in which human labor is embodied in commodities available for exchange (production) to the phase in which surplus value is realized by those who own and sell them (consumption), quite different beliefs, values, and meanings, will accompany the process. These differences ensure a sharp and fundamental contradiction in the culture of advanced capitalist societies. Such differences are the result of the very different relationships and practices that accompany the creation and production of material values from those that structure the process of their distribution and allocation.

In attempting to develop an adequate theory of socialization in advanced capitalist societies, it is clearly important to recognize the complex and fractured nature of the dominant ideology. This can only be done to the extent that class reductionist theories of ideology are rejected. There is no unitary ideology belonging to a dominant class that must be mediated "downward" to subaltern groups, through all of the mechanisms of ideological transmission (school, family, mass media, etc.). Chantal Mouffe[6] has argued that the persistence of this type of reductionism is the result of previous shortcomings in Marxist theory—its lack of understanding of the nature of ideologies and of the way in which we are constituted as subjects: "The prevailing conception—which manifests the general problematic of class reductionism—[is] that each class has a paradigmatic class ideology."[7] She continues: "The mistake of class reductionism is to reduce all social relations to social relations of production or to their ideological and political conditions of reproduction."[8] In contrast to this formulation, Mouffe notes that actually each individual is a participant in a series of different social relations and is therefore the locus of a plurality of determinations to which correspond a variety of subjective positions.

Radical theorists of education have persistently and overwhelmingly concerned themselves with "cultural production" in their study of schools. In so doing they have implicitly subscribed to a formulation of the socialization process that ignores the way each individual is a participant in a series of different social relations and is therefore the locus of a plurality of determinations. This overlooks the point made by Ernesto Laclau that the subjectivity of social agents is constantly changing because it is not a homogeneous subjectivity but a constantly recreated unity.[9] Laclau maintains: "The subject is permanently decentered insofar as the contents of his or her consciousness cannot be referred to an internal organizing core . . . but depend on specific forms of articulation which transcend the subjects themselves."[10]

The tendency to view the dominant ideology as a noncontradictory, essentially unified body of meanings, values, and assumptions has as one of its consequences the nonrecognition of this decentered subjectivity. The great majority of studies, in emphasizing the connection between schooling and the workplace (the productive phase of the circuit of capital), pay small heed to the important contradictions that actually attend bourgeois culture. For those concerned with education and the transmission of a dominant ideology, the inattention to this has meant a one-sided view of the culture. It is a view that obfuscates the extent to which such culture is a complex, conflict-ridden domain of human experiences. Far from being a structure of congruent, harmonious elements, the ideology that is mediated downward is pervaded by contradictions and antimonies that pit values, beliefs and meanings, and the apparatuses in which they are materialized, against each other. Without grasping this I do not believe it is possible to fully deal with questions that pertain to schooling and the process of socialization.

It is surprising that critical studies of education have assumed the uniformity of the dominant ideology. Given the pervasive nature of the cultural crisis in the United States—one that penetrates every social group—it would seem unlikely that anybody could identify, even within the "official" ensemble of values and meanings, with a consistent, noncontradictory way of understanding the world, or to a culture that offers a firm and coherent "guide to life." Such a view is little less than absurd in a world in which, by a great number of accounts, experience and meaning face each other with increasingly chaotic dissonance. It should, however, be recognized that one area where radical theorists of education have begun to make clearer the implications of the cultural contradictions of capitalism has concerned questions of gender socialization. Work in this area has pointed to fundamental contradictions in the socialization process. It has pointed to conflicts and dislocations existing within the transmitted system of significations—what we have referred to as horizontal conflicts in the culture. Feminist studies of schooling have begun to insist that we look at the dissonances in bourgeois ideology as girls are socialized at home and at school. These studies have added significantly to the sense of the schizophrenic quality of the socialization process. The split between the "private" values of domesticity and femininity, and "public" achievement (which, as we will see, is related to the broader division between production and consumption ideologies) permeates and afflicts females throughout the social order (though, of course, not identically in every social group).[11]

The significance of the attempt to redress the limited view of the dominant ideology, culture and the socialization process is not simply of theoretical value. It is precisely such a view that has facilitated the distorted view of education and educational history found in Christopher Lasch's influential work, *The Culture of Narcissism*.[12] While developing themes from other studies of culture in capitalist society, the work provides an account of schooling in America that, to a great extent, has buttressed the arguments of conservative and New Right critics of education during the 1970s and '80s. Given the radical posturing of Lasch's book, its conservative educational argument becomes apparent only after a careful review of the text, and an attempt to locate his argument in the broader parameters of the cultural analysis of capitalist society. New Right ideology must be understood as an outgrowth of the cultural crisis of this society; the disintegration, conflicts, and disjunctions that mark the ideology of dominant meanings and values. In this regard the work of the German social theorist Jürgen Habermas, systematized in his book *Legitimation Crisis*, provides an indispendable examination of the tendency toward contemporary crisis in advanced capitalist societies.[13] Habermas's work provides a model for attempts to integrate the crisis at the "system" level (the economic-political) with crises that have appeared in the cultural domain. With great insight, he links the increasing need for political-administrative interventions in the market with the effects of these interventions on the "taken-for-granted" meanings, assumptions, and values of the dominant culture. Whatever the weaknesses of this account in its tendency to hypostatize the distinctions between the "levels" of the social analysis, Habermas provides an important opening towards the development of a theory of socialization grounded in the political economy of advanced capitalist society. In this view schooling must be regarded as one part of a contradictory process of socialization that has become the unavoidable outgrowth of capital's own contradictory economic logic.

Origins of the "Motivation Crisis"

Thomas McCarthy, in his commentary on Habermas's three "moments" of crisis, notes that whereas his rationality crisis (see chapter 5) is concerned with economic or administrative tendencies, the focus of both Habermas's motivation and legitimation crises are socio-cultural in orientation. They are both, as he puts it, concerned with "disturbances in the delicate complementarity between the requirements of the state apparatus and the occupational system, on the one hand, and the interpreted needs and legitimate expectations of the members of society on the other."[14] While legitimation problems arise from changes resulting from expanded state activities, motivational problems result from changes in the sociocultural system itself. The core of the argument concerning Habermas's motivational crisis is the view that "the socio-cultural system is changing in such a way that its output becomes dysfunctional for the state and the system of social labor."[15] In particular, the view that the central motivational patterns required for the stability of advanced capitalist society—the "syndromes of civil and familial-vocational privatism"—are being under mined.

Among Habermas's arguments for the demise of those components of bourgeois ideology directly related to our patterns of privatistic motivation is, as we noted earlier, the erosion of the belief in achievement ideology: the belief that rewards should be distributed on the basis of individual achievement. As means to allocate rewards and to distribute gratification, Habermas argues that both the market itself and the process of formal schooling have increasingly lost their credibility as fair mechanisms for distributing life opportunities. Neither appears to satisfy the preconditions of achievement ideology which requires "equal opportunity to participate in a competition that is regulated so as to neutralize external influences."[16] It has been recognized, in the case of the market, that social force is exercised in the forms of economic exchange. In the case of schooling Habermas pinpoints more specifically the reason for a breakdown in achievement ideology. We will consider these reasons later when we look at the implications of the motivation crisis for education.

In addition to the decline of achievement ideology, another key element of the privatistic world view—"possessive individualism"—has also become problematic. As advanced capitalist societies reach a level of social wealth in which it is no longer simply "a question of averting a few fundamental risks to life and satisfying basic needs," the determination of individual preference systems becomes more complex and more unclear.[17] The constant interpretation and reinterpretation of needs can, despite massive manipulation, lead to preference systems that are dysfunctional for the political-economic system. In addition, the quality and conditions of life in complex urban society become ever more dependent on the shared aspects of the infrastructure (such as transportation, leisure, health-care, education), areas that are less subject to differentiated demands and private appropriation (that is to say, either we all have clean air or no one does, and so on). Moreover, as leisure pursuits acquire increased importance, so needs that cannot be satisfied monetarily expand.

Habermas argues that the dominant culture contains three important elements which, despite their quintessentially bourgeois nature, are incompatible with the preservation of traditional beliefs or values. These he refers to as "scientism," "post-auratic art," and a "universalist morality."[18] The growth of science and technology, he says, and the spread of scientific-technical modes of thought, have proved to be incompatible with, for example, religion, the fatalism of the lower classes, and traditional civil attitudes: "Traditional attitudes or belief," he asserts, "cannot withstand the demand for discursive justification established by modern science."[19] Those traditions, he continues, which fostered civil and familial privatism are being "non-renewably dismantled" by the spread of an ethic of "rationalization" and an expansion of the "authority of science" (encompassing, as they do, a critique of arbitrary structures of prejudice or belief). What Habermas calls post-auratic art has produced, for the first time, a counterculture "arising from the center of bourgeois society itself and hostile to the possessive-individualism, achievement and advantage-oriented lifestyle of the bourgeoisie."[20] Disregarding the aura of classical art and asserting its radical autonomy from society, modern art "expresses not the promise but the irretrievable sacrifice of bourgeois rationalization. . . ."[21] The counterculture produced by way of this art contributes to the divergence between the values of the cultural system and those required by the political and economic system.

Finally, says Habermas, liberal capitalism gave, for the first time, binding force to a strictly universalistic value system. Such universalism compels the adoption of a communicative ethic in which the only norms that may claim generality "are those on which everyone affected agrees (or would agree) without constraint if they enter into (or were to enter into) a process of discursive will-formation."[22] Unlike the system of "formalistic ethics" which preceded it and was restricted to a domain of private morality, Habermas notes that only a communicative ethics is universal, and also guarantees autonomy (it implies both a consensus on values as well as respecting individual will and consciousness). As a result, says Habermas, the privately oriented motivational patterns essential to "formal" democracy are threatened with disintegration—a threat that can be documented in the spread of the syndrome of withdrawal and protest. Communicative ethics as well as experimental countercultures (in which post-auratic art is incorporated) are today determining typical socialization processes among segments of the society. They have, in Habermas's words, achieved "motive-forming power." Such developments in the cultural system make it increasingly difficult to ensure what he refers to as a conventional outcome of adolescence. The decreasing probability of such an outcome is supported, Habermas argues, by the following indicators:

> (1) expansion of the educational system is lengthening training periods and making possible for increasing proportions of the population a psycho- social moratorium in early adolescence (from the thirteenth to the sixteenth year) and an extension of this phase (in extreme cases, to the age of 30);
> (2) improved formal schooling of cognitive capacities increases the probability that dissonances between proffered patterns of interpretation and perceived social reality will arise and intensify the problem of identity;
> (3) development of egalitarian family structures and spread of child rearing techniques typical of the middle classes promote processes of socialization that tend to burden youth with adolescent problems;
> (4) loosening of sexual prohibitions made possible by pharmaceutics works itself out (as does temporary liberation—differentiated according to social strata—from directly economic pressures) in such a way that

socialization processes free of anxiety, with an expanded scope for experimentation, become more probable for adolescents.[23]

Consumption and the Decline of Achievement Ideology

Fundamental to Habermas's claims of a motivation crisis in advanced capitalist societies is his assertion concerning the erosion of achievement ideology. Central to this is his argument concerning the increasingly problematic nature of the relationship between occupational success and formal schooling (the primary means through which this ideology is mediated). Habermas argues that the schooling version of achievement ideology can only claim credibility for itself if the following conditions are met: equal opportunity for admission to higher education; nondiscriminatory standards of evaluation for performance in school; and synchronous developments of the educational and occupational systems.[24]

He notes that while educational justice, in terms of opportunities for admission and standards of evaluation, may have increased in all advanced capitalist countries since World War II, a countertendency can be observed in the other dimensions. There is increasing disharmony between the expansion of the educational system and opportunities available in the occupational structure. The connections, he notes, between formal schooling and occupational success are becoming looser. There can be little doubt, in the United States for example, that this is the case. Indeed, as Michael Harrington has shown, the declining "payoff" in schooling has already reached critical proportions:

> In 1980, for instance, between 20 percent and 21 percent of the labor force will hold degrees, but the share of professional and technical workers... in the economy will be between 14.9 percent and 15.4 percent (in 1960, 10 percent of the labor force had finished college and professional and technical workers were 11 percent). Another projection estimates that, in 1985, 2.5 college graduates will be competing for every "choice" job, thus generating a "surplus" of two hundred thousand degree holders.[25]

At the same time, Habermas notes that "intrinsic motivation to achieve is less and less supported by the structure of labor processes in spheres of labor dependent on the market. An instrumentalist attitude to labor is spreading even in traditional bourgeois vocations (middle- and higher-level employees, professionals)."[26] It is an argument for which there is now ample evidence in the United States. Despite the increasing length of education as well as intensified competition for occupational positions, the reality of white-collar or professional work in many spheres falls far short of its promise. There has been what Stanley Aronowitz and others have called a "proletarianization" of white-collar labor.[27] Such work is increasingly fragmented, monotonous, and bureaucratized. While the opportunity to work "downtown" and wear a suit and tie still hold their attraction over the conditions of manual work, the former is less and less associated with the kind of autonomy or intellectual opportunity suggested by the long years of educational training. Such changes have significantly undermined the motivational value of the achievement ideology of schooling with its demand for investments of present time and energy (deferral of immediate gratification) in exchange for the promise of future reward.

Given the connection between schooling and achievement ideology, the wider sociocultural changes described by Habermas also indicate an erosion of those values and beliefs apposite to educational institutions. Certainly his claims concerning the "reinterpretation of needs" so that they become dysfunctional to the political-economic system portends an important schism in the motivational structure of capitalist society. Indeed, this has been the thesis of a number of social commentators in the United States during the last decade. Daniel Bell, for example, a conservative critic, notes that from about the 1920s on, the traditional notions of bourgeois morality and values have been under attack from cultural attitudes spawned by the rise of mass consumption society. The emergence in the United States of the consumption-oriented society with its emphasis on spending and material possessions undermines the traditional system of values that emphasized thrift, frugality, self-control, and impulse-renunciation. In place of a culture concerned with how to work and achieve, the focus is now on how to spend and enjoy. Bell argues that despite "some continuing use of the language of the Protestant ethic, the fact was that by the 1950s American culture had become primarily hedonistic, concerned with play, fun, display and pleasure—and, typical of things in America, in a compulsive way."[28]

The abandonment of Puritanism and the Protestant ethic creates, says Bell, an important contradiction in the norms of the culture:

> On the one hand, the business corporation wants an individual to work hard, pursue a career, accept delayed gratification—to be, in the crude sense, an organization man. And yet, in its products and its advertisements, the corporation promotes pleasure, instant joy, relaxing and letting go. One is to be "straight" by day and a "swinger" by night.[29]

Bell argues that the transformation of society and the erosion of the traditional bourgeois ethic were aided by a number of social inventions that facilitated a consumption-oriented culture. Among these were the spread of installment buying which broke down the old Protestant fears of debt; the development of marketing "which rationalized the art of identifying different kinds of buying groups and whetting consumer appetites," as well as mass production on an assembly line.[30] In addition to the availability of automobiles which allowed escape from the repressive sanctions of small town society, the introduction of movies offered "a window on the world, a set of ready-made daydreams, fantasies and projection...."[31] And the use of intense advertising and planned obsolescence ensured that selling "became the most striking activity of contemporary America. Against frugality, selling emphasized prodigality; against asceticism, the lavish display."[32]

In a culture that applauded immediate gratification, fun, and consumption, the idea of installment selling struck at the very notion of saving or abstinence which is at the moral heart of the Protestant ethic: "Being moral meant being industrious and thrifty. If one wanted to buy something one should save for it."[33] For years, writes Bell, such was the grim spectacle of middle-class morality that people were afraid to be overdrawn at the bank. By the end of the 1960s however, the banks were strenuously advertising the services of cash reserves that would allow a depositor to overdraw up to several thousand dollars. No one, he says, need be deferred from gratifying his impulses at auction or sale. The hedonistic values of the consumption culture have all but destroyed the Protestant concern with work, and the Puritan emphasis on a forbidding attitude towards life. In place of the traditional virtues of industry, thrift, discipline, and sobriety, the contemporary world of hedonism is a world of fashion, photography, advertising, television and travel: "It is a world of make-believe in which one lives for expectations, for what will come rather than what is. And it must come without effort."[34] While within the traditional culture gratification of forbidden impulses aroused guilt, now failure to have fun and successfully pursue pleasure lowers one's self-esteem. The contradictions, described by Daniel Bell, between the culture of production and the culture of consumption (the former emphasizing the values of work, perseverance, and discipline, and the latter, relaxation, pleasure, and gratification) have been paralleled in a number of studies which focus on the effects of the division of labor in capitalist society.

Eli Zaretsky, for example, describes how the split between production and consumption contains within it a second split: that between our personal lives and our place within the social division of labor.[35] He locates these splits in the historical development of capitalism. As capitalism developed, Zaretsky argues, the production functions performed by the family were increasingly socialized. Production within the family (housework, child rearing) developed since it was no longer viewed as integral to the production of commodities. At the same time, Zaretsky suggests, the family acquired new functions in the realm of personal life. It became the primary institution in which the search for personal happiness, love, and fulfillment takes place:

> By splitting society between "work" and "life", [capitalism] created the conditions under which men and women looked to themselves, outside the division of labor, for meaning and purpose.... The organization of production around alienated labour encouraged the creation of a separate sphere of life in which personal relations were pursued as an end in themselves.[36]

Zaretsky argues that the creation of a separate sphere of personal life was also shaped by the special needs of capitalism in the early twentieth century. Intensifying proletarianization, he suggests, and deepening economic crises created increasing labor unrest and class conflict, as well as the growth of the socialist movement. Beginning in the early twentieth century, a significant minority of American capitalists saw the possibility of integrating labor within a capitalist consensus through raising its level of consumption; and the family, no longer a commodity-producing unit, received new importance as the focus of the mass consumption market. As a result, American domestic and personal life is now governed by an ethic of pleasure and self-gratification previously unknown to a laboring class. Working people now see consumption as an end itself, rather than an adjunct to production. Zaretsky suggests that this is often expressed within the middle class as "life-style"—a word that is often used to define one's prerogatives regardless of the demands of "society." Such changes in capitalism, he asserts, have caused a profound democratization of the idea that it is good to live well, consume pleasurably, and enjoy the fruits of one's labor. It has vastly extended the range of "personal" experience available to men and women. At the same time, mass consumption retains an abstract and passive mode—the purchase and consumption of commodities:

> Taste, sensibility and the pursuit of subjective experience—historically reserved for leisure classes and artists—have been generalized throughout the population in predetermined and standardized forms of advertising and other means.[37]

Above all, Zaretsky makes clear that the emergence of the culture of consumption as the dialectical opposite to that of production in bourgeois society, was inextricably linked to the intensified concern with personal and domestic life in such society. As work, underemployment, and rationalization have come close to destroying people's understanding of their part in the system of production, leaving them feeling little meaning or value in what they do, so it has reinforced the tendency to look to personal life for meaning and to understand personal life in purely subjective terms:

> The isolation of so much of modern life from the sphere of necessary goods production gives it its "abstract" character. Both "society" and personal life are experienced as formless, with no common core, in inexplicable disarray.[38]

It is clear that the development of capitalism created a sphere of personal life, centered around the family and underpinned by the ethic and imperatives of consumption. It has led, according to Zaretsky, to a personal life characterized by subjectivity—the search for personal identity outside the social division of labor. Such separation ensures the increasingly intense, and tense, nature of personal life in capitalistic society:

> This new emphasis on one's personal feelings and inner needs, one's "head" or "life-style," to use contemporary formulations, gives a continued meaning to family life and at the same time threatens to blow it apart.[39]

Zaretsky argues that as it became increasingly cut off from production the contemporary family has become a "well of subjectivity" divorced from social meaning. To compensate for the rationalization and impersonality in our productive life, the family has become a "world of vast psychological complexity." The internal life of the family has attempted to be a "haven in a heartless world"—an arena dominated by the search for personal fulfillment. Indeed what distinguishes developed capitalist society, asserts Zaretsky, is the stress on individual development and uniqueness which, unlike previous civilizations, characterizes not just a handful of individuals prized for their special qualities, but all of society:

> The bourgeoisie made its revolution on behalf of a specific property form—private property—which it already possessed. But the only "property" that the proletariat possesses lies within itself: our inner lives and social capabilities, our dreams, our desires, our fears, our sense of ourselves as inter-connected beings. Reflecting the "separation" of personal life from production a new idea has emerged on a mass scale; that of human relations and human beings, as an end in themselves.[40]

Following a similar line of analysis the English sociologist Arthur Brittan refers to the process by which individuals find meaning and identity outside of the bureaucratic world of work as "privatization."[41] While Brittan notes that the concept of privacy has been around a long time ("The slogan 'An Englishman's home is his castle' is resonant of a bourgeois style of life."), its more contemporary meaning is associated with the emergence of a consumer orientation in western capitalism. Indeed, the "separation of spheres" (work from consumption, personal life from society) has become the linchpin for analysis of the family and of women in modern society. The separation of the family from production and social life has left an emotional battleground in which women have found themselves in an increasingly isolated and exploited situation. Of course, as Brittan notes, such privatization is supported by a vast advertising industry which has made it the key to providing individual fulfillment:

> Advertisers sell privatization—they sell the means whereby individuals isolate themselves from the demands and obligations of political and social relationships; they sell the glorious picture of the "good life" lived by beautiful people in suburban utopias.[42]

The Culture of Consumption—Interpretations and Possibilities

The pivot of the privatization argument is the belief that capitalism has been fundamentally transformed from an economy of production into one of mass consumption. Such a view suggests a notion of culture in capitalist society in which the conflict between the ethic of production and that of consumption has been resolved in favor of the latter. The impulse towards pleasure, gratification, and fun (to whatever extent these are, in Marcuse's terminology, repressively sublimated) has become the defining feature of contemporary bourgeois society. Such a view is indeed found in the conclusions of writers as diverse as Alain Touraine, Christopher Lasch, Richard Sennett, Herbert Marcuse, Ralf Dahrendorf, and Kenneth Galbraith. The French sociologist Alain Touraine,[43] for example, argues:

> We are witnessing the weakening of cultural expressions bound to a particular social group. Nothing could be clearer than the decline of traditional "worker culture." . . . For the mass of semi-skilled workers, participation in the culture is no longer based on professional life or traditional social roles but on consumption of items and products produced for the entire society.[44]

Such arguments must be seen as part of the larger discussion concerning what is sometimes called the "new working class" thesis in western society. The thesis contains a view of society in which traditional working class divisions, loyalties and ideology have declined to be replaced by a "middle-class" consumption ethic in which the private individual is encouraged to retreat into the confines of home and garden. Such a retreat, as has been described by Herbert Marcuse, is fueled by a culture whose internal dynamic is the stimulation of an "insatiability of wants."[45] Marcuse has been, undoubtedly, the most influential of those theorists who have argued that the culture of consumption has become thoroughly pervasive in advanced capitalist society. For Marcuse the pursuit of gratification and pleasure has been made indivisible from the desire for goods and consumer durables. Advertising creates an insatiable appetite for the items produced by the capitalist economy. Such is the nature of the integration of consumer goods and individual wants that the great mass of people in contemporary society are caught in a web of false desires and illusionary satisfactions. The atmosphere of hedonism and release that appears to saturate capitalist society offers only the fantasy of individual freedom and personal expression.

More recently the thesis that a consumption-oriented culture has become dominant in American society is found in Christopher Lasch's influential work. Indeed its title, *The Culture of Narcissism*, has almost become emblematic of such a viewpoint.[46] According to Lasch the cultural ethic in American society must be seen to have undergone a fundamental transformation. The "production" culture of work, deferred gratification, self-discipline, industry, moderation, and avoidance of debt has been overturned. Its place has been taken by a "present-oriented hedonism" and an ethic of pleasure (though, Lasch asserts, contemporary hedonism originates not in the pursuit of pleasure but in a struggle for interpersonal advantage):

> In an age of diminishing expectations, the Protestant virtues no longer excite enthusiasm. Inflation erodes investments and savings. Advertising undermines the horror of indebtedness, exhorting the consumer to buy now and pay later. As the future becomes menacing and uncertain only fools put off until tomorrow the fun they can have today. A profound shift in our sense of time has transformed work habits, values and the definition of success. Self-preservation has replaced self-improvement as the goal of earthly improvement....[47]

For Lasch the culture of narcissism has invaded every area of our social lives. The deterioration of the educational system, for example, reflects the waning social demands for initiative, enterprise and the competition to achieve. The decline of critical thought and the erosion of intellectual standards reflect the ascendance of a hedonistic culture which has encouraged a pedagogy of easy indulgence. Like Marcuse, Lasch argues that the American economy, having reached a point where its technology was capable of satisfying basic material wants now relies on the creation of consumer demands:

> In a simpler time, advertising merely called attention to the product and extolled its advantages. Now it manufactures a product of its own: the consumer, perpetually unsatisfied, restless, anxious and bored. Advertising seems not so much to advertise products as to promote consumption as a way of life. It "educates" the masses into an unappeasable appetite not only for goods but for new experiences, and personal fulfillment.[48]

The erosion of the culture of production and its transformation into one concerned with subjectivity, consumption, and personal life find expression in other studies, though in terms more positive. While these studies have emphasized the extent to which a consumption-oriented culture is a repressive and alienating phenomenon, other writers have noted what they see as its liberating or humanizing effects. Perhaps the most prolific and influential of these has been Theodore Roszak. In a recent book Roszak speaks of our passing through a revolution, though one concerned with more than the traditional demands of bread, work and physical security:[49]

> Behind these obvious and absolute necessities—but no less fierce in its demands—there stands an appetite for personal recognition, for the recognition of each of us as a special and significant event in the universe, a center of delicate sensibilities and radical originality. On a scale that has no historical precedent, we are becoming interesting to ourselves and to one another as beings who carry unexpected destinies into the world.[50]

In strong disagreement with the assertions of Lasch, Bell and others, of the rise of a pathological narcissism, Roszak claims that the new "personalist sensibility" challenges the orthodox culture; the "sensitive quest for fulfillment," he says, "must not be confused with the riotous hedonism of our consumption economy." Their critical perspective fails to distinguish a true revolt of the people on behalf of the human need for personal growth, and against "massification," assigned roles, restrictive social routines, institutions (work, education, government, corporations) that seem to have been designed for *everybody* in general, but for nobody in particular. In place of the traditional sublimated virtues—self restraint, dutiful citizenship, the work ethic, (and above all) deference of needs, Roszak detects the inauguration of society "whose every imperative and policy must yield to the demands of personal fulfillment."[51]

While Hans Dreitzel in his study of the "Political Meaning of Culture" warns against the dangers of drawing general conclusions from the California scene (Roszak lives in the San Francisco Bay area), he concurs, nevertheless, that the search for a new personal and communal identity is spreading within the middle class as well as among working-class youth.[52] Nor, according to this writer, can the decline in traditional bourgeois values, especially those associated with capitalist production, be viewed as merely the switch from one form of repressive social order to another. Viewed as a liberating tendency, the counter-cultural movement of the '60s has spawned an increasingly pervasive rejection of traditional bourgeois standards—standards organized around the centrality of production—technocratic and instrumental rationality, the temporality of industrial society ("tyranny of the clock"), bureaucratic attitudes, life planning, and career mobility. The declared goal of the counterculture movement, asserts Dreitzel, was a reorganization of our private lives around the values of spontaneity, fantasy, solidarity, communal experience, and a noninstrumental aesthetic approach to nature. The youth movement of the '60s, argues Dreitzel, "initiated a general search for a new integration of the moral, religious, and aesthetic dimension of life which threatens the psychological credibility of the industrial system."[53] Such a search has undermined the motivational structure of bourgeois man, and the ideology of productive life in the capitalist industrial system.

At the core of what Dreitzel views as the decline of bourgeois "economic man" is the crisis of "instrumental rationality." It is this rationality which underpins "the development of the scientific world view [which has] provided the bourgeoisie with the instrumental attitude towards nature which became the basis of its economic achievements."[54] The ideology of production in capitalist society rested on a concept of nature which "stripped of all magical projections" became a mere resource for exploitation. While, says Dreitzel, it is today difficult to comprehend how the culturally dominant classes were satisfied with economic progress as the central goal of their worldly existence, it is necessary to recall the miserable material conditions of life before the industrial revolution:

> The achievements were enormous: for a period of about a hundred and fifty years every generation could experience a substantial increase of material well-being over the past generation. The moment such compensations became scarce the old problems of how to meaningfully interpret the natural boundaries of life become pertinent again.[55]

It is Dreitzel's thesis "that with decreasing growth rates in all industrial societies and with increasing psychological pauperization the future of culture will be mainly a reinterpretation of our relationship to nature."[56] He suggests that the beginning of this development can be seen today in the growing ecological consciousness, increasing public debate on issues of physical and mental health, and the rise of "syncretistic" religious movements which emphasize a cosmological equilibrium between nature and consciousness:

> The psychological misery which is the cause of the general search for a new basis of authenticity, is the subtle revenge nature has taken against a culture which has celebrated its purely instrumental relation to nature in the great achievements of scientific medicine and the technological creation of artificial environments.[57]

For Dreitzel the culture of production in bourgeois society has unleashed its own antithesis. The consciousness associated with this antithesis is, he believes, likely to grow in the ensuing crisis of the world-wide economic system. Despite the political failures of the New Left and the short-lived and unique character of the May 1968 events in France, they provided brief moments "when the expressive aspects of modern life won a short-lived victory over the instrumental aspects...."[58] The "sensualization of reason," the "spiritualization of nature," spontaneity, community, and subjectivity had begun the historic process of transforming the culture of production—achievement motivation, instrumental rationality, the domination of man and nature by man, and the reification of human relations and activity. It would, increasingly, Dreitzel predicts, open a gap between the shattered old values and the not-yet-established new ones.

Whatever the more obvious limits of its methodological approach, support for Roszak and Dreitzel is provided in the studies undertaken by Daniel Yankelovitch and his associates.[59] Like them Yankelovitch argues that the "new consciousness" which developed in the 1960s on the campuses and in the counterculture has now worked its way through large sections of the middle class and parts of the working class:

> By the seventies ... most Americans were involved in projects to prove that life can be more than a grim economic chore. Americans from every walk of life were suddenly eager to give more meaning to their lives, to

find fuller self-expression . . . . The search for self-fulfillment has developed into a prime source of energy in American culture . . . . The life experiments of self-fulfillment seekers often collide violently with traditional rules, creating a national battle of moral norms. Millions of Americans are hungry to live their lives to the brim, determined to consume every dish on the smorgasbord of human experience.[60]

The challenge to traditional norms, says Yankelovitch, has found a variety of expressions in the larger society—in the women's movement, in the consumer, environmental and quality-of-life movements, in the greater acceptance of sexuality, in the emphasis on self-help, in a new preoccupation with the body and physical fitness, and above all, "in a search for the 'full, rich life' ripe with leisure, new experience and enjoyment as a substitute for the orderly, work-centered way of earlier decades."[61]

Education and the "Culture of Narcissism"—Propaganda for the Right?

The hopeful prognostications of these latter writers do not reveal the precise relationship between the rising expectations of self-fulfillment, the development of a personalist sensibility, and the existence of a consumption-oriented culture. Whatever is the exact nature of this culture, it stands on one side of a societal divide, on the other side of which is a culture of fundamentally opposing values and beliefs. The dominant culture in contemporary society is neither unitary nor monolithic, but characterized by the deep fissure that exists between the values of production (discipline, restraint, deferral) and consumption (pleasure, gratification, and subjectivity). This division, I believe, must be fully incorporated into any model that purports to understand the nature of schooling in America. Failure to do so has contributed to the functionalist explanations of schooling so common in the recent literature and an inability to assess and politically confront the relationship between schooling and the notion of a "culture of narcissism."[62] Such a notion, whether applied to issues of the family, sexuality or education, divides left critics to such extent that it reinforces reactionary concerns and anxieties. Within this context, Christopher Lasch's popular and influential psychosociology of American life in the '70s must be analyzed as paradigmatic. His work, while striking a radical social posture, feeds the rhetorical appetites of conservative and New Right critics of education in the United States in the current period.

Like Bell, Lasch describes an America in which the production values of bourgeois culture have been replaced by those of consumption:

> The growth of bureaucracy, the cult of consumption with its immediate gratifications, but above all the severance of the sense of historical

continuity, have transformed the Protestant ethic while carrying the underlying principles of capitalist society to their logical conclusion. The pursuits of self-interest, formerly identified with the rational pursuit of gain and the accumulation of wealth, has become a search for pleasure and psychic survival.... In the resulting state of organized anarchy... pleasure becomes life's only business....[63]

The demands of the mass-consumption economy, argues Lasch, have made the work ethic obsolete even for workers, and the "propaganda of consumption" has educated the masses into an unappeasable appetite, not only for goods but also for new experiences and personal fulfillment. Industry, moderation, and self-discipline, have been replaced by a cult of immediate gratification, and "present-oriented" hedonism (albeit that such hedonism is a fraud and disguises an often vicious and exploitative struggle for power). Economic man, argues Lasch, has given way to the psychological man of our time—one who "demands immediate gratification and lives in a state of restless, perpetually unsatisfied desire."[64] Changes in American life have carried the logic of bourgeois individualism "to the extreme of a war of all against all, the pursuit of happiness to the dead-end of a narcissistic preoccupation with the self...."[65] The Happy Hooker, he says, stands in place of Horatio Alger as the prototype of personal success.

It is within the context of a society in which the apparatuses of mass promotion attack ideologies based on the postponement of gratification that Lasch's notion of schooling is situated. His critique of American public education turns on two major assertions: the historical demise of a "basic education" concerned with the development of a disciplined and critical intelligence; and the tendency of public schooling to have become organized around experiences that reflect and nurture the narcissistic proclivities of the wider culture. Lasch, it seems, dates the latter tendency from the reforms of the progressive era which (together with the rise of an educational bureaucracy, and the installation of a differentiated system of industrial recruitment), saw the introduction of courses, programs, and activities that were fundamentally concerned to keep the student reasonably contented, while engaged in an undemanding program of study.

The establishment of this indulgent pedagogy continued through the 1940s reaching its apotheosis in the educational reforms of the 1960s. Evidence of the spread of its methods, says Lasch, and of its disastrous effect on students' minds abound:

> Under cover of enlightened ideology, teachers (like parents) have followed the line of least resistance hoping to pacify their students and to sweeten the time they have to spend in school by making them as painless as possible.[66]

And at the door of these effects (the "steady dilution of intellectual standards") could be laid, above all, the body of progressive educational theory and practice: in the early part of the twentieth century, the emphasis on experience and real activity; in the '40s, "education for life adjustment"; and in the '60s, free expression, relevance, "schools-without-walls," the open classroom, tailoring education to the needs of the individual.

Not surprisingly, given Lasch's view of the modern American school as a place of easy indulgence, the notion of authoritarianism as a pervasive characteristic of such environments is dismissed as only "allegedly rampant." Any other conclusion would, of course, be incompatible with his view that school, as an institution of cultural transmission, has been shaped by the narcissistic character of our culture, and thus attempts to do little more than provide ready gratification of students' whims. School, according to this view, being the embodiment of a narcissistic culture, must be characterized by the absence of any form of discipline. And yet it surely requires more than Lasch's brief assertion to adequately refute the sometimes powerful, often eloquent, and certainly voluminous account of American schooling that has accumulated during the last twenty years, which has drawn attention, again and again, to precisely this aspect of the educational process. The account, extending from the admittedly more sentimental writers of the 1960s to the more analytical and dispassionate ones of recent years, amounts to what is a view of the classroom quite contrary to that suggested by Lasch: frequently regimented and despotic, pervasively authoritarian, and usually demanding a chronic repression of present interests, concerns, or needs in the name of some future reward.

Far from having severed its links to the culture of production and the development of bourgeois "economic" man, education, with its emphasis on investing for the long-term, is its quintessential expression. It continues to be the very embodiment of that notion of delayed gratification which is central to traditional bourgeois values. Studies in the "hidden curriculum" of schooling have, for example, made quite clear how individuals are socialized to the important distinction between "play" and "work"—a distinction central to the constitution of such values. In this, play, with its notions of immediate gratification and personal satisfaction, is subordinated to work, an activity undertaken for overwhelmingly extrinsic purposes (compulsion, fear, social advancement)[67] In this process school plays an important role in the training of alienated forms of social activity (especially those associated with production). Nothing written by Lasch in his chapter on education undoes the penetrating impression created by a multitude of studies in which school appears as a stultifying and unsatisfying environment, one whose legitimacy derives not from the reified and abstract activities undertaken there, but simply from its claim to reward present self-discipline (repression) with future gratification.

It may be that Lasch, in his eagerness to paint a picture of American history in which there is a clear rupture between the earlier (and apparently now defunct) production-oriented values of capitalism (such as self-discipline and restraint) and the now dominant consumption values (instant gratification, hedonism) has created an inaccurate version of educational history—a version in which the past is romanticized and the present distorted. Despite significant changes in the institutional forms of schooling it may be that, at least as far as pedagogy is concerned, continuity rather than fracture is the watchword. In the studies undertaken by this writer, for example, of radical criticism of schools produced both in the first decades of the twentieth century, as well as in the 1960s and '70s, it is the frequent similarities in the descriptions of classrooms that are most apparent: the emphasis on authoritarian regulation, the unrequited needs of students, the absence of free expression, spontaneity, or cooperative human endeavor, and a curriculum constructed around remote instrumental criteria.[68] If "progressive education" stood for (or, indeed, brought about) an emphasis on immediate gratification and individual indulgence, as is suggested by Lasch (and is, hence, responsible for the erosion of educational standards), its successes are less apparent than he seems to assert. Lasch, it appears, in the mold of more conventional conservative commentators, has set up straw men whose alleged successes have undermined all that is most valued in public education. Indeed, for those of us more sympathetic to aspects of progressive educational reform we could only wish that schools had, in fact, entered an era in which they addressed individual needs, indulged students' interests or concerns, valued free expression and spontaneity. Alas, despite Lasch's history, this in no way describes schooling in American society which remains firmly embedded in the matrix of traditional bourgeois virtues—discipline, restraint, achievement, and an emphasis on future salvation (or, at least, graduation).

At the core of Lasch's reconstituted conservative critique of schooling is not only his attack on the reforms promulgated by the student movement of the 1960s, blacks, women, as well as other liberal and radical critics of education (all parts of his "progressive" erosion of educational standards), but also the attempt to propose as their replacement a return to traditional or "basic" forms of educational curricula. Through his attempt to identify such curricula with an education oriented towards the development of a critical intelligence, Lasch obfuscates what is the fundamentally conservative nature of his proposal. Not that I am suggesting here some cynical or devious intention in his analysis. More likely is that his attack "on the proposition, long embedded in the practice of schools, that academic standards are inherently elitist and that universal education therefore requires the dilution of standards" is sincerely held, but deficient in an understanding of the ideological nature of school knowledge.[69] To dismiss, for example, the proposals for a culturally pluralistic approach to curriculum as merely another example of the narcissistic erosion of standards is to miss the very real social and political consequences associated with the organization, selection, and dissemination of knowledge in school. Such arguments, as well as Lasch's assertions concerning other reforms (such as programs in black history, women's studies, the movement for "relevance" in education) are misleadingly dismissed as but more examples of anti-intellectualism, and the demand for undisciplined indulgence. It is a position that precisely misses (or ignores) the pedagogic context from within which such reforms were generated—one that deplored the uncritical, trivial, and scholastically remote nature of the curricular traditions that have chronically dominated education—the very traditions that appear to so impress Lasch.

In essence, Lasch's assimilation of the "basic" curriculum to notions of intellectual exertion and critical inquiry (despite his assertions of its applicability to all, not just to a cultural elite) in no way detracts from the fundamentally conservative nature of his argument concerning schools. It represents radical posturing while actually making proposals that differ little from the, by now, familiar strictures of "back-to-basics" advocates and New Right educational policy makers. His assertion of the need to return to "excellence" as the goal of education is the sadly familiar rhetoric that has underpinned the historical litany of racist, sexist, and class-biased selection procedures used in schools—one that can only ensure the maintenance and reinforcement of educational, cultural, and economic hierarchies. The mobilization of Lasch's social analysis to condemn the educational reforms of the '60s and early '70s fits precisely the arguments promulgated by conservative critics of education who have associated these reforms with what they view as the dangerously permissive character of that period, while advocating a "basic" education in the name of serious and disciplined intellectual endeavor. Lasch, in assigning the movement of the '60s to this culture of narcissism, vindicates, unwittingly or otherwise, those who, while appearing to applaud real intellectual inquiry, are, in fact, the advocates of authoritarian pedagogic relations, despotic regulation of students' lives, and a curriculum remote from human experience.

It may well be, however, that the real analytical weakness of Lasch's study is that in associating the reforms or attempted reforms of the 1960s with the final ascendancy of a culture oriented around the values of consumption, he has failed to recognize the presence of elements of "negativity" (in the sense suggested by members of the Frankfurt School). He has ignored the crucial dialectical character of culture and cultural change. So that while he may be correct in associating the rise of a consumerist mentality with, for example, falsely liberating pursuits and the "banality of pseudo self-awareness," this tells only a part of the story. It must also be recognized that the emphasis on freedom, choice, satisfaction, and self-fulfillment, also raises expectations and demands that continually threaten to go beyond (or even, in more extreme situations, be turned back against) the palliatives offered by the consumer culture. It is, in other words, a culture that continually produces and must continually resolve (if it is to survive) the contradictory moments of its own promises and expectations. Thus, while education in this period might be drawn in the direction of what Lasch calls "pseudo-emancipation," it must also be recognized that the demands that compel such change may also unleash aspects of a more genuinely liberating pedagogy. And, while Lasch is not entirely inaccurate to point at the examples of "creative alienation" and "mind-emptying ideology" of the '60s, it may be less convenient for him to remember that education, during this time (and unlike the preceding decade) also saw the upsurge of a critical, politically aware pedagogy—one not merely rooted in some psychedelic fantasy (as he would have us believe), but in the very real struggles of minorities, women, and the antiwar movement, as well as against (and this must be emphasized) the very consumer society that had nurtured it. The student-led uprising in France in 1968 was the most dramatic and far-reaching example of this tendency. It was, however, certainly not an isolated event in terms of the concerns and issues raised there.

The ascendance of a consumption-oriented culture is neither an unassailable mode of domination, or a force that securely ensures its own legitimation. In the sphere of education, an ethos which promotes the rise of pseudo-emancipatory practices may also encourage the presence of a genuinely critical and liberating pedagogy. The difficult task—and the one that Lasch does not even begin—is to recognize and distinguish each.

Cultural Crisis and the Schools

There is little reason to believe that the many descriptions from a decade and more ago asserting that schools in America are, for the most part, grim, joyless places dominated by "mindless" procedures and authoritarian practices, are any less accurate now than when written.[70] Indeed, more recent work suggests that the opposite is the case. The renewed emphasis on "traditional values," "basics," and testing has, if anything, made most schools increasingly repressive environments. What continues to be crucial to successful schooling (and successful socialization) is the willingness to forego one's own concerns, interests, desires, for the ones determined by those in authority. As Aronowitz points out, it is precisely the willingness to enter into a relationship of exchange with those in authority—to undertake activities now that offer little intrinsic satisfaction for the promise of future reward—that characterizes so much of the experience of both education and adult work. If, as Bell claims, "deferral" is the very essence of the production culture, then school surely is its quintessential expression. We do no more than admit this when we stress to students that, first and foremost, education ought to be seen as a future investment. Indeed the present crisis of public education may be understood as related to its declining value as an investment; schooling no longer seems to pay off. Contrary to so much of contemporary experience (not the least of which is the media obsession with overnight successes and sudden stardom), school is perhaps the last significant cultural institution committed to the Protestant mythology in which work is presented as the precursor to success.

Nor is the emphasis on work and the commitment to deferred gratification the only characteristic of schooling which connects it to a production-oriented culture. It is also true that, whereas the consumption culture emphasizes notions of individuality, subjectivity, and personal taste, such standards are far removed from the explicitly bureaucratic nature of schooling. It has become increasingly clear the extent to which successful schooling in America demands conformity to generalized forms of behavior, standardized expectations regarding academic pursuits, and adherence to impersonal procedures (not the least of which is a uniform regulation of all individuals' activities by the clock). Those who succeed at school do not do so by virtue of the depth of personal expression, creative originality, or individual "style," but through their ability to conform as closely as possible to the expectations of teachers and administrators. The much celebrated Individualized Education Plan (IEP) clearly reflects this bureaucratic ethos. Its goals are frequently highly circumscribed, minutely fragmented and quantifiable, excluding a concern with imaginative, creative or divergent thinking. Through the IEP (no less than with other techniques) education is a process in which students attempt to come as close as possible to the outcomes already anticipated by the teacher. It replaces a process that is open-ended and exploratory with one that awards conformity with predetermined answers.[71] There is little way in which such education can be seen as a subjectively oriented expression of individuality.

Indeed, in contrast to the values of a culture oriented to the promise of self-fulfillment, the bureaucratic, production-oriented values of contemporary education stand in stark relief; as opposed to concerns with holistic experience and personal meaning, schools emphasize the fragmentation of tasks and actions arranged in rationalized measurable quantities. Such concerns do indeed permeate every aspect of the educational process from the forms of highly routinized, "teacher-proof" curriculum packages to the "competency-based" evaluations of student knowledge; from the linear and segmented forms of reading instruction, to the rationalized measures of efficiency through which teachers are held accountable for their teaching. As studies of the hidden curriculum make so clear, school emphasizes predictability, control, and a concern with organizational efficiency at the cost of human satisfaction. Individuals are expected to see themselves not as "centers of radical originality" but as passively-determined players in a hierarchically ordered institution, engaging in tasks that frequently appear as disconnected and having only an instrumental rationality (that is, being a means to some end that is external to the task itself, such as a grade or diploma).

It is apparent even from this brief resume of the nature of schooling the extent to which it is at odds with other elements of culture in contemporary society, and to what extent the reproduction of culture in this society is fraught by fundamental disjunctions and conflicts. While among the apparatuses of cultural transmission school may be closely identified with the reproduction of production-oriented values and behavior, other apparatuses are engaged in the transmission of values that are their antithesis. TV, movies, popular music, and fashions, for example, powerfully disseminate the culture of consumption; against school's emphasis on deferral is the insistence on immediate gratification; in place of the concern with future investment and career planning is the demand for present satisfaction and "letting things happen"; and instead of discipline or restraint is a demand for spontaneity or "letting go." And in place of the disconnected abstractions of schoolwork are experiences related in some way to the existential anxieties of the young (the cloth from which the language, forms of expression, and pastimes of popular youth culture are cut).

Given these kinds of conflicts many of the predicaments faced by schools become comprehensible. School has indeed become a central battleground for the "hearts and minds" of today's youth. It may indeed constitute the final bulwark for the socialization of the young into the work-oriented, instrumentally motivated values of traditional bourgeois society. Given the depth and intensity of the divisions that now pervade American culture it must be less than surprising that the process of cultural transmission in schools (especially high schools) is resisted or treated with the ambivalence that it is. We speak here of the violence, vandalism, and apathy that have become, and continue to be, endemic to American education. School and the popular culture face each other in a relationship of increasing confrontation and dissonance, each being the focus of values, beliefs, and behavior that are the very antithesis of the other. To be young in America is to be the focus of a process of socialization that is, at best, schizophrenic and, at worst, irreconcilable.

It is within this context that the conservative movement in education during the last ten years must be placed. While its focus is education, its real meaning must be found in the wider tensions generated by this cultural schism. Though we believe that schools remain a bastion of the production culture, the claims of conservatives to perceive an undermining of the school's commitment to this culture is not without some foundation. As I will argue later the "basic skills" movement, for example, with its demand for a "return" to a clearly demarcated hierarchical epistemology and an authoritarian pedagogy must be seen, in part, as a reaction to educational change that gained momentum in the 1960s—change related in no small way to the emergence of what was earlier referred to as a personalist sensibility. The increased stress on the concept of individualization in instruction provides a case in point.[72]

A commitment to the epistemology and pedagogy that follows from this individualistic sensibility violates the norms of discipline, conformity, and authority that are associated with traditional learning. It encourages, instead, a stress on subjectivity, diversity, and self-expressiveness. Such an emphasis contradicts the production values traditionally associated with schooling. Of course, the notion of "individualized learning" more frequently receives quite a different, and much less liberal, interpretation (Individualized Education Plans, for example, are more often exercises in behavioral engineering with an extreme stress on doing preselected activities in prescheduled times). Despite this, the concerns of those on the Right toward the infiltration of notions of subjectivity and expressiveness into education are not merely overzealous reactions to the "radical sixties." Such notions, with their inevitable demands for greater choice, freedom and personal control, and the erosion of the fixed hierarchies of subject matter, are likely to be even more firmly resisted by their opponents as school becomes increasingly beleaguered and embattled in the sea of consumer and personalist culture. The increasing demand for discipline, testing, and curriculum offer little in the way of immediate satisfaction; all enforce school's role as an agency that socializes individuals into the values of deferred gratification and an acceptance of hierarchical authority. School, in short, has become the most visible symbol of those attempting to resist the final erosion of production culture. It has become the public battleground for the struggle to resolve the contradictory nature of culture in contemporary bourgeois society. Theories of cultural reproduction and schooling which ignore this struggle will fail to understand many of the tensions and conflicts, as well as the possibilities for change, that characterize present-day education in the United States.

"Civilization" vs. "Culture"—Toward a Radical Negativity

By way of a final note it should be stated that these antinomies that lie at the heart of bourgeois culture formed central concerns in the cultural studies of the Frankfurt Institute of Social Research. In particular, the distinctions between the domains of consumption and production carry some of the elements of "negativity" that were so characteristic of the Frankfurt School's critical theory. By "negativity" was intended those human expressions or practices that contain "human yearnings for that 'other' society beyond the present one." Thus, for example, while social contradictions persisted unreconciled in reality, the utopian harmony of art always maintained an element of protest against the pressure of dominating institutions, religions, and the like, no less than it reflected their objective substance. One of its most influential members, Max Horkheimer, noted that:

> We cannot blame people that they are more interested in the sphere of

privacy and consumption rather than (in) production. This trait contains a Utopian element: in Utopia production does not play a decisive part. It is the land of milk and honey. I think it is of deep significance that art and poetry have always shown an affinity to consumption.[73]

While warning of the danger of seeing the dichotomy of "sub-structure" (production) and "superstructure" (consumption) as permanent features of society and not as characteristic of a certain historical moment, Herbert Marcuse, the most prominent member of the school, argued that the continued separation of production and consumption was part of an unfree society. In his *One Dimensional Man* Marcuse noted that in the present situation the real threat comes from cultural tendencies that imply the premature reconciliation of contradictions at the level of popular consciousness. Such apparent reconciliation characterizes the pseudoliberation of modern culture in which mass-consumption society poses (falsely) as the embodiment of a culture in which production is oriented around the satisfaction of human needs.

Despite the incorporation of this repressive realm of consumption it still needs to be distinguished from the equally coercive (though qualitatively separate) realm of production in capitalist society. While the latter contains the ascetic moment in bourgeois culture (the work ethic, impulse restraint, duty, delayed gratification), consumption, with its demand for happiness and self-fulfillment contains a critical element in its focus. Consumption, as Martin Jay points out, however conspicuous, still means a protest against the asceticism of traditional bourgeois culture. Such a distinction parallels what Marcuse refers to as the segregation in the values of bourgeois culture—between those of the mental and spiritual world as an independent realm considered superior to "civilization":

> Its decisive characteristic is the assertion of a universally obligatory, eternally better, and more valuable world that must be unconditionally affirmed: a world essentially different from the factual world of the daily struggle for existence, yet realizable by every individual for himself "from within".... [74]

The work of Marcuse and others in the Frankfurt School makes clear the complex dialectic of values contained within contemporary culture: on the one hand, the world of "production"—work, the transformation of nature, and the social struggle for existence; on the other hand, the private and personal domain of consumption—leisure, human fulfillment (however distorted by the false needs of mass consumption), and the quest for meaning.

The divisions described by the Frankfurt School have continued to receive the attention of more recent social observers. Stanley Aronowitz, for example, argues that in the conditions of modern capitalism, the trivialization of labor and work activity have meant that the self is only realized in the world of leisure.[75] Labor, he says, retains a completely alien character as the purpose of production is removed in consciousness from its historical context, and the notion of self-transformation and expression of humanity through work is thwarted by the instrumental character of labor. The reasons for the maintenance of the split are clear:

> If workers become imbued with the notion of production for its own sake, that is, if they expect to measure themselves as well as others by what they produce rather than by its material reward, then the critique of capitalist society becomes devastating.[76]

The split between private life and labor, consumption and production, says Aronowitz, is a necessary mechanism by which the culture makes palatable the dissatisfactions arising from the boredom and frustrations of work. It makes it possible to accept the inevitability of alienated labor. Consumerism as an ideal has developed, he says, precisely as the older religious belief in the work ethic has declined. The sanctity of production is not now offered for its own sake but, instead, as a purely instrumental activity—a means, he suggests, rather than an end of human action. And yet the attempt to buy the allegiance of workers—especially young workers—through the promises or lure of leisure and consumption by no means ensures a fully harmonious motivational structure. Here Aronowitz differs from Marcuse in the latter's tendency to overemphasize the system's capacity to entirely incorporate currents of opposition within the culture:

> Far from being simply a new form of the old repressive swindle, the new lifestyles and modes of consumption, along with their reflections in the capitalist cultural industry, also contain the anticipation of something new, something which transcends the existing system. More specifically, the seemingly superficial pseudo-satisfactions offered by mass culture signify also forms of satisfaction which attempt to escape from the realm of mere appearance and become reality. In this second sense, they represent an impulse that cannot be completely stabilized as is suggested by the continual and general increase in frustration characterizing American society, even at times of political quiescence.[77]

It is precisely such frustration that is mirrored in the increasing levels of apathy, alienation, and hostility found among the school population. The growing disinclination towards schooling is the inevitable consequence of the cultural contradictions produced by the system—disintegrative tendencies held in check, in the last instance, by the coercive and threatening pressures of the labor market. In the next chapter this exploration of the intersection of education with a complex and contradictory culture continues. The focus shifts, however, from the process of socialization to the formation of educational policy.

3

Education as a "Complex Unity"

Educational Legitimacy and the Hegemonic Culture

IT HAS BEEN FREQUENTLY noted that the tendency to see the state as simply an appendage of the economically dominant class is the product of a determinist understanding of Marxist theory. Such a view sees all that is encompassed by the term "superstructure"—ideology, culture, and the state—determined by the economic "base." Central to this idea is what Raymond Williams refers to as "the notion of an external cause which totally predicts or prefigures indeed totally controls a subsequent activity."[1] Whereas, Williams argues, it is possible to understand by determination the notion of setting limits or exerting pressure, it has become more commonly used in the sense of prefiguration, prediction, or control. The result is the notion of a superstructure—and of education as a part of that superstructure—which is simply the reflection, the imitation, or the homologue of the economic base.

This view has been criticized by Antonio Gramsci, Raymond Williams, Nicos Poulantzas, and others. Williams, for example, through his work on culture, education, and artistic expression, has sought to deny the proposition that if the ruling class is bourgeois all ideas must be bourgeois.[2] He argues, instead, that culture and education are constituted through a dynamic process in which the ideas and outlook of a dominant class vie with those from other sources—traditional or "residual" ideologies, as well as the "oppositional" or "alternative" notions and practices of subordinate social groups. Williams surveys the development of English education and concludes that it can only be understood as the result of a complex interaction of ideological influences and perspectives arising from diverse and conflicting social interests.[3] Williams's work amplifies Gramsci's concept of hegemonic domination in which the ability of the dominant social classes to absorb diverse ideas and practices makes this domination such a powerful and resilient phenomenon.

It is in relation to this notion of ideology as a "complex unity" that the state in capitalist society must be reconceived away from the simplistic role mentioned earlier, towards one in which it is no longer an entity that is external to the competition between classes and factions. As Nicos Poulantzas argues, the state itself embodies and expresses the structure of groups or factions that compose the dominant class, as well as those comprising the subordinate classes whose demands must, in some way, also be accounted for.[4] This is the price of hegemony. The state has the important function of legitimating an ideology in which all groups feel they have some access to power and believe they may achieve some expression of their values. The state, in other words, through the process of political and ideological compromise, is able to maintain the continuity and cohesion of the entire social formation. Nowhere is this process of compromise so apparent as in the schools. The schools are, perhaps, the foremost example of the way in which institutions of the state contain practices and ideas that are the expression of diverse social groups and classes. They offer the most vivid examples of the way hegemony may be maintained through the incorporation of ideologies representing not only dominant or ruling social groups, but also intermediary or subordinate ones. The schools can no longer be seen as a simple instrument of social control, manipulated at will by a ruling class; they contain, instead, a complex unity of interests and values that reflect the ongoing struggle between groups and classes in society.

The process of legitimation that occurs through hegemony implies going beyond a version of socialization that represents a straightforward training of subordinate classes in the values, meanings and practices of a ruling class. The ideology and culture of bourgeois society is far more than the "isolable meanings and practices of the ruling class ... which gets imposed on others."[5] As Raymond Williams argues, if it were merely a process of training, manipulation or socialization, the dominant ideology in society would easily be thrown off or discarded. It would present itself as having an "onion-like reality" with layers that might be peeled off easily. The notion of a dominant culture being something more than the values and meanings of the economically dominant class is rooted in the conception of hegemony elaborated by Antonio Gramsci; it is central to this notion of culture or ideology that it is not merely an instrument of domination, but also legitimation. It

> supposes the existence of something which is truly total, which is not merely secondary or superstructural, like the weak sense of ideology, but which is lived at such a depth, which saturates the society to such an

extent, and which, as Gramsci puts it, even constitutes the limits of common sense for most people under its sway.[6]

The constitution of cultural hegemony, then, suggests the incorporation of alternative meanings, values or perceptions of the world. In order to ensure hegemony, culture must be something more than the product of a single dominant group. It must contain values, meanings, moral and aesthetic judgments that arise from the whole field of human experience, including those of subordinate groups. Only in this way can culture be viewed or felt as anything approaching a legitimate expression of human experience—a symbolic region which successfully mediates and constitutes a good part (if not the full range) of this experience.

By ensuring that the dominant culture reflects not only the meanings and practices of the dominant class, but also those of other groups or classes, hegemony ensures the active consent of those in subordinate positions in society. It ensures the effective legitimation of the class structure and the consequent relations of domination and subordination. Williams notes that the dominant culture, as a complex unity, contains not only the meanings, values, and practices of the ruling class, but also those that have survived from pre-existing forms of society, as well as new meanings and practices which are created alongside the dominant culture. The former (what Williams calls the "residual" culture) represents a

> reaching back to those meanings and values which were created in real societies in the past, and which still seem to have some significance because they represent areas of human experience, aspiration and achievement, which the dominant culture undervalues or opposes, or even cannot recognize.[7]

These may include, for example, certain religious values as well as ideas derived from a rural past. New meanings, values, and practices that are in the process of being created are referred to by Williams as "emergent." Since no culture expresses the total range of human experiences, energies or intentions, the question of what aspects of emergent practices or meanings are to be "reached for, and if possible, incorporated, or else extirpated" depends on whether, or to what extent, the dominant class has interests at stake.[8] The dominant culture must decide whether particular practices are "alternative" or "oppositional"; the latter—that is those that clearly challenge what is dominant—must be effectively and rapidly incorporated. While Raymond Williams asserts that the line between the two rests on a simple theoretical distinction, it is, in reality, a very narrow one; it is between someone who simply finds a different way to live and wants to be left alone with it, and someone who finds a different way to live and wants to change society in its light.

What must be emphasized in understanding the meaning of a hegemonic culture is that it represents not the meanings, practices, and values of a single class, but that it is a composite structure containing elements emerging from different social groups. Hegemony (active consent of those ruled) is ensured by addressing not only the dominant social interests but also those of other interests. The culture must be viewed as containing compromises and concessions by dominant groups, though never so much that the fundamental character of the social structure is threatened. In looking at the nature of education, it is possible to delineate a complex structure containing the interests and concerns of a variety of social groups. In the United States it is possible to distinguish, for example, the extent to which corporate interests have ensured an educational system which is strongly vocational, utilitarian, and professionally oriented. However, (and this has sometimes been ignored by revisionist historians or critical theorists of education) educational practices must be set within a structure of meanings and values that reflect the ideology of prebourgeois aristocratic social formations. The latter is reflected in the persistence of nonvocational goals—the notion of the "educated" individual developed through exposure to an appropriate academic and liberal curriculum. To whatever degree such goals may have been limited by encroaching vocational and utilitarian concerns it is necessary to recognize the extent to which schooling is still influenced by notions having to do with the transmission of a select body of ideas, knowledge and belief which are regarded as constituting the cultural "heritage," and representing the fund of superior "cultural capital." In addition to the influence of residual culture in education, it is also possible to identify characteristics of an emergent culture. Notions such as student relevance, choice, and participation have formed important and recurring educational demands. These demands have frequently emerged during periods of radical social upheaval—upheavals which have had as their central thrust equalitarian and democratic claims. In the next sections we will look briefly at the influence of both residual and emergent cultures in the structuring of the curriculum in American schools. Any attempt to adequately describe the form of contemporary education must, I believe, incorporate their influences.

Culture and Civilization—The Aristocratic Influence

The separation between the experiences of the everyday or material world and those associated with education received its first theoretical formulation in ancient Greece and reached its most extreme form in the English public schools (where any activity considered remotely vocational was anathema). While it is an educational form that is closely associated with the ideology of the aristocracy, it is still a fundamental characteristic of American education. Experiences that provide the matrix for education are held not to occur in the world of work, of community, political life, or family, but behind the doors of special institutions. The organizing principles of academic knowledge underline its separation from human experience and everyday social reality—its compartmentalization and structuring, its abstractness, and the reliance on literary and symbolic experience.[9] School itself often appears to represent the antithesis of genuine human activity. The experiences of the classroom are almost always vicarious, symbolic, and abstract—"make believe" activities in a "make believe" world. Indeed, despite the recent popularity of correspondence theories in which home, school, and work are viewed as providing an essentially unified or corresponding set of experiences, for many, if not most, students, the experience of school is one of massive discontinuities. It is pervaded by the feeling of its unrelatedness to the life of the individual. Nor should the phenomenon be limited to the domain of the poor or working class. It is increasingly an overtly displayed symptom of middle-class youth.[10] For many students it may be the essential discontinuity of experience, not correspondence, that marks the relation between life at home, at school, and at work. Despite the often stultifying and alienating nature of work, for many it is preferable to the unreality of the classroom. Such a perspective also makes clear the infinite preferability to young people of television as a medium of communication over the textbooks of the school room. As Caleb Gattegno expresses, it is "a medium that brings home life in the raw, not signs and symbols that one has to interpret."[11] Or at least it appears to.

The distinction between "educational" and "noneducational" experiences rests on the separation that, as we have seen, has historically existed between man's activity in the realm of "culture" and that in the realm of "civilization."[12] While the latter contained activities in the daily round of existence (work, community, family), the former was viewed as representing the crystallization of man's imaginative efforts to grasp the nature of our social and natural world. Such a distinction forms a central element in the account of the history of modern culture given by Herbert Marcuse. In what Marcuse calls the period of affirmation, a sharp distinction was developed between the mental and spiritual world on the one hand and the material world on the other.[13] This rift, in an intensifying form, is characteristic of our culture. As it intensifies so there is an increased need to express in terms of the "inner" life what can no longer find a place in external social life:

> The concept of the soul in its romantic version becomes the concept of that portion of the personality which strives to fulfill necessarily unexpressed and unachieved desires. The soulless regions are the regions of material life; the soul seeks an ideal beauty and an ideal happiness which cannot be real. When finally the bourgeoisie are only able to preserve their own social and economic order by politicizing it through and through and subjecting the individual wholly to the demands of that order, then this realm of the inner in which the individual has preserved a small area of

private freedom from the external demands of bourgeois life must come under attack.[14]

It is also a distinction made by Raymond Williams between culture as a body of intellectual and imaginative work (what is sometimes referred to as "high culture"), and the term used in its anthropological sense, as a whole way of life.[15] The limited definition traditionally applied to culture has its origins in the historical separation between mental and manual activities. This separation was underpinned by the division of society into classes. Those occupying the dominant social positions applied a hierarchical value structure to the activities performed. The practical and functional were separated from, and relegated in status to, intellectual and aesthetic concerns. The notion of culture was attached to the latter activities, while the former—the material reproduction of society—assumed the character of a commodity, engendered contempt, and sometimes paternalistic concern.

Education reflected these distinctions in its abstract, scholastic separation from activity and experience in the real world. While the individual in bourgeois society was constantly having to engage in tasks that would legitimate his position, the aristocratic "gentleman" was able to command deference from social inferiors not for what he did, but for who he was—an individual "cultivated" by his exposure to the appropriate intellectual and aesthetic experiences. Such experiences constituted a realm entirely distinct from those contained within civilization. Where the influence of aristocratic ideology has survived, the important characteristic is that the educational institution (school, college, university) provides a set of experiences (the transmission of "culture"), that enables the graduate to command deference from his social subordinates, not simply for what he can do but, more fundamentally, for who he is. It is, to this day, quite enough to have gone to Yale, or be a "Harvard Man" to claim one's social position. What matters is the type of person emerging from these institutions, not the vocational credentials he carries. As we shall see below, this is only the extreme expression of the more pervasive ontology associated with "being educated."

While little remains of the aristocratic notions of a liberal education devoted to "knowing for its own sake," where education is traditionally conceived of in its developmental (nonvocational) sense, it is sought, not in the world of our everyday social experience, but in an academic curriculum which provides experiences sharply separated and qualitatively distinct from it. The consequence of sharply differentiating "educational" from "noneducational" knowledge was explored by some of those associated with the "new" British trend in the sociology of education. Michael Young, one of its initiators, argued that one must reject

> the assumptions of any superiority of educational or "academic" knowledge over the everyday common sense knowledge available to

people as being in the world. There is no doubt that teachers' practices
... are predicated on just the assumption of the superiority of academic
knowledge that is being called into question.¹⁶

It is argued that by ensuring that educational experiences are seen as neither readily available nor accessible (that is, except through specialized agencies—predominantly, those of the state), education may be used to restrict or regulate the entry of an individual into the class structure. The hierarchical arrangements of educational experience facilitate the unequal distribution of cultural "capital" and the reproduction of the division of labor. As Young and others have documented, activities that are most dependent on manipulation of abstract symbols ("bookish" knowledge) are furthest removed from applied or actual field experience. They are generally characterized by the most status (the superior prestige of the academic curriculum over vocational areas such as home economics or technical drawing). At the simplest level, even out of school excursions—field trips—are generally conceived as expendable or frivolous educational activities, "add-ons" to serious school work.

While its effect on curriculum is of undoubted significance, the separation of "culture" and "civilization" has, in my belief, implications for education even more consequential than those perceived by the British sociologists. It buttresses the separation of activities undertaken for their intellectual, aesthetic, or self-actualizing values, from those simply utilitarian or functional. It underpins the view that what exists for the majority of us as the daily round of human activity can be of little or no educational value—tasks that are predominantly instrumental, rather than socially or personally enriching. It is a view that has supported the historically impoverished nature of much human activity and experience. The overcoming of the separation between "culture" and "civilization" would require a radical extension of educational experience into everyday life. Education would need to become coterminous with our wider social experience so that activities which comprise our economic, communal, familial, or political life would be pursued, fundamentally, because of their self-determining or self-actualizing possibilities. In seeking to implement a radical extension of educational experience into everyday life, we would need to reconsider the structure of our social institutions: work, for example, which is for the majority of people, no more than an instrumental activity, would need to be reorganized to ensure its creative and developmental possibilities; politics, likewise, which for most individuals is represented by the perfunctory experience of the ballot box would need to become an ongoing participative process. In this respect, the argument for the democratic management of our social and economic institutions becomes increasingly an educational one. The emphasis in the organization of such institutions would move from a concern with efficiency and bureaucratic rationality to the possibility of providing experiences that are intellectually, aesthetically, or emotionally enriching.

The legacy of aristocratic ideology also includes a view of culture that asserts the possibility of a comprehensive view of human knowledge or understanding. It is a view that is reflected in a holistic educational perspective. It eschews narrow understandings or specialized concerns. While the content of curriculum following from such a perspective has been, and persists in being, one of contention, a view of "all-round" human development informs it. It is a belief that has placed it, at times, in the same camp as progressive educators struggling to stem the tide of vocationalism and utility. This is particularly apparent in the current effort to maintain a commitment to a general or liberal arts curriculum in higher education in the face of increasingly functional and utilitarian demands. The cultural claims, however, that flow from this educational tradition today ring hollow indeed. Stirring promises of a well-informed and democratically empowered citizenry confront the reality of a culture in which "educated" people know more and more about less and less. Education, as Norman Birnbaum notes, is "something narrowly symbolic—devoid of an infusion of instinctual energy and lacking an emplacement in routine."[17] He continues:

> The development in the family, neighborhood and workplace of partial or limited systems of meaning, often without direct relationship to the larger structures of society or the movement of higher culture, has had terrible consequences. Precisely as higher culture has become infinitely more complex, more inhabitants of industrial society have become culturally more constricted or impoverished. The theoretic possibility of a qualitatively new human mastery of the environment remains. In practice, the higher culture which could liberate new potentials is encapsulated in forms of organizations which effectively deny this possibility.[18]

Education for "Life" and "Culture"—The Bourgeois Compromise

Bourgeois ideology, with its philosophy of utilitarianism, has had a fundamental effect on the nature of education. There has been a relentless movement towards a specialized, vocational, and instrumentally oriented curriculum and pedagogy. This movement has formed the cornerstone for the studies of the revisionist historians in American education. At the same time, however, the notion of a school system in which the curriculum, through differentiation and specialization, has become entirely utilitarian or functional, appears not to be entirely accurate. American education, for example, has never approached the kind of specialization found in European education. While in no way ignoring the social selection process characteristic of American schools, this is a far more generalized differentiation than the close articulation with specific occupations intended by those corporate leaders and sympathizers described, for example, by Joel Spring, in his history of education in the early twentieth century.[19] Indeed, if we are to judge by the present level of demand to make education "useful," to introduce "applied" studies, and to teach job and "life" skills, the school curriculum is still far from being entirely utilitarian. Nor has the school always successfully articulated with the occupational structure. Despite the introduction of institutions such as the junior high school, and practices like vocational guidance, described by Spring as part of an accelerating process of differentiating students for occupational purposes, it is clear that the needs of the corporate structure have not been the only determinants of school organization and curriculum. The "career education" movement of our own time is but one more attempt to solve the perennial problem of the under- and oversupply of skilled or professional workers.

A fundamental problem in the analysis of Spring and other revisionist historians is the absence of a dialectical perspective in their studies. The overwhelming impression is of a mechanical determinism where each aspect of the educational system is the mirror image of the economic process. There is little sense of the way in which educational ideas, in the era of bourgeois domination, contain contradictory ideological impulses. Thus, for example, we may note that out of the ideology of liberal capitalism emerges not only the corporatist ideas of Herbert Croly but also the radical liberalism of T. H. Greene. Indeed, much of the revisionist scholarship overlooks the centrality of this bifurcation in bourgeois ideology—a separation that is rooted, ultimately, in the class divisions of capitalist society. The tensions that result from these are manifest throughout the structure of society, and have formed an enduring aspect of the social and political history of our civilization. While the bourgeois class came to power with the demands for individual freedom, democratic rights, and equality, such demands rapidly became the nemesis of a part of that class which had more to gain from an authoritarian and hierarchical stabilization of the existing contours of power, wealth, and opportunity. In our own era of monopoly capitalism important transformations of bourgeois ideology have taken place so as to ensure its continued congruence with corporate needs and goals. Central to these has been the ascendance of a calculative-instrumentalist rationality and a version of individualism that is expressed through success in climbing the bureaucratic occupational ladder.

At the same time, however, such versions of bourgeois ideology have not been exhaustive. Petit bourgeois demands for independence and a freedom unfettered by social institutions (usually those of the state rather than business) have continued to be a constant theme of American social life. Indeed, as a number of recent writers have suggested, the period of the 1960s has given a powerful and enduring impetus to such tendencies. Notions of individual autonomy, antibureaucratic values (such as humanistic concerns with the "whole person"), self-sufficiency, and expressiveness, have become increasingly pervasive aspects of the contemporary culture.

In what ways such tendencies are related to the social class nature of the society are not immediately clear. The recent emergence of a massive social category employed in white-collar and professional roles in the bureaucratic structure of both government and business may be an important ingredient in this development. The peculiarity of this social and occupational group is that it is composed of individuals whose educational preparation and professional socialization have raised expectations of work in which notions of autonomy, flexibility, self-regulation, and personal growth are significant features. Such notions have often been sharply divergent from the actual experience of bureaucratic settings—frequently characterized as manipulative, rigid, authoritarian, and alienating. While the individuals in this category readily classify themselves as middle class, their growing emergence may well lead to a continued exacerbation of the tensions that are a part of bourgeois culture and ideology, and increasing contradictions in the expectations associated with lengthy schooling. Such contradictions are already apparent in the political domain where there is evidence of a breakdown in some of the typical left and right ideological categories.

The ideology of contemporary society thus maintains a demand for educational activities that are both corporate-integrative *and* enhance the free development of the individual. To ignore the chronic demand by educators for an "individualized curriculum" and a pedagogy that is organized around notions of individual needs is to lose sight of an important and permanent tension in American education—one rooted in the bifurcation of bourgeois ideology and the structure of class society. This tension might go some way towards accounting for the differences in climate between schools at different levels—for example, the more child-centered elementary school versus the bureaucratic high school. The former, with its greater distance from the occupational structure, has secured a more developmental orientation, while the latter is compelled to emphasize the calculative and institutionally integrative. The pragmatic philosophy of John Dewey may certainly be understood as the quintessential attempt, in liberal-capitalist society, to resolve the contradictions between education's corporate-integrative and individual-developmental impulses.

In the enthusiasm to subsume all aspects of education under the needs of the corporate economic structure, it was, for a long time, necessary to dismiss important, if less tractable, phenomena. Education was viewed solely in terms of the process of schooling (or what is referred to as "the hidden curriculum"). Little effort was made to demonstrate how the traditional academic curriculum (certainly a central aspect of educational practice) corresponds with the needs of corporate capitalism.[20] Such a correspondence is difficult to demonstrate. While it is clear that education in the United States does reflect the dominant bourgeois ideology, its character cannot be understood as a mere reflection of it. As I have earlier argued, education, like other social practices, contains not only responses to the dominant ideology, but also ones reflecting residual ideologies as well as emergent ones. Nowhere is this more clearly demonstrated than in the technical tracks of the comprehensive high school, or in the vocational school itself. These institutions represent anomalous and generally inefficient attempts to resolve contradictory ideological demands. While, on the one hand, they come closer than the academic curriculum to providing real activities and genuine experiences to students, they are still encapsulated in organizational forms that ensure that they are no more than simulations. It is a clear consequence of the division of labor and the separation of culture and civilization. It is this separation which compels all that is designated as educational to be located in socially isolated institutions. It is clear that if the issue were merely one of technical skill or proficiency nothing would surpass actual field training. Indeed, given the rapid rate of technical change, only at field sites is it possible to receive the kind of "state-of-the-art" experiences that are immediately useful. In short, the purpose of the vocational track or school is not so much technical training as it is socialization of individuals towards their (inferior) positions in the social division of labor. The status differentiations between vocational and academic tracks is reflected in the low morale and antipathetic attitudes so characteristic of technical or trade schools. This viewpoint is supported by the French sociologist Nicos Poulantzas in his analysis of schooling and the division of labor. The main purpose of the capitalist school, he says, is "not to 'qualify' manual and mental labor in different ways but far more to disqualify manual labor (to subjugate it) by only qualifying mental labor."[21] While schools divide students between those fit for mental work and those suited to manual labor, training for the latter does not really take place:

> The worker does not acquire his basic professional training and his skills in school (they cannot be "taught" there), not even in the streams and apparatuses of technical education. What is chiefly taught to the working class is discipline, respect for authority, and the veneration of a mental labour that is always "somewhere else" in the educational apparatus.[22]

Poulantzas argues that the vocational training programs in schools (which in all countries are overwhelmingly filled with the children of working-class families) are far less effective as actual programs of technical preparation than as means of reinforcing a particular ontology. They legitimate the differences between those with or without the capability of engaging in "mental labour." Most of what goes on in school via the curriculum does not represent a direct training for work—it is intended to locate an individual on one side or the other of the mental/manual division of labor.

The distinction that the present process of schooling makes between mental and manual labor maintains and continues the heritage of previous ideologies. In particular, it perpetuates the separation between culture and civilization inherited from aristocratic ideology. It is, however, an impoverished notion of culture laying only hollow claim to providing a comprehensive understanding of the human polity. The formal system of education reflects this notion in the increasing loss of conviction that surrounds its claims to provide intellectual, aesthetic, moral or other kinds of development. Education in its cultural or developmental sense has become little more than the "inculcation of a series of rituals, secrets, and symbolism . . . whose main purpose is to distinguish it from manual labor."[23]

Goran Therborn discusses these notions and their implications for the capitalist organization of work. He says:

> The principles of capitalist organization of the work process were formulated with unsurpassed candour and explicitness by Frederick Taylor, architect of the so-called Taylor system of "scientific management": "The manager assumes . . . the burden of gathering together all of the traditional knowledge which in the past has been possessed by the workmen and then of classifying, tabulating and reducing this knowledge to rules, laws and formulas. . . . All possible brainwork should be removed from the shop and centered in the planning or lay-out department."[24]

Therborn notes that this subordination is distinct from the precapitalist, feudal, or mandarin contempt for manual labor. What the bourgeoisie sets against manual labor is not the possession of general culture (or good breeding or manners), but specific forms of mental labor—specialized and technical knowledge. In the final analysis, it is necessary to understand the purpose of education in bourgeois society as combining both the inculcation of rituals, secrets, and symbolism that is so important to maintaining the mystique of mental labor, and the dissemination and formation of specialized and technical knowledge.

Social Democratic, Working-Class, and Populist Influences

Perhaps the most significant of all educational reforms enacted in the 1970s was Public Law 94–142, "The Education for All Handicapped Children Act."[25] Despite the accommodation of this law, in practice, to the regressive influences of bureaucratic and stratified forms of schooling (see chapter 4), it must, in many senses, be viewed as a reform that contains a strong assertion of social-democratic ideology. The concept of mainstreaming in particular—a key aspect of the special education law—most clearly reflects such an ideology. Mainstreaming stems from a concern with reducing the process of labelling children with handicaps or special needs. Such labelling was seen as producing a number of adverse effects on children. These included the stigmatization and victimization of individuals who, once categorized, are expected to conform to stereotyped notions of behavior and ability. In order to reduce such labelling and categorization, schools are mandated to educate special needs students in "the least restrictive setting." The latter refers to situations in which, to a maximum degree possible, handicapped individuals are "integrated" with their non-handicapped peers.

Mainstreaming represents an affirmation of those values concerned with the presence of community in our social lives. It advances the notion of the public school equally accessible to the offspring of all members of society, and providing experiences which facilitate shared values and meanings. Education is viewed here as an agent of moral socialization. It promotes group identification by participation in the rituals of school life. It is this function that advocates of mainstreaming have emphasized: by integrating handicapped and special needs students into the main body of the student population, hitherto excluded individuals will join the life of the community—they will become full members of society.

The concept of mainstreaming draws its impetus from the image of man as citizen in liberal-democratic society. It is as a citizen that man expresses his commitment to a community of shared values and rights. And it is through the institutions of the state (political, legal, educational) that the community is embodied. While our socioeconomic lives are characterized by private concerns, competing interests, and inequalities, these are juxtaposed with a state that, in principle at least, is viewed as a public domain of shared obligations, mutual interests, and equality of rights. It is just such a perspective that has been espoused and advocated by social-democratic ideology (reformist socialism in Europe or welfare-state liberalism in the United States). Such ideology has sought to mitigate the conflictful, hierarchical, and divisive experiences of the capitalist market, with the gradual expansion of state institutions that would provide an increasingly extensive field of democratic and social rights. The social-democratic view has, for the most part, accepted this fundamental division of society and the coexistence there of a public (state) domain concerned with communal obligations, and a socioeconomic domain of private concerns. This is in contrast to the Marxist view which seeks to abolish this public-private division.[26]

The demands by the handicapped contained in the special education law represent the renewal of a struggle to ensure that the concept of the communal is more fully realized in the institutions of the public domain, and especially in our schools. While previous struggles of excluded and discriminated-against groups have formulated their demands mainly in terms of equality of access to schools, these demands have gone farther. Not only are school systems mandated to ensure free access to their institutions (and thus the opportunity to share in the life of the school), they are also mandated to ensure maximum possible access to educational programs (to ensure the opportunity of sharing in the life of the classroom). No educational reform has gone further in attempting to provide experiences which facilitate shared values and meanings among diverse populations of students. By placing students who were once excluded or separated from their peers into closer proximity with them (in the classroom, school, or extracurricular activity), there is the possibility of providing a commonality of experience for all students. It is out of this that the proponents of mainstreaming hope for a greater degree of shared understanding and cooperation between individuals and groups.

Mainstreaming is in that tradition of social policies pursued by subordinate and excluded groups demanding a domain of responsibilities and rights separate from the criteria of the marketplace. Such policies, whether in the fields of health care, education, housing, or nutrition, have been framed by values that emphasize equal treatment, mutual obligations, and solidaristic experiences. These are values that have been persistent features of working-class political concerns in western capitalist countries (more so in Western Europe than in the United States). In the field of education it is precisely for these reasons that the realization of comprehensive forms of schooling have been permanent demands of social-democratic parties in Western Europe. Parallel to the integration and mainstreaming movements in the United States, the goal of "comprehensivisation" in England, for example, pursued by the British Labour Party, was that of breaking down the social segregation that occurred when students were sent to separate (college preparatory or vocational) schools, and providing instead the opportunity for students to develop a shared culture.[27]

All such attempts at modifying schooling so that they emphasize fraternal experiences, rather than divisive ones, ultimately founder on the basic contradiction of trying to provide egalitarian, solidaristic spaces in contexts that have overwhelmingly opposite characteristics. In schools students continue to separate themselves socially, and fill positions in a status hierarchy that anticipates their adult roles in the occupational and class structure. Despite the significance of such educational reform, its limits are coterminous with those of social democracy or welfare-state liberalism; in each there is the difficulty of sustaining institutions or practices characterized by democratic, fraternal, and egalitarian values in a larger social system generally marked by their absence.

It may certainly be argued that mainstreaming, the comprehensive school, and the social-democratic ideology from which they spring are more compatible with a corporate perspective concerned with providing individuals a view of society which is marked by its fundamental unity and organic nature, rather than by conflict and division. Such educational policies present no real challenge to the dominant interests or beliefs, and are fairly easily incorporated. Such possibilities are less evident in some of the curriculum and pedagogic reforms initiated during the 1960s, and which were organized around a cultural principle that might be termed populist. Central to these reforms was the influence of demands for a greater degree of equality in American society—demands that were fueled by the civil, economic, and social struggles of minorities and women, and by the antihierarchical and antibureaucratic concerns of the student movement. The cultural and educational revolt that resulted from this equalitarianism was focused on what Daniel Bell describes as "an attempt to eclipse 'distance'— psychic distance, social distance, and aesthetic distance—and insist on the absolute presentness, the simultaneity and immediacy, of experience.[28] The result was the attempt to reconcile "culture" and "real life," assimilate politics and culture, and eliminate the traditional hierarchies that restrict who may participate in the making of culture, what may count as culture, and who is able to appreciate it. In all, says Bell, "there was a 'democratization' of culture in which nothing could be considered high or low—and a world of sensibility which was accessible to all."[29] There was a movement towards eliminating the separation between those practices, meanings, symbols, and knowledge traditionally associated with culture from those that are a part of civilization. Included in the latter were the practices, meanings, and knowledge associated with the "daily round of existence"—work, community, family. As a result, culture is no longer seen as connected only to the abstract, the symbolic, or the past; it is concerned as much with the life presently lived, and the language, concerns, meanings, values and practices of those living. Nor is the street, the factory, or the neighborhood to be considered any less a part of the cultural environment than the more traditional sites of cultural transmission— schools, art galleries, museums, theatres, and concert halls.

In an earlier paper exploring the relationship in the United States between radical movements, ideology, and educational ideas, I argued that during periods of profound social upheaval a "radical educational mode" emerges which challenges the dominant educational beliefs.[30] Such, I believe, is the case during the early decades of the twentieth century, as well as during the period of the 1960s and early '70s. I have suggested that the particular structure of educational ideas that emerges may be understood as the expression of an ideology which is concerned with the establishment of more egalitarian social relations; the democratization of power, resources, and culture; and emphasizes the values of social solidarity and collectivism. While such ideology has traditionally been associated with working-class movements, it is clearly not limited to them (it may also, for example, be identified with the student movement of the 1960s). The radical educational mode is evidenced in a number of other situations, such as the Leninist period of the Soviet revolution, in France in May 1968, during the Chinese Cultural Revolution, and generally, where there is a profound challenge to institutional hierarchy and social inequality.[31]

It is suggested that the structure of educational ideas that emerges as a product of such situations contains (among other things) the following elements:

> (1) Change in the rigid separation of education from other human activities; that is, the attempt to move educational experience out of the classroom and into the activities of work, community, politics, family.
> (2) Related to the above point, abstract ("bookish") knowledge and the unrelatedness of academic concerns are challenged by forms of knowledge grounded in daily life and common experience.
> (3) The notion of education as primarily nonvocational, having a broad humanistic concern (not a training for technical or specialized skills).
> (4) Education as the means of producing a wider social consciousness and awareness.

For those operating within the radical educational mode, the activities of workplace, home, and community become important experiences in the educational process. The classroom is no longer an exclusive or even superior repository of educational knowledge. Such a perspective is the effect of equalitarian values which compel the transformation of our understanding of culture—and, as a result, education. In situations where there is a movement to limit or eradicate hierarchical social relations, there is, at the same time, an inevitable challenge to the prevailing notion of culture. No longer is it identified only with the intellectual or aesthetic concerns of a minority; it is perceived as representing (in Freire's words) all human creation. Culture exists, then, wherever man makes the world the object of his knowledge, submitting it to a process of transformation, altering reality. The workshop as well as the museum become repositories of culture. Culture—and education—become synonymous with the entire range of human activity and social experience. The street, the factory, and the town hall become included as the loci of culture and are the legitimate sites of educational experience. Education in the radical mode, unlike previous traditions, no longer reflects or affirms the opposition between culture and civilization. It represents, instead, its synthesis and unity.

My own study of the American socialist movement between 1900 and 1925 provides an especially vivid illustration of the emergence of this educational ideology. In the early part of the twentieth century, the new "industrial" education, as demonstrated in the Gary School Plan, or the experimental "work schools" in the new Soviet republic, embodied this concern with the interrelatedness of human activity. While some in the American socialist movement remained tied to a return to a traditional or classical curriculum as the proper goal for a radical educational program, most of those on the Left supported the new industrial education. One of them commented:

> The school today is an unnatural life calculated only to prepare one for future work. It has no relation either with home or society.... Today, so

called education ends with the classroom instead of all life being an education.... For education to be of value it must present a unity in the things taught.... The pitiable ignorance of our population of anything to be found in the country, and of our country folk of great manufacturing establishments, and of the majority of our whole population of any part of actual life outside the narrow confines of their own work, must be a source of wonder to future generations....[32]

For those educators on the Left such education embodied a number of elements contained in the radical educational mode and consistent with their general ideology: 1) It demonstrated the concept of an interrelated entity, in which the activities of each individual or group could be seen as vital to the rest; 2) The education was a broad, nonvocational one, concerned with the development of the individual through exposure to a wide variety of experiences and activities; 3) It sought to overcome the division of labor by connecting education with the practical activities of the real world. In relating the acquisition and use of knowledge to social experience and genuine human goals and concerns, the historical separation of theory and practice could be overcome; 4) The opposition between cultural and vocational education was overcome, the latter no longer a narrow, specialized concern excluding intellectual and aesthetic involvement, and the former redefined away from its abstract, scholastic character to embody the entire range of social activity; 5) In making the acquisition and use of knowledge instrumental to the real goals and needs of students, the structure and organization of knowledge are changed, away from rigidly defined forms of subject areas towards the interrelating of disciplines and perspectives.

This view of a radically democratized culture was to be found later, in the multitude of educational ventures and experiments of the late 1960s and early '70s that were characterized by their attempt to extend and to broaden the notion of what constitutes educational experience, or counts as educational knowledge. These included curricular, pedagogic, and institutional demands which had, as their unifying thread, the attempt to reduce the distance between the educational experiences of the classroom and those found in the life of the student, in his or her home and community. Changes in the curriculum reflected a shift towards an exploration of contemporary social experience (encapsulated in the often trivializing notion of "relevance"); a concern with issues of sexual, moral, ethnic/racial significance; a widening of literary instruction into contemporary themes and an inclusion of studies in other communication forms (TV, movies); and attempts to provide a more integrated approach to school studies, as in teaching organized around interdisciplinary learning rather than traditional subject divisions.

In addition to the widely heralded proliferation and diversification of curriculum around issues of personal and social relevance was the emergence of programs that focused upon, and offered direct experience of, the local community (the "school without walls" being, perhaps, the best noted example of these). Such alternative programs frequently embodied the claim that the traditional school did not constitute the only, or even the best, site for education and that education could be had in many other areas in which human beings engaged their world (and where they created culture). Indeed, from the perspective of these programs, school was seen as suffering from its cloistered unrelatedness to the real world outside. In that most visible and notorious symbol of the educational reforms of this period—the alternative school—many of the populist cultural tendencies merged: an emphasis on contemporary social issues; a pedagogy that often included direct, out-of-the-classroom experience; and an exploration of students' particular cultural/social and personal identities. If only for a few years, there was not a worthwhile public school authority without its educational programs containing, in one form or another, a curriculum that gave expression to notions of a radically democratized culture—programs that were, in no small way, directly supported and promoted by agencies of the state.

Conclusion

In this chapter I have attempted to provide some illustrations of the manner in which educational policies and practices in United States society must be regarded as much more than the response to imperatives set by any single dominant social group. It is this view that permeated and supported much of the earlier critical analysis of schooling in the United States, a perspective which obfuscated the far more complex and dynamic nature of educational reality. I have tried here to describe the way in which the state, in order to maintain its appearance as an entity representing the popular or national will, is compelled to recognize claims and demands from a diversity of social groups (including those in subordinate and intermediary as well as dominant positions). Educational policies, therefore, can be understood as neither monolithic nor reducible to the interests of a single social class. Instead, we have noted reforms which express petit-bourgeois concerns with self-sufficiency and possessive individualism, social-democratic demands for an organic social structure, populist notions of a democratized culture, and traditional or residual concerns about the meaning of being educated. Nor do such policies and practices enter or leave the public stage at clearly appointed and unopposed moments; they appear, or are replaced, as the consequence of struggle, conflict, and the mobilization of political and cultural capital. The state—and education—is no less a site of social conflict than is the area of production; the social formation is a complex unity composed of relatively autonomous levels, all of which are characterized by conflicts and contradictions.

The structure of education in the United States must be understood as a composite of cultural tendencies (though not fully formed world views) representing competing social classes and groups. It is the result of a complex interaction of ideological perspectives and influences, and reflects the weight or balance of social forces arrayed throughout the society. This, it must be emphasized, is not to deny the validity of the work of revisionist historians in revealing the way in which capital has come to have a central influence over education in the United States. To this influence, however, must be added the effects of other social groups in the forming of American education. Such groups may form part of the "power bloc" that dominates society, or (to a much more limited extent) be part of the subordinate or intermediary social strata. The resulting structure of educational practices and purposes is not a static or immutable one. With the continuing struggle between social interests, the structure of education undergoes continuous shifts in emphasis, intention, or purpose. Thus, in recent times, elimination of curricular electives, pass-fail grading, emphasis on the basics, and increasing vocationalism in education must be located within the shifting nature of the cultural (and political) compact underpinning hegemony.

The hegemonic structure of bourgeois society, reflected in the composite character of education, ensures a far more powerfully rooted system of meanings, values, and practices than one that is merely imposed by a dominant class. At the same time the attempt, through these means, to ensure a culture, and an education, that is perceived or experienced as legitimate generates significant contradictions and conflicts in the resulting cultural and educational form. While the desired effects of hegemony may include both legitimacy and effectiveness, this is not now the case. The attempt to ensure a legitimate structure of education through the inclusion of, or compromise between, separate and sometimes opposing interests, purposes, and meanings also makes for a structure that is, in some fundamental ways, ineffective. And such ineffectiveness ensures an erosion of the very legitimacy it was intended to support. The resulting structure of education is one that is widely experienced as seriously flawed.

To view education as an expression of cultural hegemony means to take seriously the view that the dominant forms of curriculum and pedagogy represent, not the imposition of a single class view of those activities, but a complex structure of diverse and sometimes conflicting social practices and ideas. For example, the vocational-utilitarian, or bourgeois, character of contemporary educational practice continues, to a large extent, to be wedded to prebourgeois educational forms. It is not for nothing that so many students (of all social classes) complain of the irrelevance of the academic and liberal curriculum and, indeed, passively or otherwise, resist them. While "basic skills," "competency-oriented" instruction, and "career" education may represent less than intellectually stimulating school experiences, they can, at least, be understood or accepted in terms of the prevailing instrumental-technical norms; whatever they may be lacking in intrinsic satisfaction, they do, at some level, appear to make sense. Such education may, at least, be perceived as useful or relevant to one's future career. It is, or is felt to be, adaptive to the techno-rational system. The same cannot be said of academic studies which purport to be the conduit for humanistic or cultural values (embedded in knowledge, beliefs, and aesthetic judgments that provide understanding, meaning, and significance to current human endeavors). While such notions may have made eminent sense in, for example, the "gentlemanly" education of nineteenth-century England, where schooling was closely identified with exposure to the select traditions of knowledge and belief in a way that would support a coherent sense of meaning in human activity, these are now increasingly unable to support such goals. Claims to an essential or coherent body of truths, meanings, and knowledge make little sense in the pervasive and deepening cultural crisis of our time, in which authentic meanings and belief disappear in the ever-widening circles of political, economic, and cultural fragmentation. No appeals by conservative curriculum critics for a return to the tradition of the "Great Books" or "Cultural Literacy" that rests on some agreed listing of facts and knowledge will be sufficient to cope with the dissonance and incoherence of meanings and belief in contemporary culture.

And while skills, competencies, and career training may appear to "make sense" within the present educational context, even they flounder on the obstacles created as a result of the ideological compromises inherent in the hegemonic process. Prebourgeois cultural notions compel the process of education to remain locked within separate and distinct social institutions. Such a separation reflects the division between culture and civilization, in which activities associated with human development and self-realization are kept distinct from the practices of the everyday world of work, leisure, family, community, and politics. The resulting separation ensures that school, for all its concern with realistic preparation for adult roles and occupational skills, remains a make-believe world filled with make-believe activities. The institutionally circumscribed nature of schooling ensures that it becomes an ever-more trivial and peripheral activity in the wider field of individual concerns and purposes.

When progressivism in education (especially apparent during periods when there are strong movements organized around egalitarian concerns) has been a significant force, a broader social context for educational experience has been accepted. The city, the community, industry or the countryside—not just the school—become the accepted context for education. Such changes are underpinned (not always explicitly) by egalitarian challenges to the selective tradition of cultural values (the elimination or redefinition of cultural capital). Even in more conservative times hegemony and the imperatives of legitimation ensure that populist cultural tendencies emerge and continue to conflict with traditional and restrictive notions of education, and give support to "de-schooled" notions of educational experience. The not infrequent calls that high school education contain more community-based instruction must be seen as an expression of more than merely typical bourgeois demands for utilitarian educational goals, but as a partial attempt to resolve the crisis of the educational process. It is an attempt to transcend cultural/ideological traditions that have defined education as fundamentally disconnected from the nonschool world of students, thereby ensuring that it remain an activity that is marked by its abstract and scholastic character. While such psoposals undoubtedly reflect the movement toward a more vocationally oriented education, they also reflect a growing recognition of the limits of schools as the matrix of educational experience. Partial de-schooling (and the use of the wider social environment as the locus of education) is clearly sought as a matter of expediency (in the face of mass apathy and alienation among students). It may also, however, represent the initial (if grudging) acceptance of the need for a radical redefinition of the nature of education in the United States.

Of course, the current formulation of educational goals and the nature of school practices cannot be separated from the social and economic crises of the 1970s and 1980s. The movement to restore basics in schools and to implement competency testing may be understood as the attempt to reassert the traditional promise of the division of labor with its clear hierarchical separation of mental and manual work. Such a separation is founded in the school's selection and affirmation of those individuals apparently possessing the capability for intellectual labor (and, of course, the exclusion and denigration of those lacking it). It is precisely upon such distinctions that the fortunes of the "new" petit bourgeoisie ride (in particular, their "special" capability for white-collar or professional work). The present educational reaction may also be spurred by economic conditions which have left an "over-production" of educated candidates for white-collar and professional positions. Such conditions have plunged schools into a crisis of legitimation. It is significant, however, that the petit-bourgeois reaction to the legitimation crisis of schooling more commonly describes the issue in terms of the erosion of educational standards, as a breakdown in the traditional measures of ability (which have underpinned the school selection process and consequent social division of labor), rather than in terms of the economic crisis itself.

The basics movement is thus supported by an ideology which resists a critical social or political perspective, preferring, instead, appeals to reactionary notions of the corrupting effects of progressive or radical educational demands. It is not altogether incorrect in its assessment that such demands may, indeed, undermine the cultural and curricular bases of the division of labor. Whether through the demands of working-class groups (in the United States, usually minorities) for a curriculum that more nearly addresses their own particular cultural experience, language needs, and social concerns, or as a result of the demand by sections of the middle class for more "individualized" or more "open" educational experiences, the traditional forms of school selection (uniform measures for the comparison of ability, common understandings of "success"and "failure") are indeed threatened.

The populist or democratic principle underlying reforms in schools during the 1960s and early 1970s did indeed begin to undermine the relationship of education to the reproduction of the class structure and, in particular, the reproduction of middle-class advantage. The expansion and diversification of curriculum during this period, for example, reduced the ordered hierarchical character of school knowledge and its clear correspondence with the distribution of cultural capital. With such changes the middle class felt itself threatened by a devaluation of its most precious resource—the ability to transmit the advantages of the division of labor to its offspring through its superior cultural inheritance. If many more people had, or could claim to have, "cultural capital" the advantages it had possessed were reduced. Those sections of the middle class who most clearly felt this threat could do no more than insist on a return to some standard through which their cultural advantage could be restored and maintained.

It becomes clear, then, that the struggle for "educational standards," "relevance" in curriculum, "individualized" pedagogy are intimately connected with the ideological struggle among social classes and factions of classes, centered around the issue of the social division of labor. All of this must be set within a framework in which the present fiscal crisis of the state has necessitated a massive withdrawal of capital from social and educational expenditures (actions that may indicate a declining sense of the significance of traditional forms of schooling among, at least, a part of the dominant economic groups in the society). While educational policy making remains the prerogative of a select group within the professional and social hierarchy of the country, it also represents the response to an agenda set, in part, by those excluded from these groups. While public policy may reflect the attempt to ensure conditions that maximize the resources and power of those occupying the ruling circles of the society, such policies have historically needed to take into account the experiences and demands of those excluded from these circles. Such a perspective does not argue for the existence of a balance of countervailing power; rather it asserts the need to understand education and other areas of public policy, not as the consequence of the unchallenged and unyielding dominance of any special group, but as the effect of the ongoing struggle between classes, interests, and ideologies.

4
Educational Reform and Liberal Democracy

THE FREQUENTLY DESCRIBED role of the educational system in reproducing the occupational structure of capitalist society is only a partial description of its ideological function. Education relates not only to economic life, but to the state. The confusion regarding this lies at the heart of critical analysis of schooling in the United States. While schools do clearly generate a differentially socialized work force inured to the experience of a bureaucratic occupational structure, they also provide experiences that ensure continuity in our perceptions of liberal democratic society. Schools must not only ensure economic socialization for their clients, but also provide experiences apposite to their political role, their position as part of the state apparatus. While the economic integrative aspect of schooling has been a prime focus of those critically examining the role of education in capitalist society, the political aspect has been ignored, or assumed to be subsumed by the economic.

We may better understand the separation in the realm of socialization by looking at the division in man's existence described by Marx in his early writings. Shlomo Avineri suggests that, for Marx, a person in modern society is divided into two distinct types of individual: he or she acts according to the norms of bourgeois life *and* as a citizen (corresponding to the division between the realms of the economic and the political). Within the latter, the individual is expected to develop a sense of universal attachments and obligations, and acceptance of the claims of equal consideration, rights, and opportunities. Such notions are embodied in the institutions of the state, including schools, in capitalist society where all, at least in principle, may invoke the equal claim of citizenship. In his bourgeois role, man needs to behave according to his egotistical needs and interests—traits that are apposite to his life in the social-economic domain. Against this notion of egotistical existence, the state represents (of course, very imperfectly) a field of democratic and classless values that are the antithesis of those other values experienced in the rest of our lives. Of course, for Marx, despite the development of the state in capitalist society, political emancipation does not ensure human emancipation: "The existence of the state as a *separate* sphere of universal values shows that all other spheres have been abandoned to particularism and egoism."[1] Despite the lack of a sustained assault on bourgeois values (hierarchy, profit, self-interest) in liberal capitalism, it is also clear that such societies do not function with entirely acquiescent or pacified subordinate classes. The universal and classless notions of citizenship may promote demands for treatment that transcends the usual criteria of the marketplace.

It is my belief that schools occupy a unique position in the institutional nature of capitalist society. They contain, at one and the same time, both the economic and the political moments of bourgeois ideology. As such, they provide experiences concerned not only with the integration of their clients into the occupational structure, but also with their integration into the political culture of the society. It is important to understand that such contradictory tendencies are the inevitable result of capitalist ideology. The state, as Bertell Ollman argues, is an illusory community as well as the instrument of rule in class-ridden societies: "This best expresses its essential character."[2] All classes, he argues, strive for political power in order to represent their special interests as the "general good."

As a result of the contradictions in the process of socialization, it is possible to predict the unstable, conflict-ridden nature of schools in capitalist society. This has clearly been the case. Schools and the educational system have occupied center stage in the ideological struggles of such societies. And unlike those at the points of production (factories, offices), such struggles have not readily stayed within the bounds of the dominant ideology. Conflicts in education have quickly spilled over into the more fundamental questions of the structure and processes of class society. In no other institutions are notions of hierarchy and equality, democracy and coercion forced to coexist in quite the same proximity. Indeed, despite the plethora of studies on the hidden curriculum, nowhere is it clearly explained why some aspects of the school experience are compelled to remain covert. It is a phenomenon that clearly reflects the illegitimacy of an institution associated with the state manifesting the ideological forms associated with the economic structures of society.

From such a perspective it is possible to see how the comprehensive or common high school may be understood as the quintessential bourgeois form of educational organization. Indeed, it is not accidental that this is the form increasingly found in liberal-capitalist societies. It makes clear the unique role of the school in having to conform to both the economic and the political values of capitalist society. Within this institution we can identify the juxtaposition of egalitarian civil and legal forms (that is, the presence of bourgeois political values) with hierarchical and unequal economic-social forms. In the comprehensive high school, this configuration is reflected in the commitment to provide equality of access to the progeny of all citizens, while dispensing differentiated forms of knowledge and educational experience (and thus economic and social hierarchy) to these same individuals. Schools provide a context for the struggle between notions of community, universal responsibilities, and collective obligations and the egotistical and unequal imperatives of the market. While schooling in capitalist society attempts to ensure social control, it also replicates the contradictory experiences of liberal capitalism. To ignore this tendency is to view human beings in the present situation as passive, normatively constrained puppets entirely inured to their present predicament. Notwithstanding the lack of a sustained revolt against the existing structures of domination, such a view surely exaggerates the extent of personal or collective compliance to prevailing social demands. Despite the relative acquiescence of students, minorities, and the working class in the present era, the miscalculations of political scientists or sociologists regarding our recent history cautions us against any premature judgment of having yet reached an "end of ideology." While its forms may change, and sometimes become less easily identifiable, social struggle and the demand for a more human society surely remain an integral part of our existence. Schooling and the politics of pedagogy or curriculum are an essential part of this struggle. It is precisely these phenomena of struggle around the demand for an extension of democratic and universal values that underpin the 1978 reform of special education. Looking at this will help to illustrate and elaborate some of the points discussed theoretically in this introduction.

The 1978 Reform of Special Education

On the opening day of school in September 1978, a quiet revolution will end. The end will not come silently, easily, or dispassionately. The officers and soldiers who led and fought the revolution will not fade away for they recognize that the passing of this revolution may merely be signaling the beginning of the next. Accompanying this end, however, will be celebration—celebration for children who are handicapped and who, since the beginning of public education in the United States, have been the victims of discrimination that often prevented them from receiving an education. On that day in 1978, it will be a violation of federal law for any public education agency to deny to a handicapped child in need of a special education an appropriate program.[3]

The dramatic and optimistic words quoted above represent the views of a proponent of Public Law 94–142, the federal legislation guaranteed the reform of special education throughout the United States. Federal special education legislation did indeed represent a significant advance for a hitherto excluded and deprived population. Despite this, the reforms reflected the limits and limitations inherent in all liberal or progressive challenges to the educational system. Such challenges must contend not merely with the constraints imposed by traditional modes of thought, institutional rigidity, and the narrow concerns of interest groups, but, more importantly, demands and imperatives set by the wider society. While educational pressure groups and innovators are important as catalysts for change, the extent of the change depends, in the final analysis, not on the perseverance and commitment of these individuals or groups, but on the parameters set by the social and economic structure. Special education reform, like other areas of educational change, may proceed only to the extent that it is congruent with the needs or goals of that structure.

The struggle for the passage of Public Law 94–142 paralleled that of other groups, discriminated against or excluded by American society, in its demand for improved and more appropriate education. Like many of these struggles, it derived its legal justification from the 1954 decision of the Supreme Court (Brown vs. Board of Education). As with other minorities, these protagonists of reform demanded educational opportunities comparable to those enjoyed by other sections of the population. These were concerned, particularly, with equality of access to public education institutions. Such demands must be understood in the context of the widespread exclusion of handicapped children from public education. Thus, for example, the statement of findings and purposes that are a part of P. L. 94–142 indicated that "one million of the handicapped children in the United States are excluded entirely from the public school system and will not go through the educational process with their peers."[4]

While access to public education has been a primary concern, it has not been the only issue. Research has increasingly made clear how special education, through misclassification and inappropriate categorization, has functioned to segregate disproportionate numbers of minority children.[5] Thus, for example, studies by the California State Department of Education discovered that although Spanish-surnamed children comprised only 13 percent of the total school population, they accounted for more than 26 percent of the students in the classes for the "educable retarded." Not surprisingly, therefore, special education legislation contained provisions relating to the process of testing and evaluating students. Such provisions speak to the need for ensuring culturally and linguistically unbiased testing. In addition, IQ testing as a basis for classifying students in need of special educational services was dismissed as simplistic and inadequate. In its place, the allocation of services and programs to children is decided through a "team evaluation" in which information and diagnoses are provided through a variety of professional sources.

The special education reform also sought to reduce the process of "labeling" children with special needs. Such labeling was seen as producing a number of adverse affects on children. It led to the stigmatization and victimization of such individuals who, once categorized, are expected to conform to stereotyped notions of behavior and ability. In order to reduce labeling and stigmatization, schools are mandated to educate special needs students in "the least restrictive setting." This refers to situations in which, to the maximum degree possible, handicapped students are integrated with their nonhandicapped peers. The process of achieving such situations is often referred to as "mainstreaming."

In attempting to ensure an appropriate education for special needs students, an "Individualized Education Plan" (IEP) is mandated for each individual. It represents a contract or agreement concerning the education of a specific student, and commits the school to providing a potentially wide range of services necessary to the education of that student. Such a plan requires regular monitoring of its implementation and demands a consideration of an individual's education in terms of his or her abilities, skills, aptitude, and interests. The plan also represents a means of ensuring that students are correctly placed in special classes, that they are not unnecessarily separated from the rest of the student body, and that there is continuous accountability of student progress.

Finally, parallel with increasing accessibility and integration of special needs students into the life of the school, the law implies an increasing integration of regular and special instructional and administrative functions. Its goal is to ensure a single educational system for all parts of the school population.

Mainstreaming and the Contradictions of Schooling

Nowhere are the contradictions of the liberal-capitalist system so clearly demonstrated as in the issue of mainstreaming. While mainstreaming has made undeniable progress in achieving the goal of placing special needs students in the same school as their nonhandicapped peers, its impact on the experience of such individuals may be far less than expected. Despite access to the same building, separation through the stratification of educational programs (in the form of tracking, homogeneous classes, or ability grouping) ensures differentiation in the key areas of a student's school experience. For special education students such differentiation invariably signifies their designation to programs, classes, or tracks of inferior educational status. The psychology and sociology of education is replete with studies that demonstrate the harmful effects of low educational status on the development of students' identity, expectations, and performance.[6]

One increasingly prevalent device that has been heralded as a means for circumventing the characteristically rigid educational stratification of secondary schools is the "resource room." It is viewed as a means of providing special needs students with additional educational services without permanent designation to a low track or class.[7] However, the resource room itself often performs the function of a track. It does so, however, in a manner more subtle than the hitherto separate or self-contained special education classroom. Where the IEP demands that students spend no more than 50 to 75 percent of their time outside of the regular classroom (usually in a resource room), this is invariably scheduled to occur during academic instruction. In other words, these students are separated from their peers precisely during the time they receive (from the school's point of view) their most significant experiences. It is, indeed, during this time that most judgments are made determining the expectations and life chances of students. It is during and through academic instruction that one is assessed to be "bright" or "dull," "intelligent" or "slow," college or trade bound. What are generally regarded by schools as comprising less important experiences—art, music, industrial arts, home economics, PE—are used to fulfill the mainstreamed time requirement of the special needs student. It is quickly apparent in the reform of special education that, even though mainstreaming does provide the minimum condition for the development of shared experiences and understanding among students, those remain secondary to the school's function of sorting and selecting individuals and providing them with expectations, attitudes, and skills appropriate to their future social and economic roles.

It is in the context of this issue that the contradictions of schooling in liberal capitalism become most apparent. On the one side is the notion of the public school equally accessible to the offspring of all members of society and providing experiences which facilitate the shared values and understanding necessary for social continuity and stability. On the other hand is the school's function of providing the differentiated experience and socialization necessary for those who will fill different positions in the social and economic hierarchy. It is a conflict that pits the Durkheimian notion of education against more critical interpretations. The former emphasizes education's role as an agent of moral socialization. Durkheim describes the way in which education promotes group identification by participation in a ritual. It is this function that advocates of mainstreaming emphasize. By attendance and participation in the life of the school, hitherto excluded individuals will join the life of the community; they will become full members of society. Critical interpretations of education, however, emphasize that it is the separation rather than the commonality of experience that characterizes schooling in America. The separation and differentiation of educational experiences (in the form of grouping or tracking) resulting from the schools' role in the organization of our economic life, constitutes the real (though hidden) curriculum of schools. It is this which forms attitudes, self-concepts, peer-identification, and life chances. Despite the increased physical proximity between students, resulting from mainstreaming, it leaves untouched the real source of students' identity and role-expectations—the educational organization of the school. While special education reform augurs the further fulfillment of liberal ideology in that it ensures a more complete *equality of access* to a public institution, it does so within the constraints imposed by a hierarchical social structure. The latter ensures that school remains a hierarchically organized institution dispensing educational (and hence social and economic) opportunities unequally.

The limits of special education reform parallel those experienced in England with the widespread introduction, during the 1960s, of the comprehensive secondary school. In that country, following bitter debate, the 11+ selection examination began to be abolished and all students in a single locale channeled into one secondary school. The goal was to break down the social segregation that occurred when students were sent to separate (college preparatory or vocational) schools. While the reform has, in many parts of the country, achieved its goal of placing all students within a single school location, educational "streaming" ensures the continuation of social differentiation. Despite a policy of integrating students of different backgrounds through attendance at one school, the truly significant organizer of social experience—educational separation in the form of ability groups and curricular tracks—was left intact.[8]

In the formation of student attitudes, expectations, and identities, the experiences resulting from the educational organization of the school, rather than mere physical proximity, are crucial. It is these that mainstreaming fails to address. Successful implementation of mainstreaming is, to an extent, dependent on the will and commitment of administrators and teachers; it is also determined by forces that go beyond the disposition and attitudes of individuals. Such forces represent the conflict within bourgeois ideology: between the concept of shared values and beliefs arising out of a common cultural experience and social situation (the political "moment"), and the school's function of providing a differentially socialized work force to occupy different roles in the occupational structure. The school experience, above all, legitimates the hierarchy of reward and prestige found in this structure.

The Comprehensive High School, Vocationalism, and the Myth of Democratic Pluralism

Implicit in the reform of special education at the secondary level is the demand that the comprehensive high school fulfill its mission of offering a comprehensive range of educational programs. This demand embodies traditional liberal-democratic values. Instead of a monolithic school entity offering a standardized curriculum to all students, regardless of whether they can succeed at it, the cry is for meeting the "individual needs" of a diverse population. Individuals different by way of race, language, learning style, aptitude, or disability ought to be able to receive, in the words of the federal law, "a free and appropriate education." Such a demand is not new. In 1908, the school superintendent of Boston argued:

> Until very recently [the schools] have offered equal opportunity for all to receive *one kind* of education, but what will make them democratic is to provide opportunities for all to receive such education as will fit them *equally well* for their particular life work.[9]

Interestingly, as David V. Cohen and Marvin Lazerson point out, during this period the ideas were difficult to oppose because the advocates of equality, of the unified curriculum, were identified with tradition during a ferment of progressive reform.

At the same time while the present emphasis on expanding vocational and occupational programs for secondary special needs students is couched in the language of meeting individual needs and in theories concerned with differential learning styles, it is probably better understood as no more than a renewal of the old academic/ vocational education tradition. Such a tradition is rooted historically in the notion of society polarized between those of its members capable of intellectual development, the growth of faculties concerned with rational judgment and decision making, aesthetic appreciation and literary skills, and those members of society capable of no more than practical-utilitarian skills necessary for work and survival. For the most part, special needs students are identified with this latter group. They are viewed as having a particular propensity for vocational education, occupational training, and "life-skills" courses. They are channeled away from an education concerned with developing conceptual or rational thought, enhancing aesthetic understanding, or nurturing critical or creative faculties. That such a dichotomous view of education and of human potentialities is rooted in the class nature of society was realized early on. It is acknowledged, for example, in the writings of John Dewey:

> Of the segregations of educational values . . . that between culture and utility is probably the most fundamental. While the distinction is often thought to be intrinsic and absolute, it is really historical and social. It originated, so far as conscious formulation is concerned, in Greece, and was based upon the fact that the truly human life was lived only by a few who subsisted upon the results of the labor of others . . . . It was embodied in a political theory of a permanent division of human beings into those capable of a life of reason and hence having their own ends, and those capable only of desire and work, and needing to have their own ends provided by others. The two distinctions, psychological and political, translated into educational terms, affected a division between liberal education, having to do with the self-sufficing life of leisure devoted to

knowing for its own sake, and a useful, practical training for mechanical occupations, devoid of intellectual and aesthetic content.[10]

Dewey's description is as applicable to our present situation as it was when it was written. As was discussed in chapter 3, there is a close connection between the differentiation of curriculum into the academic and vocational and the definition that society has traditionally applied to the notion of culture. In class-divided societies, those occupying the dominant social positions have applied a hierarchical value structure to the activities performed. The practical and functional were separated from, and relegated in status to, intellectual and aesthetic concerns. Education (as distinct from vocational training) reflects these ideas in its abstract, scholastic separation from activities and experiences in the real (nonschool) world. Indeed, the term academic, in its pejorative use, implies exactly this. Our society, no less than previous ones, distinguishes between the values of mental and manual activities. Those performing or preparing for the latter generally hold inferior status as compared to the former. They are assumed to be capable only of work and the more basic requirements of survival in society, not of intellectual reason, aesthetic appreciation, or creative activity.

In recent times, we have witnessed an increasing drive to obtain vocational training opportunities for special needs students at the secondary level. Such a drive is seen as embodying progressive educational ideas concerned with meeting individual needs and encouraging curricular diversification. It is viewed as effecting educational change that embodies the liberal notions of democratic pluralism and equality. Such a view mystifies the real nature of the reform. The increased vocationalism of secondary education for special needs students represents no more than a renewal of traditional notions of education in general, and special education in particular. It represents the continuation of a view of human potentialities and abilities that are, for some groups, highly circumscribed. It reinforces a view of certain groups of students, including special needs students, as beings better fitted for "training" than "education," fixed at the level of concrete operations rather than abstract thought, able only to benefit from the most specialized and restrictive learning experiences. Ultimately, it represents a further illustration of the function of the education system in producing and reproducing class society. Paradoxically, it should not be assumed that the institutions most responsible for vocational education, the vocational-technical schools, readily admit special needs students. The present economic situation ensures competition for training programs in skilled employment and the exclusion of students through the operation of selective admissions criteria and the limitation of places. Special education students are often left with pathetically inadequate "work-study" programs preparing them to fill roles at the lower end of the working-class occupational ladder as unskilled or surplus labor.

While "student diversity" and the notion of "meeting individual needs" are the rhetoric that has accompanied curricular change in the area of secondary school special education, it is hard to regard the public high school as embodying the values of democratic pluralism. The voluminous critical literature over the last fifteen years makes emphatically clear that each person's capacities, interests, aptitude, abilities, and background are not equally respected and provided for. Indeed, the literature has forcefully argued that the American high school most often nurtures an atmosphere of competitive individualism, penalizes deviancy, awards conformity, and legitimates authoritarian relations.[11]

In implementing special education reform at the secondary level, an increasing number of schools are attempting to deal with the need for curricular and instructional diversity by introducing "alternative" programs. Such programs are primarily an attempt to deal with those students who, from the school's viewpoint, represent trouble. Terminology for describing them is legion. It includes the "potential dropout," "reluctant learner," "juvenile delinquent," "disruptive student," and the "behaviorally disordered student." These are generally students who are described as having problems of social adaptation or adjustment, or seen as emotionally unstable. Programs constructed for these students contain elements developed as part of the alternative school/radical school reform movement of the 1960s. These include a concern with the affective as well as cognitive development of the student, an environment that facilitates student input into the decision-making process, the opportunity for community-based learning, and an emphasis on cooperative instead of competitive values. However, unlike the ideology within which the original alternatives were created—rejection of the prevailing school curriculum, pedagogic relations, and administrative structure—these schools are seen as no more than transitory appendages to the traditional high school. They do not represent a rejection of the dominant form of education or schooling. Instead, they emphasize their role in preparing hitherto recalcitrant students to re-enter the "mainstream" (the traditional high school). They are careful to regulate entry into these schools so that only categorized special education students are included. It is possible to argue that through this approach it is the "pathology" of the students rather than that of the school system or method of instruction that is emphasized. By seeing the alternative program as transitional—an opportunity to "shape-up"—the problem is seen as being located *within* the student. It emphasizes the aberrant or deviant nature of the students who attend such schools. It is the individual's "problem," "disability," "handicap," that is emphasized, not the limitations or inadequacies of the instructional environment or educational process.

The use of alternative schools in the context of special education anesthetizes the attack on traditional schooling that alternative education represented at an earlier time. In attempting to understand or explain student "failure" through such means it is useful to refer to what William Ryan calls "blaming the victim." Such an ideology defines the "problems" of society in terms of the dispositions, attitudes, values, or culture of those who represent society's deviants—the poor, unemployed, those on welfare, school dropouts. In defining the origin of problems as residing "inside the skins" of individuals, we may ignore the way in which the instructional process or social structure systematically generates such problems. Thus, failure in the traditional school situation is not viewed as the result of an environment that systematically alienates and excludes a significant section of the student population. Instead, such students may be labelled "learning disabled," "emotionally unstable," or "socially maladjusted." We may see their problems arising from an indolent or apathetic disposition, broken homes, learning problems, mental retardation, or other handicaps. In all of these ways we are able to ignore the educational process that often is responsible for school failure. Just as the unemployed represent, for the most part, not an indolent group but the product of economic policies deliberately designed to maintain a level of unused productive capacity, so schools are organized around the competitive principle which ensures a normal distribution of success and failure. In such a situation those assigned to the latter group may develop attitudes of hostility or aggression, be disruptive or uncooperative, or become unmotivated and apathetic. Such students do, in part, become classified as special needs and may be assigned to an alternative situation which will accommodate them. While such programs do, at least, encourage innovative or more humanistic responses to individual needs, they also maintain the stigma of a separate education, and the labeling of students as deviants from the norm.

Special Needs: The Social Construction of an Educational Category

Despite the attention given to vocational education and alternative programs in this chapter, it must be emphasized that they do not, at this time, represent the primary vehicle for the instruction of special needs students at the secondary level. The resource room represents the dominant institutional arrangement for special education at all levels of public education. Despite the use of elaborate diagnostic tests and procedures, much of the instruction in the resource room is of a general remedial or compensatory kind. Special education teachers in high schools consistently complain of having kids "dumped" there for reasons that have little to do with specific learning or handicapping conditions. Such students are, in their words, individuals who are "turned-off," "behaviorally disordered," or unable to cope with the academic work. The remedial nature of much of the instruction in the high school resource room serves mainly to reinforce the low expectations (and low self-image) of many special needs students. It also ensures that those who use the room are stigmatized as being intellectually deficient. (In many high schools I have visited, students readily identify the special education resource room through terms such as the "retard room," "romper room," and other similar epithets.)

The whole notion of curricular diversification in special education is predicated on the ability to assign students, in some objective manner, to appropriate learning environments—indeed, that it is possible to establish accurately whether students belong to the category of special education. While, during the past few years, a large body of research has established just how unscientific are much of the tests and measurements used in education (that IQ, in particular, is biased in favor of the cultural, linguistic, and social dispositions of the children of the middle class), special educators have not lost their belief in the ability to evaluate, diagnose, and prescribe differentiated educational programs for students. Recognizing the problems of objectively evaluating students, the federal legislation contains a strong emphasis on the need to accurately assess the skills and aptitudes of children, though in ways that circumvent traditional forms of testing. Such an evaluation seeks a more comprehensive view of the child than previous tests. It is, however, far from certain that such an approach will overcome the cultural and class discrimination associated with previous methods. As has been shown by a number of researchers, special education is traditionally a catchment for disproportionate numbers of poor, black, Hispanic, and working-class children.[12] Mental retardation and emotional illness are labels long used to obfuscate the chronic hostility and exclusion shown toward such students. In Massachusetts, four years after the introduction of the state special education reform law, Chapter 766, a report stated that minorities are two or three times more likely than whites to be enrolled in special education classes.[13] My own experience in high schools leaves me in no doubt that the category of "unmotivated student," with its dubious etiology of mental disturbance, social maladjustment, or learning disability, represents the major focus of special education programming in secondary education.[14] Indeed, of the 12 percent students in Massachusetts who are categorized as special needs students, only about 2 percent possess severe or profound disabilities. The remaining 10 percent comprise students who, especially at the secondary level, are seen as academically unsuccessful, or display behaviors which are regarded by the school as hostile, antisocial, or deviant. Such students come disproportionately from black, Hispanic, or working-class backgrounds. For many students, the designation "special needs" represents less the discovery of an inborn handicap than the final official seal on a chronic process through which deviancy is constructed from the interaction of the student and the educational environment.[15]

Individualizing Instruction: The Process of Incorporation

The concept of individualizing instruction is regarded by many advocates of Public Law 94-142 as an essential aspect in reforming special education. This is especially true at the secondary level. Since keeping the handicapped student in the regular classroom is a central goal of the educational reform, it is believed that all teachers ought to have both the commitment and skills necessary to deal adequately with the special needs of each student. It is widely believed that teachers ought to be able to devise individualized modes of instruction oriented to students' particular aptitudes, interest abilities, and styles of learning. From my experience in secondary schools it is clear that such individualization takes place only rarely. This result, however, must be seen as a product of more than teacher inflexibility or tradition-bound instructional methods. It is the consequence, instead, of the overall culture of the high school. Such a culture motivates creativity, originality, and independence only rarely; for the majority of students passivity, obedience, and conformity are the required traits. The degree of passivity and obedience required increases as one "descends" through the levels of academic performance. Thus, it is in the classes and programs for those functioning at the lowest academic level (which generally includes special education) that authoritarian pedagogic relations, rote learning, and drill dominate the classroom (what are sometimes euphemistically referred to as "structured" learning experiences). The characteristics of such a classroom environment preclude the notion of individualized instruction. Such instruction requires not the authoritarianism and rigidity found at this level, but flexibility and latitude; it requires a degree of autonomy in place of rote learning and activity and movement in place of passivity.

This failure to provide a genuinely individualized form of educational experience is properly understood only by apprehending the manner in which meanings and practices are reinterpreted, diluted, or put into a form which supports or at least does not contradict other elements of the dominant culture. This "incorporational process" is at the heart of the Gramscian notion of hegemony. In following this approach to the understanding of an effectively dominant culture, school is seen as an important (though, of course, not the only) site for the continual making and remaking of culture, and, more specifically, the process of selecting, organizing, and integrating human experience. Such an approach takes us a long way from the "transmission belt" view of the ideological process and the school's role in it. In a similar vein, Raymond Williams notes the "alternative meanings, and values, the alternative opinions and attitudes, even some alternative senses of the world, which can be accommodated and tolerated within a particular effective and dominant culture."[16] In understanding the ideological role of school, we must recognize its active involvement in selecting and incorporating cultural notions—notions that are constituted by a range of meanings and practices wider than those simply or easily congruent with the ideological imperatives of present-day corporate capitalism. Indeed, they may include some, at least, that are "alternative" or even "oppositional" to the dominant ideology. Individualization of instruction, drawing on liberal democratic ideals, provides an especially illuminating example of the way in which potentially liberating dimensions of these ideals are effectively absorbed and incorporated.

The ideology and culture of bourgeois society itself has been, and continues to be, an important source of oppositional and alternative meanings and values. Liberal-democratic ideology is far from being simply a source of legitimating ideas and values for the capitalist mode of production. Notions of individual rights, self-determination, and equality have been, and continue to be, ideological rallying points for those concerned with the partial or even fundamental reform of the social and economic system. Indeed, the perennial attempt to move education towards a greater recognition of the individual as the center of the instructional process or the definer of the educational purpose cannot be dismissed as merely an alternative road to the imposition of ideological domination (as some conspiratorial or Marcusean views of progressive education would have us believe). It reflects the real tensions that have historically pervaded liberal-democratic ideology— between the imperatives of a hierarchical and bureaucratic social order that regulates human behavior and experience on the basis of class, sex, race, and age and the promise held out by such ideology for individual freedom, autonomy, and self-determination. It is within this latter context that there has historically developed resistance to, or a radical rejection of, the imperatives of corporate capitalism (a resistance that has moved to both the left and right of the political spectrum—the petit bourgeois notions of "rugged individualism" and the "self-made man," or the radical insistence on the right to define our own needs or identity; the latter so important, for example, in the movements for the liberation of blacks or of women). It is within this context, too, that the educational demand for individualized instruction must, at least in part, be set. Such a demand has emphasized creativity, self-awareness, subjectivity, and self-regulation as moments in the process of individuation. What Zvi Lamm refers to as individuation connotes an act of liberation from the existing culture in which the individual actualizes his unique personality and crystallizes his unique identity.[17] Its purpose is the emergence of an autonomous and authentic individual, not one socialized to the acceptance of a given social order or conforming to its institutional prescriptions. While such tendencies within bourgeois ideology pose threats of significant dysfunctionality to the smooth running of a bureaucratic or corporate system, they cannot be extirpated without a radical and dangerous transformation of the society which gives rise to them (fascism being one such result). A more effective, and less costly, means to accommodate these tendencies has been through the more subtle, but certainly powerful, process of hegemony in which the individualistic aspects of bourgeois ideology are incorporated into the constellation of dominant meanings and practices. This has meant the apparent assertion of meanings and practices associated with the idea of individuation, while effecting, in practice, a dilution or reinterpretation of the notion so that it has become accommodated to corporate goals and purposes.

The clearest sense in which the related educational concept of individualization has been incorporated into the hegemonic culture is in the way that its usage has been restricted, in large part, to limited or marginal populations. To require individualized learning is often to mark one as "exceptional" or "special." Implicit in this approach is the rarely articulated notion that "normal" students require no particular attention to their individuality. What marks normal children is their ability to become part of the undifferentiated or corporate whole. This is the conceptual underpinning to the myriad of descriptive studies that characterize the American classroom in terms of its concern with conformity, rebelliousness, or exceptionality. More broadly, it illustrates the process of incorporation through which a potentially threatening notion is accepted, but employed in highly restricted circumstances. It is a response to a destabilizing aspect of ideology that takes the form, "This is a good idea, but, of course, it's not for everyone."

It is intriguing that the two populations for whom individualized learning is especially reserved belong either to the group categorized as the handicapped or designated by the title, "gifted and talented." While, as we will describe below, the actual individualizing practices are sharply differentiated for these two populations, its restricted identification with these exceptional groups undermines the generalizability of the notion to the entire educational community.

Despite this, the appeal of individualized instruction resonates strongly with the philosophical/psychological notions of a significant section of those involved with the schooling process—parents, teachers, and teacher-training instructors. Such concerns are especially strong at the lower grade levels. However, here again, the identification of the concept of individualization with younger students supports its association with a limited component of the whole—usually those who are in some sense perceived as deficient in their emotional, intellectual, or even physical development.

To a large extent, official mandates for individualized instruction have been restricted to those designated as in need of special services for the handicapped or disabled. The effect, however unconsciously arrived at, is one in which individualization becomes a remedial device for those seen as in some way deficient or underdeveloped. Far from being a pedagogic practice that serves to affirm the self, individualization becomes part of an elaborate process of negative categorization. The need to engage in learning through a distinct or particularistic approach becomes an emblem of inadequacy. To be normal is to need no distinctively organized or transmitted educational experience. While this is not the place to pursue its implication, the hegemonic incorporation of individualized learning through its restriction to a population generally perceived as deficient or disadvantaged speaks powerfully to the ontology of normality and deviance in our society.[18] It illuminates the means by which the corporate mode of human organization assumes a shape that is morally and aesthetically dominant. To require special, distinctive, or particularistic treatment becomes the mark of disablement. To be otherwise is to assert that one needs no special considerations, it implies one's ability to "keep up," "fit in," be "in step." It is clearly not far removed from the military ideal in which the self may be eliminated from the calculus of organizational concerns. Indeed, it is precisely because of the implicit challenge to such a world view embedded in the notion of individualization that its incorporation becomes of vital concern to those concerned with the maintenance of existing forms of human organization and social relations. There can be no more powerful means to this than through a school process that strongly identifies it with those who are categorized as mentally deficient, emotionally disabled, or physically handicapped. While the state wraps itself in the flag of humanistic policy making, it ideologically encircles the challenge of radical liberalism.

Individualization, the Differentiation of Meaning, and Correspondence

While the notion of individualized learning is preeminently attached to only certain specifically designated populations (particularly the young, the educationally disadvantaged, the handicapped, and the gifted), its meaning and practice for them are not uniform. In particular, the notion of individualization for gifted and talented students has associations and meanings quite different from those of the other groups. In this respect the process of hegemony is not merely concerned with smothering or absorbing potentially subversive or destabilizing elements in the total ideology or culture; it also fulfills the needs to successfully utilize (exploit) emergent notions, ideas, behaviors, which may have a functional value to the dominant interests. Of course, such attempts to utilize the "emergent" culture require that its immediately dysfunctional characteristics are held in check. And this is not easily achieved. Thus while the development of a genuine youth culture since the Second World War has been a boon to the myriad of corporate and entrepreneurial interests who benefit from the exploitation of an adolescent market in music, fashions, and the like, it has also nurtured the alienation of the young from established social, moral, and aesthetic norms, which sometimes explodes in a radical form. The youth-oriented market both coopts and sustains generational rebellion. Even as it channels the frustrations and alienation of the young, it also contributes to the continuing crisis of legitimacy in institutions such as the school. There is, in short, no guarantee that the process of incorporation is ever entirely successful. Indeed, hegemony must be understood as a never fully complete process. It is always an after-the-effect attempt to accommodate emergent behaviors, perceptions, and tastes.

Individualization may be of considerable value to the successful reproduction of the division of labor and hierarchical social relations—of course, only when the notion has been defined and interpreted in ways that ensure the careful selection, or extirpation, of possible meanings with which it may be associated. Correspondence theory has alerted us to the specific personality traits and behaviors required within adjoining layers of the corporate hierarchy and the way in which these are produced and reproduced through the hidden curriculum of the classroom. At the higher levels of the corporate structure the ability to perform autonomously, and with some degree of self-managing and self-initiating behavior, is necessary to the successful functioning of the organization. In addition, such individuals must be able to manifest some degree of creative and problem-solving talents. At these higher levels of the organization, education or socialization for mere obedience or conformity would be functionally inadequate. Workers in these positions must be prepared in ways that ensure an ability to perform beyond simple or mere dependence on regulations or conformity to preexisting norms. Clearly, such needs are facilitated by instructional and curricular experiences that allow for the development (in some degree) of individuals able to approach the working situation with independence and criticality. It is precisely at the higher levels of the academic hierarchy (advanced placement classes, honors classes, and classes for the gifted) that, under the rubric of individualization, such behaviors are permitted or encouraged in the classroom—through independent research, self-initiated projects, opportunities for "free" reading. In addition, the classroom allows more opportunity for the expression of student opinions and ideas, a process which is continued and developed at the "better" colleges and universities.

The concept of individualization utilized here is precisely an example of the way the hegemonic process is able to select from a variety of possible meanings in the emergent culture so as to ensure its functionality with existing notions and arrangements or at least to mitigate its potentially destabilizing effects. In this case, individualization in education is defined in a way that is most useful to corporate interests and needs, while extirpating or selecting out the more radical possibilities. Its form is one that encourages freedom to act, think, or choose all within clearly prescribed boundaries. Indeed, it is not so much autonomy that is encouraged as the internalization of already prescribed norms. Whether in the classroom or office, individuals are not so much expected to pursue activities or tasks that promote the development of their unique capacities, interests, or potentiality, but those that are congruent with organizational values and norms. Individualization is encouraged only in so much as it fosters a more efficacious implementation of corporate or bureaucratic imperatives. Autonomy, freedom of choice, self-initiated behavior, and creativity are encouraged only within the parameters of demands set down within the authority structure of the organization.[19] It is clear we have travelled far from notions of genuine self-determination or self-realization that have informed the radical-humanist tradition in education.

It may well be (as commentators on both sides of the Atlantic have noted) that the appeal of open education, with its notions of individualized learning, to predominantly middle-class and professional parents may not simply reflect their more "liberal" dispositions (though this cannot be simply dismissed), but indicates a knowledge about occupational life that is unavailable to working-class families.[20] In particular it is the need for professional and managerial employees to be able to internalize organizational goals and to be able to act "autonomously" rather than needing precisely elaborated organizational rules and regulations. It is also probable, however, that the appeal of individualized learning in these social groups is an example of the ambiguity of ideas and practices that is a linchpin of a hegemonic culture. Educational practice, while in actuality well accommodated to aspects of bureaucratic and corporate reality, contains sufficient latitude to support interpretations considerably more antipathetic to such realities (such as the hostility among these groups to typical bourgeois divisions between work and play, or the dominance of instrumentalism over expressive attitudes in everyday life). Like the emperor's new coat, individualized learning is able to take the form that whoever is viewing it most prefers.

The hegemonically necessary obfuscation of "individualization" is also apparent when its meaning at this level of the academic hierarchy is compared to its meaning at the lower end of the school order. Here it is not a matter of the conflation of the notion of autonomous behavior to that of conformity to the internalized norms of the organization, but its assimilation to externally validated controls. The major instrument for such assimilation is the Individualized Education Plan (IEP). It is the institutional crystallization of liberal educational ideology with its emphasis on the individual—his capability, aptitudes—as being at the center of the educational process. Indeed, where it is used by conscientious teachers, administrators, and parents, it has been a significant tool for focusing educational resources on a student's particular circumstance or need. At the same time, however, the uniformly behavioristic formulation of the IEP ensures that its hidden agenda is anything but individually liberating. Its pedagogy is one in which "individual needs" are matched to precisely formulated goals, procedures, experiences, texts, and schedules. The particular interpretation of individualization that is embodied by the behavioristic orientation of the IEP ensures a very different experience for those students than the ones we considered above: instead of flexibility, the emphasis is on rigidly prescribed procedures; a controlled and regulated schedule in place of relative latitude and opportunity for discretion; and an emphasis on convergent and circumscribed results that may be unambiguously defined and measured, rather than the relatively open-ended problem solving or project work of the higher level classes. The overall result is a learning experience that is controlled, restrictive, and closely supervised. Its typical expectation (being able to answer so many questions, by a particular date, at a prescribed level of accuracy) ensures a notion of individualized learning that stresses conformity with the already anticipated results of those in authority.

By juxtaposing these two dissimilar interpretations of individualized learning, it becomes clear how the hegemonic process includes the assimilation of very different practices to a common educational pretext. Quite different pedagogies are apparently conflated to a common theoretical (and discursive) understanding. Nor is such differentiation merely a matter of confused terminology. While individualization at the higher levels of the academic hierarchy are congruent with expectations in terms of occupational roles (relative autonomy of those in professional and managerial positions), at the lower end of the order (which usually included those having an IEP), the behavioristic formulation of the education program corresponds to job roles which are closely supervised and regulated, and contain tasks which are often minutely fragmented and circumscribed.

The Psychologizing of Educational "Deficiency"

Where individualized instruction for students of low ability is employed, the result may be a more flexible approach to the pace of work, criteria for grading, and instructional techniques. It infrequently, however, results in the development of new curricula oriented to the particularistic experiences and needs of students. It rarely produces a concern with the phenomenological world of specific students, sensitive to the cultural peculiarities of language, race, sex, or social class. The pedagogic emphasis in individualized instruction has rested preponderantly on a consideration of the "how" of learning, rather than on the "what" of it. The context for considering poor ability, school failure, and deviant behavior, within the remedial framework of individualized instruction, has become largely a psychological one connected to cognitive development or "learning style." The latter, in particular, has become the primary theoretical perspective available to teachers in pre- or in-service training. Thus the emphasis in working with deficient or disadvantaged students becomes, fundamentally, a concern with the suitability of the modality through which knowledge is presented in the classroom—its appropriateness to the specific learning style of the student. Teachers are urged to diagnose the learning problems of students and address to them through a more flexible use of teaching styles (substitution of visual methods for auditory ones such as the occasional replacement of books with tape recordings, oral responses to tests rather than written ones).

Despite the relative humanization of instruction that follows from such a perspective, it also represents a fairly distinct element in the hegemonic absorption of individualization. With the help of recent educational and psychological theories concerned with notions such as learning disabilities and learning styles, the understanding of school failure and inability remains primarily situated at the level of the psychological. Despite accumulating evidence concerning the distinctly unbalanced social distribution of special needs students, the application and formulation of individualized instruction is governed by theories of brain dysfunction, perceptual inadequacy, or cognitive underdevelopment, not by notions of cultural/social experience. The assimilation of the significance of individualization to psychological explanation compels education, ultimately, to focus on the methods or techniques of instruction rather than on the nature of the curriculum. In so doing, it allows us to avoid important political, epistemological, and social questions about the nature of the knowledge transmitted in school. Such questions must inevitably raise issues connected to the type of knowledge or experience that are sanctioned as validating ability and intelligence and those that are not. It must raise the issue of "cultural capital" in which the differentiated social experiences of students are accorded very different kinds of treatment or recognition. The work of those engaged in developing a critical phenomenological approach to curriculum provides an important alternative to the dominant psychologistic mode of accommodation to the perceived deficiencies of certain students.[21] From such a perspective a *genuine* individualization of educational practice would need to recognize the differentiation of cultural experience which gives rise to diverse forms of knowledge and intelligence. Such diversity, whose respective rationalities or meanings are context bound (and hence not easily comparable), is not at all amenable to the usual hierarchical orders of intellectual recognition congruent with the unequal distribution of income and status. It raises the question, ultimately, as to what extent genuine individualization would be reconcilable with the usual hierarchical orders of evaluation and assignment found in schools. The present disproportionate attention to the psychology of learning and techniques of teaching, as opposed to the sociology of the curriculum and the nature of knowledge, is an important means by which individualization, while remaining on the agenda of "progressive" educational concerns, loses its radical potentialities.

Schooling, Individualization, and the Ideology of the New Petit Bourgeoisie

Finally, in considering the hegemonic incorporation of the notion of individualization in education, we need to return to the view of social relations transmitted through the school process. In this respect the type of individualism contained in "progressive" versions of schooling is probably best understood as belonging to the ideology of what Nicos Poulantzas describes as the "new petit-bourgeoisie"—the massive group of white-collar, middle-class, salaried employees who work in corporate or governmental bureaucratic institutions.[22] It is a group that, because of its numerical significance in all advanced capitalist societies, has formed a focus for much recent sociological work on class consciousness and affiliation. Erik Olin Wright has noted the important ideological differences between the "old" and "new" petit bourgeoisie:

> The individualism of the new petty bourgeoisie . . . is a careerist individualism, an individualism geared towards organizational mobility. The archetypical new petty bourgeois is the "organizational man," whose individualism is structured around the requirements of bureaucratic advancement.[23]

Such a view of individualism must be sharply contrasted with older kinds of petit-bourgeois ideology which have stressed the notions of individual autonomy, economic and social independence, controlling one's own destiny. Such tendencies find their mythic expression in the rugged individualism of American folklore or, more recently (and, of course, with some significant deviations), in the notion of unconstrained individual freedom associated with the counterculture. All have images of man as standing outside, or even against, the organized establishment of society. Notwithstanding variations in the educational philosophy of teachers or administrators (where some, at least, may maintain Rousseauian aspirations for children) schooling, to a great extent, represents an accommodation of the individual to the ideology of this new petit bourgeoisie. Such an ideology can be understood as organized around a hierarchical image of society. In this, society is viewed as a ladder in which the steps represent a series of levels differentiated according to the lifestyles and prestige of its members. Social ascent or descent is a function of the relative degree of ability, determination, and perseverance possessed by each individual. What man achieves, finally, depends primarily on what he makes of himself. The purpose of social activity is to maintain a progressive improvement in consumption standards, and an ascent in terms of the prestige of one's life-style.

Schools are a major conduit for this middle-class image of the social order and, in particular, the view of individuality that underpins it.[24] They emphasize a view of the social order that is hierarchical, consisting of ascendant, contiguous, finely graduated levels of recognition and opportunity. Access to such levels is a function of individual perseverance and ability. In school students are encouraged to view the separation of tracks and ability groups as a system of relatively fluid distinctions which do not represent fundamental or insurmountable divisions so much as they constitute a continuum of experiences that are separated quantitatively rather than qualitatively. Within the context of these social relations, individualization in school is not a matter of the development of the unique expression of individual abilities and potentialities, but of the utilization of skills or knowledge in the quest for organizational mobility. It represents less the assertion of an autonomous, expressive, and self-determining individuality than an accommodation of the self to the imperatives of a bureaucratic structure. In this conflation of individuality and organizational mobility or bureaucratic position, the incorporational process achieves its most penetrating effect.

Conclusion

This discussion of individualization illustrates that cultural domination cannot be understood as the mere imposition of ideas or beliefs on a subordinate social group. In reality, the blend of culture and ideology contained by contemporary society exists in a considerable state of flux and tension, with the process of incorporation a continual attempt to absorb and stifle the dysfunctional moments. Such moments are the inevitable and perennial effect of alternative or oppositional meanings, values, and judgments that emerge from the total range of human experience and practices in our society. Thus, if individualization is a pedagogic concept of considerable appeal, it may be so because it resonates with aspirations, needs, and concerns that arise out of existing human practice (and are, to a large extent, repressed or inadequately expressed through the social order). At the same time, despite its emergence as an oppositional or alternative notion, the lack of a genuine self-awareness or critical consciousness allows it to become incorporated, transposed, and ultimately transformed, so that what starts out as an assertion of human liberation becomes turned back on itself as a means of further repression or accommodation. Present conservative nostrums, both in school and out, must not be seen as mere manipulation or imposition (false consciousness in its conspiratorial sense), but rather as the successful mobilization of genuine human concerns and needs around mystifying and obfuscating responses to the conditions which have spawned them.

This perspective views schooling not simply as a conveyor belt for the delivery of the dominant ideology, but as a terrain of contested, conflicting, and contradictory ideologies. Despite the fundamentally successful transmutation of oppositional challenges within and against dominant ideological notions, school, perhaps like nowhere else in bourgeois society, brings us face to face with the dialectic of liberal-democratic ideology—an ideology whose noble ideals and ignoble practices provide a continuing source of radical (cultural, if not political) ferment. Individualization then must be seen as a focus of some of the tensions that underlay this ferment—a source of purposes or intentions that are in no simple way congruent with the bureaucratic or corporate institutional order. More fundamentally, it is the crystallization of a structure of feelings that develop within the matrix of bourgeois values, meanings, and judgments, and find some resonance in the humanistic or progressive ideology of teachers and educators. Such feelings are no less grounded in the experience of bourgeois society and life than other, more reactionary, bureaucratic or authoritarian values.

For those of us who have been seeking to expose the repressive and alienating structure of feelings typically associated with school life, there is always the danger of viewing this institution as a straightforward process of totalitarian cultural or ideological domination. My attempt here has been to contribute to an understanding of this domination in ways that emphasize its dialectical nature. The pedagogic experience contains no simple or uniform ideology of repression (and is one reason teachers and other educators often find it difficult to identify fully with this interpretation of schooling). Instead, I have suggested a view of school as a complex field of sometimes discontinuous or oppositional ideological moments which must be actively selected, affirmed, and actualized by educators. It is a view in which human intentionality (shaped predominantly around notions of individual educational "needs") is in continuous interaction with (and accommodation to) the objective imperatives of the social structure and institutional forms. The repressive nature of schooling cannot be understood as a simple result of the human values held by educators (these may indeed be progressive or humanistic), so much as a product of the particular ideology—meanings and practices—that becomes embedded in the institutional context of schooling.

While I have sought in this chapter to emphasize the way in which the wider society limits and defines the possibilities of educational change, I do not wish to suggest futility in pursuing such change. Clearly, special education reforms contain the claim for basic civil rights with respect to an excluded and deprived population. Equally, the struggle for passage and implementation of special education legislation is a challenge by an oppressed minority to prevailing values and beliefs. It is a challenge to the dominant ideology posing important questions about our notions of deviancy and normalcy. The reform, too, makes the claim for progressive change in educational practice and pedagogy. Schools become compelled to see the student, his concerns, aptitudes, and needs, as being at the center of the instructional process, not the reified demands of the formal curriculum or course content. In this respect, we may see more clearly to what extent schools meet their official commitment to the well-being of all individuals. The familiar rhetoric of "meeting the needs of all students" and "equality of opportunity" is highlighted against the reality of the schools' role in selecting, categorizing, and preparing students for their anticipated roles in the social and occupational structure. While special education reform may not radically change education, it helps make clearer the contradictions between liberal-democratic educational ideals and the schools' role in the corporate structure.

Finally, while rejecting a notion of social reform that sees education as the primary agent of change, it would nevertheless be wrong to exclude it entirely from the process of social change. In reflecting the wider ideology, it contains the parameters of choice, the possibilities of change, and the definitions of reality that shape the demands, expectations and perceptions of individuals. Education becomes, at times, the focus for the expression of tensions and conflicts arising out of our wider social experience. The attempt at reform, in special education or in other areas of the field, becomes the attempt to resolve issues arising not simply out of education itself, but out of the broader social domain. While it is incapable, alone, of resolving these issues, attempts to do so must not be seen as merely exercises in mystification or futility. The struggle for progressive educational change serves to focus and stimulate demands for the genuine fulfillment of democratic ideals that frequently receive only formal or limited recognition in American society. It is possible to suggest that it is in these latter demands that the passage and implementation of Public Law 94–142 finds its true significance. In chapter 5, I continue the investigation of the tensions within, and around, the liberal-democratic state and their relationship to the currents of recent educational change.

5
Crisis of the State and Educational Politics in the '80s

I HAVE ARGUED THAT in attempting to understand the nature and direction of educational policy making in capitalist society, few contemporary analysts have taken seriously the role of the state in the process and the conjunction of interests and ideologies which educational policy, at any moment, inevitably embodies. Instead, the overriding impression created by many of those engaged in the development of a critical understanding of schooling has been one in which education is the very nearly unmediated expression of those occupying a dominant position in the social and economic order. Educational policies are frequently seen as the pure, unalloyed product of those holding economic power.

Such a view of educational development is rooted in a simplified and overdetermined notion of ideology in class-divided societies. To a great extent education, like the rest of the ideational superstructure, is seen as an entity determined by a single social group (or, at least, fractions of that group). Culture, from this perspective, is conceived of as a structure of beliefs, values, meanings, and practices which are the "reflection," "echo," or "sublimate" of needs or imperatives set entirely by a ruling class. Ideology becomes nothing more than the rationalization of the power of the class, and culture a process by which the nature and dynamics of the society within which it is located remain obscured.

Such a unidimensional view of the relations between class, power, and ideology has been severely challenged—not least by those who have noted the positivist implications of this schema.[1] It has also been demonstrated that such a view of ideology frequently lends itself to an understanding of the social process that is reductionist or conspiratorial.[2] Domination by ruling groups appears to be maintained by what Nicos Poulantzas refers to as "mendacious mystification."[3] It is certainly the case that frequent utilization of such a view of ideology, in attempts at developing a critical view of schooling, has led to a notion of educational change that is strongly determinist, and educational policies that are uncompromisingly monolithic. Such a view suggests that schooling is an unremittingly coherent, functional, and rational process (within the terms set by a dominant social class). It is a view that, despite its appealing simplicity, avoids the more complex, and frequently incoherent, nature of educational policies in capitalist societies. Instead we are attempting to develop an understanding of educational policy making in which it is seen constituted by the complex relations between class, power, and ideology. Educational policies, far from being some unalloyed product of the interests of a single dominant class are instead the mediated compromise of diverse class imperatives, interests, and ideologies. Educational policy making in this case is located in a notion of ideology that is reworked so as to divest it of its monolithic, determinist, or conspiratorial character.

It is precisely here that Gramsci's notion of hegemonic domination is so significant. Rather than representing the unmediated product of a single, "totalitarian" social class, able to impose its ideas, sensibilities, meanings, and values throughout the consciousness and practices of society, hegemony suggests a view of ideological domination at once more fluid, more adaptive to external social pressures, and open to the incorporation of diverse cultural meanings and practices. For Gramsci, it is the state in capitalist society that has the crucial responsibility for mediating and incorporating this diversity of social interests and ideologies.[4] For understanding the present educational landscape this perspective is vital. It is necessary to show how policies are formed out of the melding of diverse class imperatives and viewpoints. It is, after all, certainly clear that, in order to effect the political mobilization needed for educational change, something more is required than a simple manipulation of belief or ideological coercion. It demands the creation of an ethos of widespread consent which is embodied in the formation of a political power bloc. In the process of hegemonic control such a bloc is formed through the inclusion or incorporation of the concerns of those in subordinate or intermediary class positions into the policies of the state. Certainly, given that the ultimate purpose of this state is the maintenance and reproduction of the existing structure of class domination, the inclusion of such concerns ultimately must facilitate rather than challenge this domination. Thus, for example, the inclusion of ideas, meanings, values, and practices belonging to a subordinate class into the dominant ideology must be executed without their constituting a significantly oppositional moment in this ideology. Of course, the incorporation of the concerns of those outside the ruling groups can only take place through a complex process of selection and transformation. Through this incorporation a widespread sense of democratic participation is sustained, and consent for state policies ensured, while the possibilities of fundamental political or cultural opposition are dissipated. The policies formulated by the state must represent a response to social concerns other than those of the dominant class, but in a form that sustains the fundamental forms of class domination.

In looking at the nature of the state in liberal-capitalist society, it makes no sense, then, to view it as simply reflecting the unmediated interests of capital. It must, in the final analysis, do this, but it must also do more. For the Swedish sociologist Goran Therborn, the state must embody two relationships:

> The State . . . must represent, that is to say, promote and defend, the ruling class and its mode of exploitation or supremacy. At the same time, the State must mediate the exploitation or domination of the ruling class over other classes and strata. The State, in other words, is both an *expression* of class exploitation and domination, and *something more* than a simple expression.[5]

In her discussion of Antonio Gramsci's view of the state, Chantal Mouffe notes that while it is "seen as the organ of one particular group, destined to create favorable conditions for the latter's maximum expansion . . . the development and expansion of the particular group are conceived of, and presented, as being the motor force of a *universal* expansion, of a development of *all* the 'National' energies . . . ."[6]

The state's claim to be serving not only the interests of the most powerful groups, but acting in a more universal capacity, is no simple illusion. Nicos Poulantzas, for example, argues that the capitalist state's particular characteristic feature is to represent "the general interest of a national popular ensemble."[7] Social policies may contain "real economic sacrifices imposed on the dominant class by the struggle of the dominated classes."[8] (Yet, Poulantzas asserts, such policies ultimately cannot call into question the capitalist nature of the state.)

There is, at the center of the studies reviewed in this chapter, a view of the state in capitalist society that follows these perspectives, one in which the state is seen as a complex phenomenon, propelled by no simple or uniform purpose. Central to it, however, is the need to accomplish two frequently contradictory ends: it must try to maintain or create conditions in which profitable capital accumulation is possible while, at the same time, trying to maintain or create the conditions for some minimum degree of social harmony. For, as James O'Connor notes, a state that openly uses its coercive force to help one class accumulate capital at the expense of other classes loses its legitimacy and hence undermines the basis of its loyalty and support.[9] It is these dual and often conflicting demands that give the capitalist state its distinct and irreducible character.

In beginning to recognize the "relative autonomy" of the state from the immediate demands of the system of production, and its need to be concerned with both accumulation and legitimacy, requires that our view of the process of educational policy formulation undergo a serious revision. No longer can educational policies be understood as merely the response to the demands of dominant economic groups or as reflecting only adjustments to the productive system. Such explanations miss the point of the need to view education as, first, a component of the state (more specifically, the "social-welfare" state) and thus bound by the peculiar and distinct dynamics of that entity. This has certainly been apparent in recent times. Conservative educational policies and reform must, first and foremost, be seen in the context of broader policies that emanate from a general opposition to the social-welfare state.

To understand the nature of recent educational policies in the United States it is necessary to see them as a response to the present crises of this state. It is in the attempt to resolve these crises that much of the future direction of education is being set. In particular, the formation of such policies is, in important ways, a response to the intensifying conflict between the two major imperatives of the state—accumulation and legitimation. The major part of this chapter considers a number of important arguments that seek to lay out the nature and consequences of this conflict and out of which may be derived what are referred to below as the "fiscal," "administrative," and "ideological" crises of the capitalist state. Only through such a focus is it really possible to understand how present, or intended, educational reforms have been arrived at. Below, the contributions of three key authors—Jürgen Habermas, James O'Connor, and Alan Wolfe—are reviewed. The social, political, and economic analyses of these writers has added significantly to our understanding of the present problems of the capitalist state: Habermas in the field of rationality and motivation, O'Connor in fiscal analysis, and Wolfe on the issue of organization and administration.

Crises of the State: Origins of the Politics of Retrenchment

For Habermas the rapid encroachment of the state into more and more areas of our social lives has undermined the traditional legitimations and motivations of capitalist society.[10] In arguing against the present applicability of Marx's critique of political economy, Habermas notes the changed relationship between the state and the economy in liberal capitalism. In particular, the latter no longer has the degree of autonomy earlier posited by Marx. Indeed, argues Habermas, it is now the state that regulates the economic cycle as a whole and ensures conditions for the utilization of surplus accumulated capital. This is done through a range of phenomena that include government credits, price guarantees, subsidies, loans, labor policy, income redistribution, "unproductive" consumption (such as armaments), improvement of the material and "immaterial" infrastructure (such as in transportation, communication, health, housing), research and development, improvement of the productivity of labor through technical education and training programs, and relief from the social costs of private production (through unemployment compensation, welfare, and ecological repair).

The result of all this, says Habermas, is a change in the "organizational principle" of capitalism. The state, under the pressure of ensuring its democratic legitimacy, is required to make good the functional weaknesses of the market and compensate for its politically intolerable consequences. This is certainly apparent in the demands increasingly made of the state in regard to such matters as environmental repair and protection, welfare programs for dependent or excluded groups, and citizens' protection from product or service abuse. Most importantly, says Habermas, the autonomy of the economic sphere *vis-à-vis* the political has given way to a "quasi-political" distribution of the social product: "There is a general awareness that the distribution of social wealth depends in no small way on government policies and the 'quasi-political' negotiation of rewards and obligations."[11] This is so, whether in government involvement or intervention in labor contract bargaining, or in the negotiations over transfer payments, or tax policies connected to the budget process. Perhaps even more fundamental is the belief that what happens in the economy (the level of inflation, unemployment, availability of credit) is no longer the uncontrollable result of a "nature-like" process, but the direct consequence of government activity: "economic processes can no longer be conceived immanently as movements of a self-regulating economic system."[12] They are subject to the control of the state and, at least in principle, to the legitimation of the democratic process.

What Habermas calls a "rationality crisis" occurs when the state, despite popular expectations, is unable to reconcile and fulfill imperatives that arise from the economic system. He notes that a number of arguments have been proposed concerning the origins of this type of crisis; these have included the assertion of the incompatibility of the collective planning of the state with the "anarchistic" interests of private capital, and the crisis in public finances that results from the government's assumption of the cost of more and more social expenses such as armaments, transportation, communications, research and development, and health care. Despite these significant problems, Habermas argues that they do not, inevitably, pose a threat to the system. He notes that the "critical threshold" of tolerance for disorganization is unclear, as are the limits of administrative negotiation and compromise with interest groups and various sections of society: "The possibility that the administrative system might open a compromise path between competing claims that would allow a sufficient amount of organizational rationality, cannot be excluded from the start on logical grounds."[13]

More threatening than this rationality crisis, claims Habermas, is the "legitimation crisis." The process of subjecting increasing sectors of social life to the administrative planning of the state produces the unintended side-effect of undermining traditional forms of legitimation:

> Rationalization [i.e., administrative planning] destroys the unquestionable character of validity claims that were previously taken for granted; it stirs up matters that were previously settled by the cultural tradition in an unproblematic way; and thus it furthers the politicization of areas of life previously assigned to the private sphere. For example, educational (especially curriculum) planning, the planning of the health system, and family planning have the effect of publicizing and thematizing matters that were once culturally taken for granted. The end effect is a consciousness of the contingency, not only of the contents of tradition, but also of the techniques of tradition. And this development endangers the civil privatism essential to the depoliticized public realm. Efforts at participation and the plethora of alternative models ... are indications of this danger, as is the increasing number of citizen's initiatives.[14]

Nor, argues Habermas, is the state able to compensate such "legitimation deficits" through conscious manipulation. The cultural system, he notes, is "peculiarly resistant" to administrative control: "There is no administrative production of meanings. The commercial production and administrative planning of symbols exhausts the normative force of counterfactual validity claims."[15] Indeed, the opposite is true; the spread of administrative interventions increases the pressure for legitimation—there is a widening circle of activities and practices that need to be subjected to public discourse and popular acceptance and express decisions made through some kind of rational consensus.

Ultimately, according to Habermas, the spread of administrative rationality spurs a third kind of crisis—one concerned with motivation as "normative structures ... no longer provide the economic-political system with ideological resources, but instead confront it with exorbitant demands."[16] Specifically, he argues, the "syndromes of civil and familial-vocational privatism," which are the most important motivational patterns for the continued stability of advanced capitalist society, are undermined by the rationalization of areas of life once regulated by tradition. Thus, for example, "achievement ideology," which is an important element of this syndrome (the idea that social rewards should be distributed on the basis of individual achievement) becomes problematic to the extent that the market loses its credibility as a "fair" medium of allocating these rewards. (Habermas notes that, while in the more recent versions of the achievement ideology, occupational success mediated through formal schooling takes the place of success in the market, this, too, has become problematic. He points at, for example, the increasingly unsynchronized developments of the educational and occupational system and to the fact that there are more and more areas in which production structures and labor processes make evaluation according to individually accountable achievement improbable.)

"Possessive individualism," another aspect of the privatistic syndrome, has become problematic to the extent that capitalist society attains a level of social wealth at which the avoidance of basic risks and the satisfaction of basic needs are no longer the principal determinants of individual preferences. And, too, the "quality of life" is increasingly dependent on "collective commodities" (such as transportation systems, health care, and education). Finally, Habermas argues, the "orientation to exchange value" (belief in the market as the way of expanding energies or allocating resources) is weakened as more and more people are engaged in work not directly connected to the market (in human services, state employment, education).

Thomas McCarthy suggests, however, that it is not at all clear that the motivational patterns associated with welfare statism, the competitive structure of the occupational and educational spheres, and the orientation to consumption and leisure have been weakened to the extent that we could speak of a tendency to a motivation crisis. Or that the growing "cynicism of the bourgeois consciousness" to which Habermas frequently refers might be described as the willingness to accede to a political order because it provides an acceptable flow of system-conforming rewards. To whatever extent such arguments may confound Habermas's thesis, the true significance of his analysis lies most clearly in its identification of the public sphere as the "new conflict zone" in organized capitalism. In particular, the assertion of the politicization (or, as he describes it, the repoliticization) of the public sphere implies expectation that greater areas of our social and economic life will be subject to rational discourse and democratic discussion, not the influence of some "hidden hand" or the power of unrepresentative authority.

The Contradictions of Capitalism and the Problem of Bureaucracy

Following Habermas, the American political scientist Alan Wolfe has argued that the central difficulty of the capitalist state is its need to be responsible for both the accumulation of capital and the legitimation of the existing social order.[17] In his history of the American state he describes the unresolved tension between these two functions: on the one hand the need to meet what he calls the imperative of "liberal" ideology that is the assurance of profitability for those who dominate the economic marketplace, and, at the same time, the need to fulfill the "democratic" demand for "some kind of popular participation and some equality of results." At the present time, Wolfe argues, the policies which have attempted to resolve or ameliorate these tensions have exhausted themselves. As a result, late capitalism is characterized by political and economic stagnation. The key terms, he asserts, that now describe western capitalist society are no longer harmony or growth, but stagnation, *immobilisme,* limited options, and *la societée bloquée.*

Societies which only two decades ago were viewed as having solved the major issues are now seen as overwhelmed to the point of paralysis.

At the center of this paralysis is a view of the state as having reached unmanageable proportions and bureaucratically out of control. Such a view, says Wolfe, is essentially correct, but it is the direct consequence of the need to reconcile the demand for accumulation with the need for legitimacy:

> So long as the state was concerned predominantly with an accumulation function, government bureaus were small and easily managed.... The need to reconcile accumulation with legitimacy changed this uncomplicated situation; out of this need the modern bureaucratic state began to grow ... the more the state was called on to regularize both intra- and interclass conflict by making authoritative decisions, the greater the inevitable bureaucratization that followed. Increases in bureaucracy stem from the tension between liberal and democratic conceptions of the state, which are channeled into public agencies that attempted to resolve it on an ad hoc basis.[18]

Wolfe notes that each failure of a public agency to routinize class conflict with finality led to demands for new bureaus. The result has been the intensification of the process by which the state has evolved into a sprawling, irrational, contradictory, and wasteful bureaucracy.

The bureaucratic and wasteful consequences of requiring public administration to resolve problems that were previously left to the market (or merely ignored), is pointed to by Claus Offe. The capitalist state, he argues, can act in two ways: distributing existing resources to all the contending parties, and creating new resources directly by participating in the accumulation process. Under the present conditions of economic stagnation, says Offe, the state is increasingly drawn into direct productive activities. This, however, (and in contrast to allocation) is incompatible with bureaucratic modes of operation:

> Productive activity ... assumes a range of questions that bureaucracies are not equipped to answer: What is the end goal of the activity? What is the most efficient way of obtaining it? How should it be financed? For this reason, the emergence of late capitalism brings about new needs that bureaucracy cannot satisfy at the same time that it encourages greater bureaucratization.[19]

In late capitalist society, Wolfe asserts, the bureaucracy has become more than unwieldy—it has become the one place to which the most impossible tasks are assigned. Where previously the market and the political process decided who got what, when, and how, the bureaucracy now decides. And caught between its political task and its depoliticized rationale, he argues, public administration in late capitalism searches for answers to its intractable task wherever it can find them, only to discover that each possible option causes as many problems as it solves.

The resulting growth of new bureaus that do not solve the problems for which they were created gives rise to both an administrative and a fiscal crisis. Wolfe argues that the simultaneous need for, but despair of, bureaucracy colors the public life of our time. The consequent confusion is reinforced, rather than ameliorated, by the practices and reforms of state policy makers. As administrators struggle to gain support for their particular concerns, so the traditional distinction between politics and administration is eroded, and the latter becomes increasingly politicized. As the monopolization of firms in the private sector eliminates competition and subjects the economy to a "thorough rationalization," bureaus within the state appear as parochial, competitive, and inefficient by capitalist criteria. The enormous disparity between the principles organizing the two sectors could not be tolerated, and the result, says Wolfe, was an attempt to organize public bureaus in monopolistic fashion. The resulting centralization ultimately did little more than contribute to the further stagnation of policy making. The creation of "super-administrative" units has, by a number of accounts, reduced innovation and risk taking and eliminated "self-generated standards of propriety."

In response to the problems created or exacerbated by centralization, the opposite notion of decentralization was proposed:

> A school of thought developed holding that approximation to a market place of allocation *within the state* was the best option. For every conglomerate department, there were calls for vouchers, local initiatives, creative federalism, and voluntary programs. Centralization and decentralization were even advocated by the same men at the same time; Richard Nixon, for example, would argue publicly for creative federalism while centralizing national power to new heights. In the confused ideological context, one must see both solutions as not being answers in themselves. The fact that political thought could swing with such abandon from one pole to the other is testimony to how intractable the problem of bureaucracy in late capitalism was becoming.[20]

The Fiscal Crisis of the State

From problems of legitimacy and the issue of administrative rationality we pass to the third area of crisis—what James O'Connor terms the "fiscal crisis of the state", that is, the tendency for government expenditures to outrace revenues. Its origins, at least on the surface, are fairly clear:

> Every economic and social class and group wants government to spend more and more money on more and more things. But no one wants to pay new taxes or higher rates on old taxes .... Society's demands on local and state budgets seemingly are unlimited, but people's willingness and capacity to pay for these demands appears to be narrowly limited. And at the federal level expenditures have increased significantly faster than the growth of total production.[21]

O'Connor's argument, however, goes beyond the simple explanation of the crisis. The categories, as he describes it, that make up the theoretical framework are drawn from Marxist economics and adapted to the problem of budgetary analysis. Like Habermas and Wolfe, his initial premise is that the capitalist state must try to fulfill two basic and often mutually contradictory functions, accumulation and legitimization.

We can, in this chapter, do more than point, briefly, at the fundamental contradiction at the heart of the budgetary process of the state as suggested by O'Connor. At one pole of this contradiction is the belief that the growth of the state sector and state spending functions increasingly as the basis for the growth of big business ("the monopoly sector")[22] and, conversely, that the growth of state spending and state programs is the result of the growth of these industries. Thus, for example, O'Connor notes the greater and greater responsibility borne by state and local budgets in providing the basic investments in physical, social, and human capital needed to ensure the profitability of big business, such as highway and transportation systems, port and aviation facilities, urban renewal projects, research and development, and technical training. Among the reasons for the enlarged role of the state, says O'Connor, is the increased pace of technological change and thus the more rapid obsolescence of capital equipment, the increased financial risk attributable to the growth of uncontrollable overhead costs, and the sheer size of many investment undertakings. Finally, there is the lengthening of the lead time before the typical private investment is in full operation and able to pay for itself.

In addition to the huge growth in state-financed social investments, monopoly capital (together with organized labor) has generally favored socializing social consumption expenditures, such as medical and health costs, workers' retirement income, and unemployment compensation. While, as O'Connor notes, unions have supported socializing these costs because of membership needs and demands for better and more comprehensive medical care, liberalized pensions, and the like, monopoly industries have supported such policies because of the burden of expensive pensions, health and insurance plans won through collective planning. In addition, however, he argues that the growth of the monopoly sector is "irrational" in the sense that it leaves in its wake unemployment, poverty, economic stagnation, environmental damage, and urban decay. And, says O'Connor, to ensure mass loyalty and maintain legitimacy, the state must meet the demands of those who suffer the costs of economic growth, or anticipate them. Thus, he notes:

> Although social security contributes to social and political stability by conservatizing unemployed and retired workers, the primary purpose of the system is to create a sense of economic security within the ranks of employed workers ... and thereby raise morale and reinforce discipline.

This contributes to harmonious management-labor relations which are indispensable to capital accumulation and the growth of production. Thus the fundamental intent and effect of social security is to expand productivity, production and profits. *Seen in this way, social insurance is not primarily insurance for workers, but a kind of insurance for capitalists and corporations.*[23]

One of the paradoxes of capital accumulation and technological change is that it enlarges the population unable to gain employment in monopoly industries. Such "surplus" population is frequently left unemployed, underemployed, or employed at low wages in the competitive sector of industry and becomes to varying degrees dependent on the state. O'Connor notes that, partly as a consequence of the deterioration of competitive sector workers' standards of living during the past two decades or so, increased numbers of surplus workers have become militant in their opposition to budgetary priorities that favor the monopoly sector:

> National movements and organizations of blacks and other minorities, women, welfare rights groups, and local insurgency movements and community groups struggling against local welfare, health and other bureaucracies have compelled the federal, state and local governments to broaden welfare standards, develop new welfare-related programs, increase intergovernmental grants, and so on. Subsidies, particularly for education, retraining, childcare, housing, transportation, and health (mainly Medicare and Medicaid) have increased. Public assistance payments, which until the 1960s were less than 2 percent of the federal budget, have mounted sharply in recent years because eligibility provisions have been liberalized, more people have taken advantage of their rights, and benefits have been raised.[24]

One side of the fiscal conflict is characterized by a huge expansion of social expenses paid for by the state, the other side is marked by the lack of adequate revenue to balance it. O'Connor argues that while the state socializes more and more capital costs, the social surplus continues to be appropriated privately. Thus favorable treatment of capital gains, together with enormous benefits of income-splitting at high income levels, reduce taxes on the rich by about one-half, and personal deductions reduce taxation still further to about one-third of potential levels under the nominal rate structure. All in all, he suggests, the average tax rate at the upper end of the income structure is probably as low as 20 percent.

Nor is it only the avoidance of appropriating equitably the available wealth to pay for social expense outlays that is responsible for the gap between state expenditures and state revenues; it is also the "private appropriation of state power for particularistic ends." The fiscal crisis is exacerbated by the host of "special interests" (corporations, industries, regional and other kinds of business interests) who make claims on the budget for various kinds of social investment. In addition to this, organized labor and workers, the unemployed, and the poor make claims for different kinds of social consumption. As O'Connor notes, most of these claims are processed by the political system and are won or lost as a result of political struggle:

> Precisely because the accumulation of social capital and social expenses occurs within a political framework, there is a great deal of waste, duplication, and overlapping of state projects and services. Some claims conflict and cancel one another out. Others are mutually contradictory in a variety of ways. The accumulation of social capital and social expenses is a highly irrational process from the standpoint of administrative coherence, fiscal stability, and potentially private capital accumulation.[25]

The result of this pursuit of particularistic ends is, of course, the exacerbation of the state's fiscal troubles.

Implications: Conservative Politics, Education, and the Resolution of the Crises

In 1981 the *Harvard Educational Review* published an extensive "report analysis" of *public and private schools* by James Coleman and associates.[26] What was especially surprising in this series of six articles was the total absence of any indication of the sociological context for such research. While the various commentators went about their task of discussing issues connected to data reliability, the meaningfulness of comparing "cognitive outcomes," or the difficulty of excluding "self-selection" as a factor in accounting for the type of pupils found in private schools, there appeared to be little awareness of the context, social or political, in which such work exists. It is an absence especially noticeable when one considered that the report was authored by an individual whose name is synonymous with the educational and social reforms of the 1960s. One surely does not need to be too much of a scholar in the sociology of knowledge to appreciate that there may indeed be some connection between the focus of Coleman's more recent report and the social, political, and economic reality which is its backdrop. Nor is this an assertion of conspiracy. It is certainly not a simple matter of who pays the bills, or which "masters" we serve (though, as C. Wright Mills so powerfully reminded us, these are not inconsequential). More important in directing our research interests is another, somewhat less tangible, force—one that springs from the circumstances that surround us and the experiences found there and within which our consciousness is shaped. It is here that questions, meanings, and perceptions are formed and from which, out of the plethora of possible research concerns, some are selected as being paramount. It is within this "ideological environment" that research reports (especially ones that receive so much attention) that question the viability of public education and lend themselves to the arguments of those advocating a "privatization" of schools must be understood. (It is not merely a matter of what research is done in a particular historical period, but which, from the enormous range available, is paid particular attention.)

Research into, and subsequent publicized discussion of, private education must be understood, at least in part, as reflecting a wider set of social concerns that are rooted in the context of a specific historical juncture and the particular human and social experiences found there. Such concerns center on the efficacy, rationality, and legitimacy of public institutions (specifically those connected to the state) during this period, and they ultimately embrace questions about the viability of liberal-capitalism with its increasing tensions between "private" and "public" sectors. In understanding the emergence of arguments concerned with the advocacy of private schooling,[27] I believe it is necessary to view it in the context of crisis, not just of public schools but of the whole public sector. Such a crisis is manifested at a number of levels, fiscal, administrative, and ideological, to which the response has been the acceleration of demands for the contraction of state institutions and programs, and their replacement by the privatized mechanisms of the market. It is a response that has been embodied in the politics of "Reaganomics" in this country or of "Thatcherism" in Great Britain. Their conservative programs proposed, and sought to implement, the view that social and economic problems are best solved, not through the interventions of the state, but in the marketplace. In a variant of middle-class populism, the proposals held out the promise of individual (and corporate) freedom untrammelled by a coercive, bureaucratically-inflated state, and in which private concerns or preferences could be fulfilled unhindered by administrative regulation.

Above, I have presented three distinct but converging analyses of the present crisis of the capitalist state. It is not so much the descriptions of the problems that give these works their radical character, but the analysis of its causes. That there is a budgetary crisis, or that a burgeoning bureaucracy has created an administrative leviathan, or that ever-expanding expectations have overloaded the state with demands and obligations can be denied by few on the political Left or Right. Conservative politics are certainly predicated precisely on these beliefs. Nowhere has this been as apparent as in the design of recent educational policies: the attempt to ensure fiscal solvency through massive reductions in educational spending; the attempt to thwart bureaucratic expansion by dismantling the Department of Education or the introduction of block grants; and the curtailment of an interventionist government stance in regard to the educational demands of groups or individuals. In many respects, the private school issue was emblematic of an ideological crusade whose goal is to reduce the scope, expense, and involvement of the public sector and to increase the extent to which social concerns are met through private means. It is a view that is supported by the characteristically middle-class perception of a state whose major interventions (in education and elsewhere) seem to be on behalf of the poor and minorities. It is these latter groups who are held to be the beneficiaries of oppressive middle-class taxation.

While conservative politics certainly appears to confront, if not solve, the problems of the state in its major dimensions (fiscal, administrative, ideological), this has certainly been more illusory than real. Conservative policies undermined the egalitarian and democratic concerns crucial to the legitimizing function of the state in a class society. While there has been no reduction in the level of state expenditures overall (though, of course, a significant reallocation of them), there also has been no attempt to ensure budgetary solvency through an effective and equitable taxing of existing wealth. The opposite has been the case. Conservative fiscal policy has not resolved the fundamental contradiction of the budgetary process described by O'Connor. Its results are deficits, the likelihood of renewed inflation, and hardship for those most dependent on social and educational expenditures.

Nor has it been only in the fiscal area that policies produced consequences in no way leading to the resolution of the crises of the state. In regard to the administrative crisis—the ever-expanding and proliferating bureaucracy that characterizes government—parallel effects can be observed. Under the guise of interventions that purported to restrict bureaucratic enlargement, the effects of policies were to reduce environmental protection, lower occupational safety or consumer product quality standards, and weaken the enforcement of civil-rights statutes. Such policies have ignored what is at the core of Wolfe's argument: regulative agencies and government interventions in capitalist society developed, at least in part, as a response to the abuses, failures, and neglect of the capital-accumulating process. In the face of the profit-seeking imperatives of the economy and the inequitable effects of the private sector, it is left to the state to maintain the levels of fairness and protection necessary for the continued legitimacy of the system. In education, as elsewhere in the society, government interventions have grown, not as a result of a malevolent conspiracy among bureaucrats, or through the indulgent whims of "liberal" politicians (the conservative view), but as a response to genuine social demands in the face of inequity, exploitation, and the violation of rights. Far from merely the capricious imposition of government officials or politicians, regulative and fiscal interventions have been a consequence of the attempt to bring some legitimacy to a system which, left to itself, would quickly reveal its inequitable, undemocratic and frequently despotic nature. In anticipating the transfer of public subsidies to private schools, for example, Guthries and Zusman speculate on its effect in establishing new government regulations:

> If a private school receives a public subsidy, does it have the right to

refuse admission to any applicant? For what reasons can a student be expelled from a publicly subsidized private school? Will regulations be imposed to ensure due process regarding dismissal?. . . . Are publicly subsidized private schools included under the collective bargaining provisions of the National Labor Relations Act? Must private schools be made to expand their governing boards to include publicly elected representatives?[28]

Such questions make clear that government intervention and administrative regulation are the necessary price of liberal capitalism; it represents the unavoidable pressure to reconcile somehow the values of democracy and equity with the privatistic and hierarchical character of our social institutions. Attempts to curtail interventions or regulation in the present social environment must lead to inevitable increases in discrimination, the use of arbitrary authority, and a decline in the equitability of opportunities and resources.

The conservative response to the crisis of the state can only produce harsh consequences for those most dependent on government interventions. Nowhere is this made more explicit than in the attempt to deal with the crisis of legitimacy. At its root, the crisis of legitimacy is a crisis of rising expectations in which the state attempts to guarantee the fulfillment of an expanding range of human demands. Indeed, we have seen that such guarantees have become requisite for the continued legitimacy of the liberal-capitalist system. The state, to some degree at least, must underwrite the failures and neglect of the private sector and hold out the promise of making good on citizens' social and economic expectations. Thus the avowed aims of conservative policy are to control such promises and to lower expectations. David Stockman's claim that "the government can no longer be expected to do everything" was an attempt to meet the crisis of legitimacy by "cooling-out" purportedly too high expectations and demands.

Nowhere were such goals more clearly demonstrated than in the 1980–81 educational policies of the Reagan administration; the projected 56 percent cut in student loans in the United States (including the proposed elimination of Social Security benefits for college students who were dependents of deceased, retired, or disabled workers); the $1 billion cut in college work-study programs that attempted to remove 250,000 job opportunities for students trying to work their way through school; and the reduction in Pell grants for needy students so as to remove a million students from the rolls.[29] Such policies have had their parallel in the policies of other conservative administrations: the Thatcher government's proposed 15 to 20 percent cut in university support between 1981 and 1984.[30]

Government policies such as these were aimed directly at a system in which (as Habermas notes) educational and occupational structures are more and more "unsynchronized." After increasingly long periods of schooling the anticipated outcomes in income and job satisfaction go more and more unfulfilled. Increasing numbers of students exit from school only to find their occupational expectations unmet as capitalist economics and democratic promises become more and more dissonant.[31] In the attempt to restore harmony, government sides with the former against the latter; the democratic state must simply promise less. Notions of equal educational opportunity notwithstanding, the intent is clear; reductions in government assistance will reduce the number of aspirants for "better" jobs, introduce a greater measure of "stability" in the professional job market, and help to resolve the legitimacy crisis by lowering the expectations of young people overly encouraged by the welfare state. Such a view, however, hides a somewhat darker reality; it is the systematic exclusion of low-income individuals from higher education, and the attempt to reconcile larger segments of a new generation of workers to an economic system which promises, if not outright unemployment, at least mass underemployment of talents, abilities, and intellect. It is the resolution of a crisis of legitimacy in which democratic and human values are unashamedly subordinated to the imperatives of the market and the maximization of profit. Chapter 6 continues the examination of the sociological roots of conservative educational policies, looking, especially, at the role of middle-class groups in supporting the policies of the Right.

6
The Making of Conservative Educational Policy

Conservative Educational Policies and the Reallocation of Wealth

IN THE FORMATION OF conservative educational policy, the incorporation of demands and the inclusion of concerns from those outside the dominant groups have been critical elements. Indeed, such policy requires the mobilizing impetus of groups located outside the ruling class. In the United States it has been the harnessing of the concerns of sections of the middle class that has constituted the real dynamic of conservative educational policy making. This has meant the selective incorporation of elements of petit-bourgeois ideology into a set of critical policy demands that reflects the unquestionably urgent frustrations, anxieties, and concerns of the middle class. While, however, policies have provided only the illusion of an adequate response to these frustrations, anxieties, and concerns, they do facilitate the real interests of the dominant class—capital. Indeed (and certainly not for the first time in history), capital, through the hegemonic absorption of middle-class fears and anxieties, has been able to construct a political "battering ram" for the achievement of its own ends.

Conservative educational policy in recent times may be understood as representing the conjunction of two distinct but reinforcing concerns:

(1) The attempt by capital to effect a radical redistribution of the national product through a drastic reallocation of "social" expenditures.

(2) The demand to more thoroughly ground (or reground) education in the ideology of petit-bourgeois values, beliefs, and social relations.

While a confluence of class concerns in the determination of a conservative educational policies is suggested, there is no intention here of asserting the existence of some kind of balance, or equivalence, in the relations between these class forces. The former (capital) is always, in the final analysis, decisive. The interests and concerns of other social groups or classes receive attention, or are accounted for, largely in the degree to which they may facilitate the interests of the dominant economic class. In other words, middle-class policy concerns receive support in the political process to the extent they are commensurate with the needs of capital. At the same time, however, the mobilization of middle-class concerns to execute state policies that are in the interests of the dominant class must not be seen as merely exercises in manipulation or mystification. What is at issue here, rather, is a complex screening, transformation, and adaptation of subordinate class concerns to facilitate or augment the power of those who constitute society's dominant social groups.

During this recent period educational policies are being formed against a background of a rapid and decisive reallocation of economic resources in the direction of capital. It is this phenomenon which constitutes the first element in the conjunction of class interests and concerns underpinning conservative educational policies. The demand for a redistribution of the social product in favor of business and away from the New Frontier and Great Society programs of the '60s was rooted in the demand for increased corporate profitability. Such profitability has declined as United States business has run into stiffer competition from capitalist rivals in Japan, West Germany, and elsewhere, and small Third World nations have begun to resist United States political and economic domination—a problem compounded by the end of the domestic boom in the 1970s, after which an extended period of "stagflation" set in.[1] As a result the American economic pie began to shrink, and the real incomes of both working people and capitalists stagnated or declined. The general corporate explanation of this, and the one strongly espoused by the Reagan government, was that a capital shortage was at the root of declining American productivity vis-à-vis Europe and Japan. It developed because Federal policies impeded capital formation; high taxes penalized the innovators and investors by holding down profits; and Washington's massive borrowings "crowded out" businessmen in the credit markets. The proper response then was to hold down, or cut back, social programs, restrain wages, and increase the return to capital. Michael Harrington notes that the apologists for these policies conceded that this might look like special pleading on behalf of the rich: "But if one treated the wealthy in a kind and decent fashion, they said, that would increase investment, which would lead to new jobs, which would benefit the workers and the poor."[2]

Educational Change and the Demise of Middle-Class Expectations

It is within this context of a transfer of wealth to capital through drastic reductions in social-educational expenditures that the incorporation and mobilization of petit-bourgeois ideology has been an important element in the framing of educational policy. Such ideology, and its related educational perspective, was crucial in the justification of a reduction of federal dollars in education. It became the means to generate the necessary electoral and political support in order to effect such policy.

In order to understand fully the mobilization of support for conservative educational policy, it is necessary to say a word about the wider ideological context within which such support was set. This context has included those traditional American virtues associated with what is called the "Protestant ethic" or the "Puritan temper." Such virtues have emphasized work, sobriety, frugality, sexual restraint, and a forbidding attitude towards life. Indeed, it has not been hard to suggest a link between the assertion of such values and the emergence of conservative educational demands. This seems especially clear in the advocacy of a return to notions of "traditional" schooling—expressed in a restricted curriculum, imposition of more pronounced hierarchical pedagogical relations, and an emphasis on greater restraint in students' moral and social conduct. Yet, while the 1970s and '80s certainly seem to offer evidence of a significant reemergence of this kind of ideology, the extent to which it has been a primary force in shaping American education must be viewed with caution. In perhaps one of the best statements on this subject, Daniel Bell, in his essay on the "Cultural Contradictions of Capitalism," argues that such traditional bourgeois consciousness has, in fact, been in a state of demise since the early part of the twentieth century.[3] Bell suggests that the 1960s did not represent the great watershed in the breakup of the traditional bourgeois value system. The counter-culture of this period, he asserts, was no more than an extension of tendencies begun several decades before, which began the breakup of "traditional" ideology. Given the conclusions of Bell and others, it becomes more difficult to accept at face value the concern with traditional values as the primary impetus for the conservative educational viewpoint.[4] The policy demands which emerged from such a viewpoint claimed to be rooted in traditional values and social behavior: the assertion that school is too easy and no longer rewards hard work; that advancement takes place as a matter of right and no longer reflects real achievement; and that school encourages an instinct of immediate gratification and enjoyment rather than an attitude of persistence and endurance. In all these cases, the interventions of the federal government are given at least partial responsibility for such change. Such notions are reinforced by wider assertions of the invasion of individual freedom by "big government's meddling" or "social engineering."

While these arguments have certainly been loudly articulated by those on the right, such appeals to traditional ideology do not tell the whole story. The class interests underpinning the demand for change in educational policies cannot, primarily, be found in the concern with traditional values and beliefs, however much they have been made to appear that way.

While not entirely disposing of the notion of traditional middle-class values as the motor of recent educational demands, the latter are much more rooted in issues connected to the reproduction of the division of labor. Present educational demands stem far more from middle-class perceptions of the erosion of its relatively privileged position in the class structure and the division of labor. The distinctions that emanate from the division of labor endow the middle class with the experience of its separateness and superiority over the working class. Such distinctions include the "clean-ness" of white collar work (as opposed to manual labor), the opportunity to work "downtown," to wear a suit and tie as well as an organization of social contacts at work that permits and encourages fraternization with the boss or one's organizational superiors—all of this quite distinct from the experience of the working class whose jobs are usually characterized by their separateness from the rest of the hierarchy.[5] At the root of this superiority is the relationship of these classes to mental labor which, as Nicos Poulantzas has argued, is characterized far more by its symbolic and cultural forms than any real scientific or technical content. He writes:

> This mental labour is in fact encased in a whole series of rituals, know-how, and "cultural" elements that distinguish it from the working class . . . . This cultural symbolism is well enough known for us not to have to dwell on it. It extends from the traditional esteem given to "paper work" and "clerical workers" in general (to know how to write and to present ideas), to a certain use of "speech" . . . . All these things, of course, require a certain training: learning to write in a certain way, to speak in a certain way, to dress in a certain way . . . . This "certain way" is always the *other way,* opposed to that of the working class. . . . The main thing in fact is to know how to "intellectualize" oneself in relation to the working class; to know in these practices that one is more "intelligent" . . . .[6]

The primary function of the school in capitalist society, says Poulantzas, is to provide a legitimate basis for making this distinction between those with or without the capacity to engage in mental labor. The role of the school, he says, is "not to 'qualify' manual or mental labour in different ways, but far more to disqualify manual labour . . . by only qualifying mental labour."[7] Most of what goes on in the school curriculum does not represent a direct training for work, but is intended to establish an individual on one side or the other of the mental-manual division of labor.

In the present situation class distinctions dependent on the division of labor have eroded. For the middle class, changes in school practices are held, at least in part, responsible for this situation. Such changes are thought to be the root of the frustrations associated with what has been referred to as the "proletarianization of white-collar work"—the mechanization, routinization, and fragmentation of such work that have steadily undermined the relatively privileged expectations of large sections of the middle class.[8] Nowhere is this so clearly evident as in the massive increase in industrial-style unionism among middle-class employees (of whom teachers are, perhaps, the most visible example). This loss of privilege is traced to the schools' "overproduction" of "qualified" graduates, and the resulting decline in market value among educated job applicants. At issue for the middle class is not merely the ability to obtain work commensurate with one's training or qualifications, but to obtain any form of roughly appropriate work.

From the standpoint of the middle class, government interventions and government-supported reforms in education, during the past twenty years or so, appear to undermine class boundaries and class advantages in American society (reflected in the decline in quality and opportunity for professional work). This has occurred as government-sponsored efforts have, it is claimed, compromised the school's role in the process of intellectual selection (hence upsetting the "natural" balance between those capable or not of engaging in mental labor). Such efforts have made school "too easy" and "too flexible" so that it no longer functions to adequately restrict or select out the "wrong" or "incapable" students (that is to say, working-class, black, or other minority students). The educational policies consequent to these efforts have, it appears, undermined the class and racial advantage of the middle class—and, as a result of decreasing selectivity in the schools, glutted the job market with qualified applicants. The result is a serious erosion of the status, opportunity, and market position of the American middle class.

Within this context of the undermining of the division of labor and the erosion of the class-related expectations and advantages are petit-bourgeois attitudes towards educational policies formed. Within this context antagonism towards the reforms of the 1960s, as well as the demands for an end of "social promotion," are constituted. In the mobilization of political opinion around the need for cuts in social expenditures, the perception is established of a link between forms of federal intervention in schools, the erosion of educational standards, and the undermining of expectations in the job market. Of course, attempts to curtail federal expenditures are done, not explicitly in the name of this last element (the restoration or preservation of middle-class advantage over the working class, blacks, or other minorities), but through their association with reforms, and innovations that appear to have undermined the quality of education. By reducing government monies, and government involvement, return to a hitherto virtuous set of educational arrangements is possible, or so it is claimed.

Nowhere has this process been more clearly apparent than in the policy concerns of those advocating a return to basics. The movement organized around this demand must be seen as, primarily, a reaction to the belief that curriculum and pedagogic changes initiated during the 1960s and '70s undermined the curricular basis of social ranking and hierarchy embedded in the process of schooling. The introduction in schools of an extended range of curriculum experiences, many of which were more directly related to the lives of the poor, minority, or working-class students, threatened the particular character of the "cultural capital" that is both the source and product of middle-class advantage. A larger and less exclusive set of symbols, meanings, knowledge, and values could be utilized as "capital," hence reducing the advantage that had hitherto accrued to middle-class life. The egalitarian thrust underpinning the orientation of such curricular reforms supported institutional changes which moved schools toward more closely reflecting the social and cultural context in which they were located (through racial integration, mainstreaming, and bilingual programs). Such changes inevitably led to a demand for a broadened version of what constitutes educational experience, or "counts" as educational knowledge or ability. All of this indicated (not without some validity) an erosion of the curricular and evaluative criteria supporting the traditional hierarchies of school, and consequent economic success or failure. It became possible (even, to an extent, mandated) to widen the criteria by which students were judged to be "intelligent" or "bright." Curricular, pedagogic, institutional, or evaluational changes did indeed work to reduce the restrictiveness of educational judgments—to make it possible for a greater number, and a greater variety, of students to be competent to engage in mental (that is, white collar or professional) labor. From this perspective, the return to basics attempts to restore the restricted universe of cultural and social experiences upon which traditional judgments of educational ability are made (such as the return to literacy as the all-important criterion of intellectual capacity). There is in such change, behind the rhetoric concerning educational standards, the attempt to resolve the current crisis of middle-class expectations—a crisis whose origins are perceived to lie in the reforms, innovations, and interventions of Great Society liberalism, and supported by tax dollars whose profligate use appears to be responsible for the decline in the living standards of middle-class life.

The extent of the erosion of existing patterns of mobility and opportunity as a result of the changes in school practices should not be exaggerated. Changes that have taken place cannot, to a great extent, be separated from the overall performance of the economy. What is important here, however, are the perception of such change and the mobilization of those perceptions around political goals which would support reductions in government social expenditures and interventions. Such interventions appear, from the perspective of the middle class, to have made school a place where anyone can succeed. The mobilization of such perceptions has contributed to the maintenance of what Colin Greer has called "The Great School Legend"—the belief that adequate and appropriate employment opportunities are linked to the opportunities for adequate and appropriate schooling.[9] It obscures what economist Lester Thurow refers to as the idea that it is not the skill and training of the worker that determine the job he or she gets; it is the job that determines the skill and training of the worker. (Thurow notes that the President's Commission on Technology, Automation and Economic Progress found that only 40 percent of the work force actually used cognitive skills acquired in formal training programs. The other 60 percent had learned all they needed to know on the job.) He writes: "The labor market is not primarily a bidding market for selling existing skills but a training market where training slots must be allocated to different workers."[10] While the decision as to who is to receive these training slots permits the reproduction of the inequalities associated with class, race, or sex (as they are mediated by the process of schooling), the salience of educational characteristics nevertheless varies with economic circumstances: "When labor is plentiful, hiring characteristics escalate; when labor is in short supply, hiring characteristics relax."[11]

Thurow's theory makes clear that the economic devaluation of education is related not to the quality of one's education (the standards or competencies achieved), but to the relationship between labor supply and job opportunities. It is this which is responsible for the fact that the "premium" attributed to a degree fell from 39 percent in 1969 to 15 percent in 1974, that 80 percent of college graduates are currently underemployed. Steven Dresch predicted: "In a traumatic reversal of historical experience, children born to persons entering adulthood in the 1950s and 1960s will, on average, experience relatively lower status than their parents."[12]

Perhaps sadder even than the illusions maintained by the association of adequate educational preparation with job success (and the resulting obsession with competency testing and the like) is the attempt to resolve the frustrations of the middle class through their support of policies that victimize the working class, the poor, and the handicapped. Conservative educational policy becomes, at root, a thinly veiled attack on the gains made during the last twenty years by such groups around the principle of equal opportunity.

Middle-class educational demands draw on, and reinforce, a view of the state in capitalist society in which it is seen as primarily an agent of the poor and the lowly. From this perspective there appears to be a fundamental bifurcation in the society, between those who espouse entrepreneurial attitudes, "getting ahead," achievement motivation, and a belief in the freedom to compete unfettered by government restrictions or control and those who demand government intervention to redress their inability to compete successfully in the marketplace of American society. Such a world view has the effect of placing the middle class alongside capital in its apparent espousal of the free market, and against collectivist interventions. It is a view that drives a wedge between the middle class and other subordinate groups—the latter, through their enlistment of government support, appearing to undermine the "fair" allocation of resources and opportunities through the market. It is this ideological alignment of the middle class and capital against the state that supports the mobilization of opposition towards federal social and educational expenditures on behalf of disadvantaged or excluded groups in American society. It is the not uncommon fate of the middle class to carry the banner for an ideology espousing an unfettered capitalism (and to share that task with a dominant class whose true interests are not so much an end to state intervention, as an elimination of interventions that restrict corporate profitability). The ideological bloc formed by the middle class and capital reflects the attempt by these groups to restore their eroding class positions through a reduction in the living standards and opportunities of working-class groups, women, minorities, the elderly, handicapped, the young, and others. It must be noted, however, that public opinion surveys have consistently pointed up the "contradictory consciousness" of middle-class people who espouse, on the one hand, an "individualistic" ideology, at the same time supporting collectivist interventions. There is, for example, no lack of support among the middle class for medicare, educational loans, veterans benefits, environmental protection, or social security.

The effect of social and educational policies that reflect a radical polarization of class interests (expressed not in direct class confrontation, but as mediated through attitudes towards the state, and particularly towards state social expenditures) creates the possibility of a significant breakdown in the hegemony secured by the postwar policies of "welfare-statism." What we are now witnessing is a fundamental decrease in the political (and social) support for the institutions and procedures which have historically underpinned the accommodation between democratic ideals and economic realities in American society. Educational policies, for example, now reflect an increasing disregard for the idea of public schooling as the means to reconcile the egalitarian and hierarchical aspects of life in liberal-capitalist society. Instead, education is likely to more unreservedly assume the purpose of an agency responsible for the differential advancement of particular social (and racial) groups. Schooling will become more clearly identified with the reproduction of class, gender and racial advantage. As the *Carnegie Report* made clear, the most serious manifestation of this is in the continued, deepening crisis of urban schooling in this country.[13]

Such tendencies will have serious implications for the maintenance of an ideology which is able to "win the hearts and minds" of those in the most subordinate social positions (as well as, of course, not halting the erosion of middle-class fortunes). The individualistic, achievement-oriented accommodation to hierarchy and inequality made possible by the ideology of schooling will appear less tenable in the face of current and prospective educational policies. Indeed, what the implications might be of such an ideological "breakdown" are hard to predict. At the least we may assume a sharp increase in dissatisfaction and alienation. Together with the more general perception of a politics that is enriching the wealthy at a terrible cost to the poor, the consequences may go far beyond this.

Political Divergences in the Ruling Class: The Educational Reports of 1983

The preceding discussion presented a schematic picture of capital that appears as a class with homogeneous concerns and a unitary political agenda. The ruling class is better described through Gramsci's notion of a power bloc which, far from being monolithic, possesses a complex, conflicting, and contradictory character. This complex nature necessitates a state that retains some autonomy within the social formation. Such autonomy makes possible the harmonizing and coordinating of the diverse concerns of the dominant class fractions, as well as compelling them to make unwelcome concessions to subordinate groups. Only in this way can the state ensure propitious conditions for the accumulation of capital in the long run. Long-run considerations imply a concern with legitimation and consent by those who benefit least from the logic of capital accumulation and a need to focus on the needs of the capitalist class as a whole rather than the fragmentary and particularistic concerns of elements within the class.

Probably nothing makes clearer the distinctions between segments or fractions of the dominant class in terms of their general ideological point of view than their contrasting attitudes toward public education and its role in the attempted rejuvenation of the American economy—contrasts that are sharply illustrated by the spate of reports on public education issued during 1983. Such divergent attitudes toward education are inseparable from their broader expectations and attitudes concerning the role of public or state interventions in the management of the economy. Thus the call for the enhanced role of public schooling in offsetting economic decline—the central imperative of many of the reports—must be contrasted with the policy decisions of the Reagan administration to restrict and reduce programs and expenditures in education (as well as in a great many other areas of public and quasi-public activity). The affirmation of the public domain (whether in education or elsewhere) must be contrasted with the notion of the private market as a means to restore the dominance of American monopoly capital in the world economy, lower inflation, reduce interest rates, and raise productivity. As we have seen, the political Right asserted that it was precisely the expansion of public/state responsibilities and interventions that has been the undoing of the system. Appealing to the strongly rooted petit-bourgeois values of the middle class, it has argued that the turning away from the traditionally American emphasis on private interests (in the free market) has undermined the initiative, enterprise, and productivity necessary to economic competitiveness. Under the rhetoric of this ideology, the Reagan government mounted its unprecedented campaign to dismantle or significantly reduce the role of the state apparatuses (especially, of course, in the welfare, human service, and education fields); to reduce the scope of public interventions in the market (in the regulation of environmental hazards, occupational safety, consumer product quality, and affirmative action); and to diminish the scope of public employment and services.

Within the framework of sharply curtailed state expenditures, education felt the sting of the retrenchment of the public sector. Early and sustained attempts to make significant reductions in the levels of federal funding in a wide variety of programs; the attempt to reduce the public education lobby by downgrading the Department of Education from its current cabinet-level position; the effort to lower the expectations of higher education for many Americans by reducing the availability of college loans; and the attempt to place renewed emphasis on private school education through the adoption of tuition tax credits—all these represent a wider political project to "solve" America's economic problems through a massive retrenchment of the public domain and an expansion of the prerogatives and resources of the private sector.

Of course, while the promulgation of these antipublic sector policies was to the immense benefit of the ruling elites and to at least some fractions of capital, the antistate rhetoric harnessed, as we have seen, wider and more popular grievances.[14] Not the least of these were the rising levels of taxation at a time of high inflation and protopopulist resentment at high-living politicians, unresponsive bureaucrats, and profligate spending of the public purse. In addition to this was a widespread feeling among the middle class—and fueled by right-wing demagoguery—that the state's major concern was a too-generous support of racial minorities and the poor. Conservative political rhetoric fed the sentiment that chronic state interventions have led to an over-concern with the less-than-able student and neglected the average or middle-of-the-road student. Such rhetoric resonated easily with middle-class fears that the state had been kidnapped by interest groups representing blacks, the poor, and other, apparently clamorous, groups. Right-wing political rhetoric, as it spoke to educational issues or other concerns, certainly utilized the antistate, antipublic sector message in its exploitation of class fears and anxieties. Diatribes against "freeloaders" and "welfare queens," as well as the more general denunciations of the bias in the orientations and concerns of the national government, harnessed class resentments, as did appeals for a return to the spirit of self-sufficient individualism instead of publicly supported dependency.

The mobilization of antistate sentiment (always a powerful sensibility in American life) in the 1970s and '80s (the Carter campaign, too, was predicated on such feelings), gave necessary electoral support to the campaign waged by sectors of capital for interventions to enhance its declining profitability. Under the impact of higher wages, increasing competition from Europe and Japan, increasing costs of raw materials from Third World countries, as well as the rising ratio of machinery costs to human labor costs, capital in America was beset by a crisis of insufficient profitability with results that were plain to see: industrial closings, lay-offs, plant relocations to other countries as well as to less unionized regions of the United States, and rising bankruptcies became the visible signs of the troubled economy. Capital's response was to support a program that would reduce both the indirect (the so-called social wage of the state, the panoply of social and educational benefits associated with the welfare state) and direct costs of labor and to make possible the extraction of a greater quantity of surplus value. Such a position meant, in the first place, a sizable shift in the distribution of the social product away from labor, the poor, the unemployed, and middle-class groups and toward the dominant corporate and elite elements in American society.

The antistate campaign (of which the attacks on the federal role in education were a part) confused rhetoric with substance. While the rhetoric of the attack on big government resonated well in the American political culture, the Reagan program meant no reduction in the overall size of the national government. More accurately, it has meant shifts in government support and expenditures. For all the ballyhoo about leaving it to the market, the fundamental Keynesian interventions in the economy remained. The state continued to be used to set the parameters for capitalist production by regulating aggregate demand, interest rates, and taxes. The huge expansion of the military budget more than offset budget cuts in social/education areas. In fact, several analysts have noted that such an expansion of the defense sector inevitably entailed greater intrusions of government into the inner workings of the economy.

Educational Reform and the Need for a State-Directed Capitalism

The response by the Reagan administration to the needs of capital by no means solved the problems of the American economy. While there were indeed a massive transfer of income from the bottom to the topmost reaches of the social structure and a further reduction in the bargaining power of workers (as a result of not only cuts in the income maintenance programs but also the high levels of unemployment), more fundamental long-term problems in the capital accumulation process remain. Such problems, as a rising chorus of spokesmen now argue, require a different set of political responses and economic policies. At the center of such responses is the need for a more activist and interventionist state. These arguments are well reflected in the reports on education which call for a renewed federal role in meeting what the *Report of the Task Force on Federal Elementary and Secondary Education Policy* called the "threatened disaster" to the nation's welfare posed by a school system whose performance falls far short of expectations. The report insisted that the national government must ensure a role of strong leadership that "guides and inspires states and communities." The National Commission on Excellence in Education (NCEE) report, while stopping short of calling for new outlays, also made clear its support for a strong federal role. The document asserted that "the federal government has the primary responsibility to identify the national interest in education."

These calls for a greater federal role in education as necessary to meeting the "national emergency" mirrored a more general assertion that the dire needs of American industry required an active interventionist state that was able to provide leadership to a floundering economy. Far from the rhetoric of decentralized responsibilities and the unrestricted forces of the market, it argued corporate needs could only be met through the centralized resources and planning agencies of the national state. The NCEE report's assertion that the federal government "must provide the national leadership to ensure that the nation's public and private resources are marshalled" mirrored the assertions concerning the state's wider role. Felix Rohatyn, an investment banker who is one of the leaders of that fraction of capital who argues the need for a strong state role, noted in the second year of the Reagan administration:

> The coming year will mark the fiftieth anniversary of the election of Franklin Roosevelt. A well-to-do aristocrat, he was incapable of standing by idly and witnessing misery and unfairness. FDR saved capitalism in this country by intervening in the name of fairness. The Reconstruction Finance Corporation, a modern version of which, I am convinced, will have to come about soon; the TVA, still functioning however controversially; the FDIC, the only present protection of the savings banks—all of these are examples of what can be created by an active government to bring relief to the poorer regions of the country, put people to work, protect savings. Although not politically fashionable today, FDR could be very fashionable tomorrow.[15]

Rohatyn's call for "vigorous intervention" by the central government included the need for an industrial and regional policy, a wage and price policy, and the assignment of all income-transfer programs related to poverty (including medicare, food stamps, and welfare) to the federal government, "to be administered nationally with national standards." Rohatyn asserted that without the adoption of such policies it might be impossible to save the free enterprise system. Robert Reich, one of the more influential economists in the development of an alternative economic policy, favored renewed government interventions in the market to "reindustrialize" America. Such interventions would channel capital into targeted industries, fund research and development, renovate America's crumbling infrastructure, improve the competitive position of home-based industries, support high-risk investment, and initiate market development. Similar calls were made by the economist Lester Thurow, who has supported the idea of a national industrial policy to coordinate capital investment and corporate expansion.

Implicit in all this was the advocacy of an intensified form of the corporate state in America—the development of what Erik Olin Wright calls "state directed capitalism." In this the state needs to become directly involved in the rationalization of production, the coordination and planning of productivity increases, and the destruction of inefficient sectors of production.[16] Business and government were to increase the extent to which their activities and purposes are pursued in an integrated, harmonious manner. Nowhere was the idea more clearly articulated than in the educational reports. Thus the National Task Force on Education for Economics Growth (NTFEEG) argued that "schools and business leaders should develop partnerships to advance school improvement."[17] Only in this way, it continued, could American public schools overcome their failure to adequately prepare students for the demands of a competitive, technologically based economy. The central thrust of many of the reports was the need to harmonize educational practices with corporate business needs in the United States. Whatever the NCEE report's apparent concern with education in the humanities, "civics," or the development of a "literate citizenry," education's relationship (or lack thereof) to business needs was its number one interest:

> Knowledge, learning, information and skilled intelligence are the new raw materials of international commerce and are today spreading throughout the world as vigorously as miracle drugs, synthetic fertilizers, and blue jeans did earlier. If only to keep and improve on the slim competitive edge we will retain in world markets, we must rededicate ourselves to the reform of our educational system....[18]

The conflict between elite groups in our society over the degree to which the state should intervene in education is part of a larger conflict concerning the extent and nature of state intervention in the economic and social system. The issue of whether the state ought to be involved was settled a long time ago. In more recent times the state fills an absolutely indispensable role in two fundamental aspects of the capitalist system. It creates conditions in which profitable capital accumulation is possible, and it ensures at least a minimum degree of social harmony. The dual role of the state generates some severe contradictions that manifest themselves in fiscal, administrative, and ideological crises of the state—crises that are expressed not only in the political conflicts between dominant and subordinate classes, but also between fractions of the dominant class itself.[19] It is within the latter context that at least some of the assertions of the recent educational reports must be located. To understand this better, I return, at least briefly, to the fundamental nature of the conflicts involving the state.

I noted earlier the way in which the growth of the state sector and state spending have functioned increasingly as the basis for the growth of big business. O'Connor, Castells, and others have noted the increased responsibility of state and local governments in providing the basic investments in physical, social, and human capital needed to ensure the profitability of big business: highway and transportation systems, port and aviation facilities, urban renewal projects, research and development, and technical training. The reasons for this enlarged role of the state have been the increased pace of technological change and thus the more rapid obsolescence of capital equipment, the increased financial risk attributable to the growth of overhead costs, and the sheer size of many investment undertakings.

The huge expenditures by the state, added to the inequitable (and, as a consequence, inadequate) system of taxation, have meant increased deficit financing, high interest rates, and inflation. The consequence of state interventions has meant different costs and benefits to different segments of capital. O'Connor notes that there is a "private appropriation of state power for particularistic ends." Such particularistic ends are disproportionately those of monopoly capital who are able, most successfully, to make claims on the budget for their own purposes and needs. Bob Jessup, too, describes how, in the corporatist conditions of late capitalism, there is an "asymmetry" in the position of small and medium capital and monopoly capital *vis-à-vis* the state:

> While small and medium capital may gain some measure of political influence in a corporatist regime, they still remain subject to the constraints of the law of value in their competition with other capitals. Conversely, to the extent that corporatist forms of representation and intervention prove adequate to realizing the various conditions of capital accumulation in late capitalism, it is monopoly capital in general that will be their principal beneficiary.[20]

Variations in the costs and benefits to different segments of capital have meant serious political differences within the class as to the extent and nature of state interventions—differences that are mirrored in the degree of support for public expenditure whether in education or in other state supported activities. Thus, for example, Castells has shown that for financial interests the fight against inflation has top priority. Financial corporations, he writes, ask for a global economic policy "to provide the structural requirements . . . to fight inflation, that is, to reduce it, to control it, to channel it before its geometrical progression is able to devastate the very foundations of the financial markets."[21] For such interests, public expenditures, especially those concerned with the welfare-education state, are likely to be viewed with less than great enthusiasm. William Domhoff describes those groups within capital who are most opposed to the interventions of the state as being

> from the smaller companies within the national corporate community, from local business communities and prosperous farm areas. They join together in such organizations as state manufacturers' associations, city and state chambers of commerce, and the National Farm Bureau Federation. They have formidable allies in the upper-middle-class professionals who have created their own organizations especially the American Medical Association and the American Bar Association.[22]

For these groups with their more short-term concerns, the demands of a massive interventionist state are felt to be a hindrance more than an asset in the accumulation of capital.

While such interests line up on the side of a decreasing state role and reduced public expenditures, other fractions of capital (including, today, elements of both high-tech industry, as well as some of the economically besieged sections of the industrial infrastructure) have begun to assume (or resume) a more favorable stance towards state intervention. For such groups the tendency toward falling rates of profit has been exacerbated by anti-inflationary policies which have meant the loss of outlets for the realization of their capital investments and reduced utilization of productive capacity. Ultimately, for these groups, only increased productivity provides an answer to their problem of strong unions and the loss of markets to foreign competition. Manuel Castells has summarized the process that results in the quest for increased productivity supported by expanded forms of state intervention:

> Capitalist accumulation relies primarily on the rate of exploitation. Therefore, the process of class struggle at the level of the overall society defines the basic characteristics of the process of accumulation. Because of the historical tendency of workers to increase their own power, the basis for the formation of capitalist profit structurally shrinks. Capital responds by developing productive forces and increasing labor productivity.[23]

To develop these productive forces and to increase labor productivity require investments in machines and human capital that must increasingly be supported by the central state which, alone, is able to provide the massive investments in scientific research, education, and the training of labor power. Such investments, says Castells, are fundamental to the development of productivity but are very expensive for capital and only profitable in the long term. While increased productivity may come from technological innovation and the enhancing of human creative powers, it may also be derived from a process of intensifying the existing work process—through speed-ups, longer hours of work, increases in production norms, and greater work discipline.

This concern with increased industrial productivity among certain sections of capital was mirrored in the 1983 reports on education. Without exception, the reports made clear that on the road to higher productivity, the state or public sector would have to be in the vanguard. Thus the NTFEEG report noted that:

> We have expected too little of our schools over the past two decades—and we have gotten too little. The result is that our schools are not doing an adequate job of educating for today's requirements in the workplace, much less tomorrow's.[24]

The Report of the Task Force on Federal Elementary and Secondary Education Policy, sponsored by the Twentieth Century Fund, stated: "We think that they [the public schools] should ensure the availability of large numbers of skilled and capable individuals without whom we cannot sustain a complex and competitive economy."[25] According to the NCEE report,

> Americans like to think of this nation as the preeminent country for generating the great ideas and material benefits for mankind. The citizen is dismayed at a steady 15 year decline in industrial productivity, as one great American industry after another falls to world competition. The citizen wants the country to act on the belief . . . that education should be at the top of the nation's agenda.[26]

Given the centrality of the productivity crisis in the demands for an improved educational system, it was not surprising that improvements in science and technical curriculum and instruction were preeminent elements in their list of reforms. The Twentieth Century Fund report, for example, called on the federal government to emphasize "scientific literacy" programs and provide advanced training in science and mathematics for secondary school students. The reports were only a small part of what is now an avalanche of new programs designed to orient schools towards training students in the use of the new electronics.

Although improvements in technical training were obviously high on the list of the educational reforms as the means to improve American productivity, it was possible to detect slightly more "old-fashioned" means to increasing industrial output. While such suggestions concerned only the behavior of adolescents in school, not adult workers, implicit in these recommendations was the desire to ensure a less lackadaisical, more disciplined work force, better prepared to accept long hours of labor, and less prone to tardiness and absenteeism. Thus there are in the reports frequent statements of the need to lengthen the school day and the school year; the need to implement attendance policies with "clear sanctions and incentives" to reduce absenteeism and tardiness; the need for increased homework assignments. Such attitudes were paralleled in the recommendations concerning teachers: the need to weaken job-security laws, introduce merit-pay systems, criticism of teachers' unions for protecting their weakest members and promoting the principle of equal pay, and the need for installing more stringent evaluation mechanisms on which would depend salary, promotion, and retention decisions. For the employees of schools as well as their students, as in industry, there was a common message— one which, in the name of higher productivity, insisted on the increased scrutiny of individual performance, a more thorough system of monitoring skill levels, and a more pervasive use of rankings in order to maximize output. While certainly there is no simply one-to-one correspondence between the practices of schools and those found in industry, the accelerating obsession with output, performance, and productivity is surely part of the encompassing *zeitgeist* of our time.

The Intensification of Social Conflict and the Effort to Preserve Hegemony

While reports on education were oriented to the needs of the corporate sector and to its problems of adequate profitability, such concerns alone cannot ensure hegemony. Hegemony refers here to the maintenance of class domination in a society through some kind of generalized consensus on the ideas and practices that apparently govern the society—a universal sense that society functions in a way that is reasonable, just, appropriate and sensible. Such control is not a simple matter of imposing one class's interests on the rest of society. If it were so, social control would rapidly appear as little more than coercion. It requires, instead, that there be some attempt to address the concerns, needs, and demands of other, less powerful, groups in the society. To ensure the maintenance of the basic contours of wealth and power in society through something other than coercion, the dominant groups must pay heed to, and make some genuine concessions to, these subordinate groups, but never to the extent that they pose any fundamental threat to the basic nature of the capitalist system. Through its role as the lever for enacting such concessions (the process of social reform) the state in capitalist society is able to maintain the appearance of a neutral arbiter of the "nation's interest"— able and willing to address the concerns of more than the elite elements in the society. The issue of maintaining hegemonic domination becomes ever more tenuous as the concern with profits, output, and productivity produce policies of brutal effect on the working class—rollbacks of wages, abrogated union contracts, and lay-offs. For some among the ruling elites, widening class divisions with the prospect of renewed social conflict and hostilities engender the need for some renewed attention to the mechanisms for continuing the ideological consensus. Reports on education, alongside their preeminent concern with the needs of the corporate sector, also state the importance of renewing commitment to notions of equality or equal opportunity. While the schools must have at the forefront of their concerns the goal of facilitating the faltering process of capital accumulation, they must (if they are to ensure the continued legitimation of the system) also speak to their role in ensuring economic and social opportunities for the broad masses of people. They must, in short, appear to serve both capitalist and democratic purposes. Thus the NCEE report added to its major preoccupation—the need to enhance industrial productivity—a statement on the government's responsibility in maintaining equal opportunity:

> The federal government, in cooperation with states and localities, should help meet the needs of key groups of students . . . the socioeconomically disadvantaged, minority and language-minority students, and the handicapped.[27]

The Twentieth Century Fund report stated:

> In proposing new federal measures to stimulate national interest in improving the quality of public education, we urge that they not come at the expense of children from low-income families or of children suffering from one or another disability.[28]

The report continued by asserting the need for federal "attention and assistance" to localities with high concentrations of "immigrant and/or impoverished groups." It also argued that categorical programs required by the federal government be paid for from the federal treasury.

The reports maintained the belief that social legitimacy rested on the state's support (or apparent support) for democratic and egalitarian ideals (more precisely, the liberal, meritocratic version of these ideals). In schools this is a matter of supporting programs that appear to enhance equality of educational opportunity. In contrast, conservatives offered a legitimacy that issued not from the attempt to resolve the contradictions of democratic expectations and the realities of the class structure, but one that came from the establishment of a unitary system of cultural values and meanings—a system built around the virtues of the Protestant ethic and the Puritan temper. It is an approach that bypasses or minimizes the concerns of social and economic justice and offers, instead, a legitimacy founded in God, America, and obedience to authority. It reduces the state's role in pursuing equal opportunity for those excluded or subordinate groups in the society, replacing it instead with efforts to impose a unified, if restricted, cultural viewpoint. Such efforts, to a great extent, speak an antiquated language badly at odds with the unleashed impulses and stimulated desires of our consumption-oriented society. They ignore the multiplicity of cultural perspectives and the ideologically differentiated landscape of contemporary society, substituting the voice of a constricted and ungenerous minority. It is clear that more than this would be necessary to paper over the widening breach in the social and economic order. (President Reagan showed himself to be a master at combining the rhetoric of popular democratic grievances with policies that favor one class. Both the 1981 and 1985 tax reform packages managed to reward the rich disproportionately as well as appearing to express working- and middle-class outrage at the injustice of the system.) More than New Right moralism would be needed to convince the broad cross-section of people of the system's viability, rationality, and justice. Whether the return to a more vigorous state intervention on behalf of meritocratic ideology will suffice remains to be seen.

Though there are educational policy differences, these generally do not radically differ from each other. Indeed what marked the educational reports most was their conventionality and ordinariness. Their reforms in no way attempted to alter the fundamental nature of curriculum, pedagogy, and institutional structure typically found in American schools. What the reports wanted was more of what already exists, rather than something profoundly different: increases in credit requirements, more lesson hours, more tests, more homework. One looks in vain for any attempt to address many of the deeper issues that have vexed educational scholars during the last fifteen years. There was no discussion of the existential nature of teaching and learning in the present culture—the meaningfulness and purpose of what it is that is learned or intended to be learned. Nor was there any attempt to engage the issue of education for citizenship—one that in this era of powerful mass communication surely demands attention to the notion of educating for a critical awareness. Nor was there any discussion of the perversions of education that are induced by the bureaucratic, credentialing functions of schooling, or the hierarchical and frequently despotic manner by which schools are frequently governed. In short, the educational reports followed a line of criticism and contention that represented little more than a tempest in a tea cup. They in no way suggested any basic divergence from the present course of schooling. The pressure to align schools more closely with business-defined industrial needs is not much more than the continuation of a phenomenon present since the inception of American public education. As a host of revisionist histories have so well described, the history of public education in this country is incomprehensible unless seen from within the context of the changing modes of capital accumulation. Finally, one is struck by the rather disturbing desire to emulate European or Japanese models of education—systems that are often noted for their rigid, class-riddled, paternalistic ways, whose curricula are marked by feudal traditions, and whose exclusivity at both the secondary and tertiary levels results in experiences of extreme personal anxiety and competitiveness.[29]

Notwithstanding all of this, one is ultimately compelled to question whether the successful adoption of the reforms suggested in all of the reports could indeed cure the ills of our economy. It is likely that the attempt to "intensify" learning through increases in the formal demands of schools would, in the consumption-oriented ethos of contemporary culture, produce further alienation from school among a great many adolescents and a heightened sense of the institution's coercive nature. Any attempt to increase the productivity of labor must face up to what a number of recent observers see as the greatest impediment to the liberation of workers' creative energies—the stifling nature of the hierarchical, authoritarian social relations of the workplace. As Manuel Castells, Martin Carnoy, Samuel Bowles, and many others have argued, only a more democratic workplace in which there is an increase in the worker's control over the means of production would unleash the energy and effort needed for a qualitative leap forward in human productivity.[30] Without this, no amount of technical training, specialized know-how, or investments in human capital provided through schooling will overcome the entropy of an industrial system run down through its unresponsiveness to human needs that go beyond the monthly paycheck or the security of a steady job. Such needs can only be addressed in the context of a workplace that takes seriously the issues of human creativity, workers' autonomy, and the self-management of the industrial process. It is an agenda for higher productivity that goes far beyond issues of educational reform, demanding changes in the forms of technology in use, as well as in the fundamental structures of our social and economic life.

7
The Dialectic of the Welfare-Educational State, I

Introduction: The Welfare State and the Politicization of Social Demands

THE POLICIES OF THE Reagan administration represented the most serious assault on the welfare state in the United States in the past fifty years. By the summer of 1981, congressional approval had been obtained to slash $140 billion from the social programs over the years 1982–84—more than half of it from the income-maintenance programs that provide low-income people with cash, food, health care, and low-cost housing. Additional social program reductions of $45 billion and $30 billion were proposed for 1983 and 1984.[1] In the field of education federal expenditures in 1984 totalled less than what they were in 1981;[2] this included a projected 56 percent cut in student loans and a $1 billion cut in college work-study programs (removing 250,000 job opportunities for students trying to work their way through school).[3]

Such policies created a significant redistribution of the national income in the direction of the topmost income holders. The programs that provided a national minimum income floor were cut back as one part of a larger strategy to increase business profits. The federal tax structure was reorganized to promote a massive upward redistribution of income: new investment and depreciation write-offs favored large corporations over small businesses—80 percent of the benefits going to the 1,700 largest corporations. Personal income and estate taxes were slashed by formulas that gave 85 percent of the benefits to those with annual incomes exceeding $50,000. Whatever the economic justification of such changes, in terms of increasing capital investments, the redistributive goals were undeniable.[4] As Richard Cloward and Frances Piven argue, an even more significant cause of the reduction in income-maintenance programs was their disruptive effects on the traditional relationship between unemployment and wage levels, between the supply of labor and the power of labor. Income-maintenance programs undermine the usual macroeconomic stabilization policies in which price inflation could be controlled through the maintenance of appropriate levels of unemployment. (This formulation is embodied in the famous Phillips Curve: when unemployment falls, wages rise; when unemployment rises, wages fall. As Cloward and Piven note in their book, *The New Class War*, the Phillips Curve is consistent with Marx's thesis regarding the industrial reserve army of labor, for it suggested that high levels of unemployment weaken the bargaining power of workers.) Income-maintenance benefits, however, support wage levels despite high unemployment. The reason, they point out, is a simple one:

> If the desperation of the unemployed is moderated by the availability of various benefits, they will be less eager to take any job on any terms. In other words, an industrial reserve army of labor with unemployment benefits and food stamps is a less effective instrument with which to deflate wage and workplace demands. . . . a labor force that is made more secure by the possibility of alternative means of subsistence is less docile, less productive and more costly.[5]

The question of discipline among workers points to the larger meaning of the attack on the programs and institutions of the welfare state. This has to do with the common business view that "the central tension of American capitalism . . . is between people's rising aspirations and the inability of the American system to satisfy them without weakening its long-term viability."[6] It is a belief that the welfare state embodies a profound and threatening change in the nature of American capitalism, a change in which, for the great majority of the population, an increasing proportion of benefits, resources, and opportunities are to be had as a matter of democratic right, not as a result of one's fortunes in the economic marketplace. It is as a result of these changes that conservative commentators warned that economic possibilities have converted "into a range of *entitlements*," that political systems are "overloaded" with participants and demands, and democracy endangered by the "excessive expectations . . . generated by the democratic aspects of the system."[7] Of course, as Cloward and Piven point out, it is not so much the overall politicization of the economy that concerns these intellectuals:

> They are preoccupied only with the intrusion of popular economic demands into political contexts. Demands for equality or for entitlements are the problem, and such demands do not emanate from the top of society. They surge from the bottom. It is not the propertied who are

overloading the system. It is ordinary people who have become too clamorous, who want too much.[8]

The attack on the welfare state has been an attempt to restrain or reduce the expanding politicization of social and economic life. It is an attempt to thwart the growing demand that increasing sectors of societal resources, benefits, and opportunities be distributed, not according to the vicissitudes of the marketplace, but as a matter of political or democratic right—a perception which has been fostered in no small way by expectations and demands arising from the system of public education.

The result is a politicization of the relations of production, as a consequence of which the idea of "fair exchange" loses its hold. There is a growing awareness that the distribution of social wealth depends in no small way on governmental policies and the quasi-political negotiation of rewards and obligations. Despite this awareness, economic growth still follows the capitalist principle in which priorities are shaped by the private goals of profit maximization. This generates a sharp tension in the whole system: since the appeal to the inherent "justice" of the market is much less credible, the legitimacy of the distribution of the social product in ways that continue to be inequitable become increasingly problematic. As Habermas argues, as government interventions spread into more and more areas of life, and increasing sectors of social life are subjected to administrative planning, the legitimacy of the system comes increasingly into question.

It is in regard to these points that so much of the analysis of the role of the state in capitalist society has been dangerously off the mark. While the emergence of the welfare state in America followed the penetration of the state by business (which made the hypocrisy of *laissez faire* transparently evident, and thus undermined the doctrine prescribing the separation of economy and polity), it is mistaken to view the programs, institutions, and policies of this state as simply emanating from dominant class interests. Contrary to such a view, the policies and programs of the welfare state frequently emerged as a result of struggle against many of these very interests. In many important respects the expansion of social, educational, and economic entitlements was won, not because of, but in spite of, dominant class interests. As Alasdair MacIntyre has pointed out, these have only been sustained through the continued struggle of the working class and popular movements against such interests.[9] This view of the state in capitalist society as a site of class conflict and a domain of conflicting social demands contradicts the conventional Marxist view in which the state is seen as little more than an instrument manipulable at will by the ruling class, or as an appendage of those economically dominant social groups.[10] The state is a terrain on which the conflicting social demands of competing classes are fought out, and on which reforms allowing real gains to subordinate groups may be made (of course, as Nicos Poulantzas notes, so long as these reforms do not threaten the basic system of domination and control).[11] In this way the state in capitalist society may appear to express the popular or national will, and maintain the loyalties of the broad cross section of the society. Only through such reforms can it maintain the appearance of what Bertel Ollman calls the "illusory community."[12] What this amounts to is a rejection of the argument that the welfare state is simply a means by which insurgent or disruptive subordinate groups may be "cooled out." From such a perspective the welfare state is seen as little more than an elaborate apparatus of social control, a mechanism by which deprived, excluded or oppressed groups may be "regulated" into conformity.[13] It has indeed been a frequent argument of left critics that the welfare state emerged out of the need to pacify and depoliticize disruptive or potentially disruptive groups. Social welfare programs appear "as part of the strategy by which the ruling class rules, through which working people are induced to cash in their political capacities ... for a pittance in material benefits."[14] While such views do, of course, contain some elements of truth (FDR was as much interested in saving capitalism as transforming it) this is only a part of the story. It is precisely in the dysfunctional (for capital) effects of the welfare state that the *raison d'etre* for Reaganomics may be found. Such effects have significantly limited the power of the market as the sole determinant of people's legitimate social and economic expectations. Political and democratic rights, not simply money or position, have emerged as increasingly important criteria for fixing one's life opportunities and circumstances.

In many of the critical studies of education in America, a parallel misinterpretation of the role of the state has been common.[15] Either implicitly or explicitly (usually the former), education in the United States has been viewed as little more than an apparatus of the state, manipulated at will by the interests of big business. From this perspective the institutional structure, curriculum and pedagogy of American education have been understood as expressing little more than the ideological and material imperatives of corporate capitalism. Radical or critical studies of education in the United States have presented schools as little more than the epiphenomenon of the economic infra-structure; the character of schooling has followed the demands of the economy as surely as night follows day. Implied in such a perspective is a notion of education which does little more than ensure a work force and citizenry totally inured to the values of corporate-capitalism, and passively compliant to the structures of social and economic domination. It is a view of schooling that does no more than ensure a normatively constrained and thoroughly pacified population.[16] Such a view stems from an understanding of the state in capitalist society in which it is seen as an unalloyed instrument of class domination, and in which all of the apparatuses of this state, including education, are little more than means of social control. This view of education finds some of its origins in a Marcusean understanding of capitalist society in which there is a total integration of all social spheres—schools, factories, universities, trade unions, the mass media as well as welfare institutions—to one unified purpose: to ensure the domination of subordinate social groups or classes. For Marcuse and for those who have, in one way or another, accepted his position, the liberal-capitalist state is simply an incipient version of the totalitarian state. It is, of course, not surprising that such a view precludes the possibility of class conflict in modern society.

In contrast, our view of the state in capitalist society argues for a very different orientation: the state is the central battleground between social interests and ideologies. The emergence of the welfare state represents the crystallization of gains achieved by subordinate groups. From this perspective, education in the United States is seen as a complex and contradictory phenomenon. While critical studies certainly demonstrate education's role in the process of social control and the reproduction of capitalist social relations, this is only a part of the story. Public education, as an essential element in the structure of the welfare state, functions also in a quite different way. The institutions of public schooling are a central focus for demands and expectations that depend not on the criteria of the marketplace for their fulfillment, but on the rights and entitlements that emanate from citizenship. Public education is a primary catalyst in the demands for an enlargement of political rights to include increasing areas of our social and economic lives. It has been, perhaps, the single most important spur to the expansion of such rights in the United States. Schooling in American society, in short, is both an instrument of domination and a focus for the insurgent social and economic claims of excluded, discriminated against, and subordinate groups in the society.

Educational Rights and the Emergence of the Welfare-Educational State

One of the most significant influences in the extension of democratic claims against the free-market allocation of services, resource, and opportunities has been the emergence of what might be called the welfare-educational system. Receiving its impetus from progressive notions of the "whole child," the assertion that the ability to learn is inseparable from the satisfaction of an individual's physical and emotional needs has permeated the popular consciousness. Successful schooling is understood as necessarily linked to the provision of a much broader set of social services: adequate health care and access to preventive treatment; the availability of adequate food and nutritional resources; the opportunity to alleviate emotional and mental distress; and the provision of an adequate home and physical environment. In short, school has become a major focus of, and the ideology of the education of the whole child a major justification for, the extension of social rights and the provisions of the welfare state.

This broadly conceived notion of the educational context is illustrated in the following statistics: In 1981, the Department of Health and Human Services spent on education an estimated 1.9 billion dollars.[17] In the same year school feeding programs (including special milk programs and summer feeding programs) had 26 million beneficiaries and totalled 4.50 million dollars. Perhaps no single educational act has done more to exemplify the welfare-educational system than the passage in 1975 of Public Law 94–142, The Education for All Handicapped Children Act. The attempt to provide an education that would give each handicapped child "an opportunity to achieve his full potential" quickly assumed the need to provide a range of auxiliary services such as counseling, physical aids, mental health treatment, and hospital care. Individualized Educational Plans prepared for the 10 to 12 percent of students meeting the criteria of eligibility under the law not infrequently (and certainly not without a struggle between parents and fiscally pressured administrators) contained mandates or references to the need for broader health or welfare provisions; such extensive care or treatment being seen as a prerequisite to successful education. (It is perhaps not surprising, given my general thesis in this chapter, that in June 1982, an increasingly conservative Supreme Court ruled in a 6-to-3 decision that federal law entitles handicapped children to a public education from which they can derive "some educational benefit." The court, however, said that local school districts are not obliged to provide services that such children need in order to reach their *full* academic potential—a clear attempt to reduce the extent of the provisions of welfare-educational services and the field of newly won social rights for this discriminated-against group.) Similar broad prescriptions followed educational programs developed through P. L. 93–145 (The Juvenile Justice and Delinquency Prevention Act) which provided "resources to develop and implement programs to keep students in elementary and secondary schools and prevent unwarranted and arbitrary suspensions and expulsions." The Drug Abuse Act of 1970, too, integrated educational and social resources in "support of ... programs for parents and others on drug abuse problems."

Nowhere, perhaps, is the institutional nature of the welfare-education system more clearly demonstrated than in the Head Start Program. The right to successfully avail oneself of the school process becomes the right to avail oneself of the broadest range of human services, benefits and resources. In addition to the explicit educational objectives, the Head Start Program objectives state the need to link the child's family "to an ongoing health care system to ensure that the child continues to receive comprehensive health care even after leaving the Head Start Program"; to mobilize community mental health services to ensure that a child and family achieve the full benefits of participation in the program; to "involve all staff, parents and other community agencies in meeting the child's nutritional needs"; and through the use of social services to "assist the family in its own efforts to improve the condition and quality of family life."[18]

The notion of educational rights has expanded to embrace a much wider and more encompassing set of social rights that extend to food, health, and other forms of assistance to the family. While many of the programs and social interventions mentioned may well be viewed as having their roots in the attempt to "regulate the poor" or control the insurgency of subordinate groups, they have also, perhaps unwittingly, given rise to drastically expanded notions of political and social rights. The accepted idea of educational rights has become the focus (especially in the 1960s and early 1970s) for a radical extension of the claims that children and young people, as well as their families, could make on the state. Educational rights underpinned by progressive philosophy have been converted into welfare or social rights; the right to be educated has become the right to be nourished, to receive adequate health care, and grow up in a secure environment. It is, of course, only a short step from this latter claim to demands for adequate job or income-maintenance guarantees for adults. Even antipollution regulations drew support from evidence concerning the harmful effects on the intellectual functioning of children (especially inner-city children) subjected to the concentrated effects of airborne lead.

Once again what we are driving at here is not the celebration of an adequately funded, fully secured social-welfare state. In the United States that has always been far from reality. We are, instead, referring to the expansion of the territory from which the battle for social and economic rights might be joined. However poorly funded, punitively appropriated, and paternalistically administered, the last twenty years or so have seen an important extension of the areas in which citizens regard themselves entitled to make social demands on the state. Under popular pressure there has been a partial democratization of the capitalist state. The assertion of educational rights has provided important momentum for the legitimation of other demands. While puritan prejudices against adult welfare dependents may die hard, it has been more difficult to resist the establishment of educational welfare provisions for the young, and to effect the political mobilization necessary to enact it.

In a previous chapter I noted that critical studies of schooling in the United States pay insufficient attention to the concept of "public" in public education. While such studies illustrate well the place of schooling in the transmission of capitalist values (hierarchy, egotism, competition), little attention is paid to the complex duality of bourgeois ideology. In the early writings of Marx the separation in the realm of socialization is noted; between man's role in modern society as "bourgeois" and his role as "citizen" (corresponding to the division between the realms of the economic and the political).[19] While, in the former, individualistic impulses rule, in the latter, human beings are expected to develop a sense of universal attachments and obligations and the claims of equal consideration, rights, and opportunities. Under liberal capitalism, our economic lives compel us to adopt the competitive and individualistic values of the marketplace, our political lives (as citizens) require us, at least in principle, to raise demands for equality, mutuality, and democracy. Nowhere are the political and economic moments of liberal capitalism so clearly juxtaposed as in the institutions of public education. Schools are both economic appendages to the market and political components of the state. They must embrace the promises of democracy and equality, as well as the hierarchical and competitive values of the marketplace.

The result is a duality in the ideological meaning of public education. While it is the clearly capitalistic aspect of schooling that has been drawn attention to, its political nature has been overlooked, or treated as simply a mystification. Once again it is important to emphasize that the significance of the political lies less in the reality of equalitarian promises fulfilled than in its role as a catalyst for the assertion of democratic rights, as an institutional focus for social (and economic) demands that run counter to the more dominant privatistic concerns of our bourgeois society. Public education provides a cutting edge for the enlargement of the domain in which an increasingly wide variety of social resources are distributed according to need or by virtue of political right, not simply as a consequence of the ability to pay, or according to one's status or class position. Public education must be seen as more than simply a means to adjust individuals to economic life. It must also be viewed as an important affirmation of the public domain in a society whose commitment here has been, at best, a tenuous one, a domain in which the distribution of resources and opportunity may be checked against democratic and equalitarian criteria rather than those of the marketplace.

Educational Reforms and the Expansion of Economic Aspirations

Above I suggested education's role as a major force in the extension of the welfare state—a key factor in the expansion of a sphere in which resources, benefits, services, or opportunity may be claimed as a matter of political right, not as a consequence of social or economic privilege. Parallel expansion of such claims is apparent also in the demands made more directly on the economic order—demands which have also been instigated, to an important degree, by the educational process. Here the expectations are for job opportunities commensurate with the growth of an educated white collar and professional class. To more fully understand this it is necessary to return to the notion of schooling as a process that is concerned, fundamentally, with the reproduction and legitimation of the social division of labor, that is, the means by which individuals are selected and validated as being capable of functioning on one side or the other of the "mental-manual" divide.

The dramatic expansion of educational opportunities during the 1960s and '70s represented, above all, the demand for, and expectation of, access to mental labor. It promised an escape from the routine, the drudgery, and the unpleasant conditions of blue-collar work and entry into a world where one could hope to have more autonomy, win more social recognition, and exercise a greater proportion of one's creative and intellectual potential. In this respect education is intimately related to the American dream of social mobility and middle-class fulfillment. Richard Sennett and Jonathan Cobb note in their study of working-class attitudes that everything in the family lives of workers they interviewed was oriented to moving their children over the "barrier" of the division of labor.[20] Crossing this line, they believed, would mean a qualitative change in their children's lives—more freedom, the opportunity to command the respect of people outside their immediate community, work that was intrinsically satisfying, and "the chance to make something of oneself." All of this is linked, it appears, to successful schooling. A typical comment, they note: "My child must be educated . . . that's the only way he can do what he wants."[21]

The expansion of educational opportunities during the 1960s, which transformed the extent of economic aspirations was a consequence of the widespread equalitarian demands of that period. Such demands had the effect of expanding economic aspirations through a process that undermined some of the traditional mechanisms of pedagogy and assessment. The educational changes that occurred issued from a number of diverse social and ideological origins. Perhaps the most visible of these were in the curriculum reform efforts of the 1960s. Such efforts were organized around a cultural principle that, for want of a better term, I have called populist. Curiously, while many of the efforts of the '60s experiments and reforms have been swept away during the era of conservatism which has followed, they continue to serve as an important focus (symbolic or otherwise) for the discontent of basic skills protagonists.

The successful schooling of unprecedented numbers of working-class and middle-class students meant entry into professional or white-collar work by large numbers of new aspirants. (By successful schooling I refer only to the acquisition of credentials and diplomas, not to the quality of intellectual, critical, or creative educational achievements.) Unparalleled numbers of individuals equipped, as they believed, with the appropriate skills or knowledge were ready to assume their rightful places on the "other side" of the barrier separating mental from manual labor. To an unparalleled extent, the economic structure became the object of widespread democratic expectations; the right to educational achievement became, on an unprecedented scale, the right to the fulfillment of economic hopes. Widening educational opportunities with their consequent occupational expectations meant greater popular demands on the economic domain. The promise held out by the reform of educational policies and practices accelerated the politicization of the economic realm; it added to the expectation of greater state intervention if expectations could not be fulfilled there through the autonomous decisions of the free market. Behind the cutting edge of educational rights and opportunities the economic order became increasingly subject to popular pressures and demands.

The Expanded State, Educational Reform and the Crisis of Bureaucratic Rationality

The period of greatest educational expansion corresponded, initially, to one of high economic growth, thus, to an extent, submerging such demands or pressures. Indeed, Reaganomics depended on its ability to convince a sizeable proportion of the electorate of the need to "leave free enterprise alone"; to return the economic order to its autonomous path. This, however, represented no simple return to the days of *laissez-faire*. The Reagan economic program was touted as a strategy (and a quick one at that) for meeting popular demands and aspirations. It was, in all probability, far less a renewal of faith in the natural right of capital to proceed in its own unhindered way, than an expedient and temporary choice of policies in the absence of anything that appeared more effective. In the long term there is little reason to assume that popular demands will be any less focused on the government's responsibilities for meeting the expectations of our economic lives. Certainly the growing extent of the dissonance between popular expectations and economic reality can no longer be hidden. Under the democratic pressures unleashed by educational promises, the implications for the relations between state and economy is one of increasingly unresolved tension. In the face of the disparities between professional and technical job training and real employment opportunities, the likelihood, at least in the long run, is for greater, not less, state intervention into the marketplace. This is especially so since many of the would-be professionals are linked to careers in the field of human service employment—an area which in every advanced capitalist society has been the overwhelming direct responsibility of the state. No amount of "supply-side" or "trickle-down" economics is likely to meet the pressure for jobs in the social services, education, or health care systems.

Habermas argues that in advanced capitalist societies the economic crisis has been *absorbed* by the state. It is the state, with its substantial number of market-replacing or complementing functions, that is now the focus of the economic crisis. It is this phenomenon that has opened the way to other kinds of popular demands, in education and elsewhere. Habermas points to what he calls the "displaced" nature of this crisis and its manifestations in the existence of chronic inflation and the permanent crisis in public finances—the latter coming about as the government budget is burdened with the cost of more and more socialized costs. The result of this transfer of the locus of the economic crisis, from the market to the state, means that the crisis no longer appears as a natural fate of society, but the responsibility of democratically elected governments. If governmental crisis management fails, he asserts, it lags behind programmatic demands that the government has placed on itself. The penalty for this failure is a withdrawal of legitimation. Of course the very process of subjecting areas of social life to administrative planning or rationality produces the unintended side effect of undermining traditional legitimations. As the state expands its activities into more and more areas of life, the accompanying "organizational rationality" destroys the unquestionable validity of matters previously taken for granted; it stirs up questions about matters that had previously been settled by the cultural tradition in an unproblematic way. Concerns that were once justified through appeals to traditional values or norms now find themselves subjected to public discourse. The result is a "politicization" of areas of life previously assigned to the private sphere:

> While organizational rationality spreads, cultural traditions are undermined and weakened. . . . Administrative manipulation of cultural matters has the unintended side effect of causing meanings and norms previously fixed by tradition and belonging to the boundary conditions of the political system to be publicly thematized. . . . [22]

Habermas further notes:

> At every level, administrative planning produces unintended, unsettling, and publicizing effects. These effects weaken the justification potential of traditions that have been flushed out of their nature-like course of development. Once their unquestionable character has been destroyed, the stabilization of validity claims can succeed only through discourse. The stirring up of cultural affairs that are taken for granted thus furthers the politicization of areas of life previously assigned to the private sphere.[23]

The end effect, argues Habermas, is a consciousness of the contingency "not only of the *contents* of tradition, but also of the techniques of tradition, that is, of socialization."[24] Cultural affairs that were taken for granted and previously outside of political manipulation now "fall into the administrative planning area" and become part of the "public problematic."[25] An example of such direct administrative processing of cultural tradition, says Habermas, is in educational planning, especially curriculum planning. He notes that whereas school administrations formerly had to codify a canon that had taken shape in an unplanned nature-like manner, present curriculum planning (Habermas' emphasis) is based on the premise that traditional patterns could well be otherwise: "Administrative planning produces a universal pressure for legitimation in a sphere that was once distinguished precisely for its power of self-legitimation."²⁶ Other examples he gives of the politicization of cultural matters previously taken for granted, can be found in regional and city planning ("private ownership of land"), in planning the health system (the "classless hospital"), and in family and marriage laws ("which relax sexual taboos and lower the thresholds of emancipation").

The subjection of deep-seated norms and values of the cultural system to administrative planning produces a high degree of uncertainty in traditional attitudes. This, says Habermas, is reflected in the demands for, and attempts at, participatory planning in an increased number of cultural spheres—school and university, press, church, theater, as well as in the increasing number of citizens' initiatives. Such developments threaten the formally democratic institutions and procedures of the public realm. The kind of "democracy" found there has been able to ensure both a diffuse, generalized, mass loyalty to the system, and the requisite independence of administrative decision making from the specific interests of citizens. The increasing demands for "genuine participation of citizens in processes of political will-formation" undermines the ethic of "civil privatism"* necessary to a democratic order that has been substantially depoliticized.²⁷ The replacement of a system of formal democracy with genuine participation in a substantive democracy would bring to consciousness, says Habermas, "the contradiction between administratively socialized production and the continued private appropriation and use of surplus value"²⁸ (more simply, it would increase awareness of the private use of social resources). It is in this erosion of civil privatism and in the demand for genuine citizen participation in the political process that there emerges increasing awareness of the deficits in the legitimizing culture. Such deficits, Habermas believes, cannot be easily compensated for through consciously directed cultural manipulation. The cultural system, says Habermas, is peculiarly resistant to such forms of administrative control. The procurement of legitimation through the commercial production and administrative planning of symbols, he argues, is self-defeating as soon as the mode of procurement is seen through.²⁹

Perhaps the most evident example in education of the existence of such a legitimation crisis has been the increasing and intensifying public debate around questions of intelligence assessment, scholastic ability, and educational competence. Such debate is a by-product of the unceasing drive for administrative rationality—a process that forces assumed and accepted cultural ideas and practices out into the political arena. It stirs up the taken-for-granted nature of cultural affairs

---

* Habermas describes "civil privatism" as "political abstinence combined with an orientation to career, leisure, and consumption"—an orientation that involves a "high output-low input" relationship between citizenry and government.

(including, of course, education) and subjects to public scrutiny those practices and theories that have hitherto been justified through their traditional, or apparently self-evident, meanings.

Thus, for example (and paradoxically), the very rationalizing forces that were the midwife of the movement for educational testing are, frequently, now also its nemesis. Such forces continue now to raise questions as to the legitimacy of the educational notions of ability, aptitude, and intelligence; they compel us to critically examine the fundamental validity or meaningfulness of such categories. Whether in the English debate over the 11+ examination or the controversy in this country around IQ and SAT tests continuing public scrutiny erodes any confident belief in the nonsituational and socially unbiased nature of educational measurements. As each new testing instrument becomes a means of social selection, so it also finds itself the subject of a public discourse that concerns its apparently inequitable treatment of some group or other in the population. This is a process in which such groups and their sympathizers have an obvious interest in debunking the scientific validity claims of the test. In the insistence on submitting such claims to public scrutiny there is a politicization of theories and practices previously entrusted to administrative elites.

Socialization and the Emerging Struggle for Cultural Power

So far, I have argued that public education has contributed to, and sometimes instigated, growing popular demands on the economic realm as well as politicizing practices previously left to administrative elites. And in its contribution to the development of the welfare state, schooling may be seen as a major catalyst in the extension of social rights. Perhaps the most visible arena, in recent times, in which schooling has been caught up in the struggle for wider democratic rights, is connected to the question of popular control of the dissemination of cultural symbols and meanings. To understand the emotional and frequently vituperative nature of this issue, it is helpful to return to the conflict emanating from what Daniel Bell has termed the "cultural contradictions of capitalism."

Bell, in his eloquent essay on this theme, describes the breakup of the traditional bourgeois value system—the ideological underpinnings of the development of the capitalist economy.[30] He notes that these underpinnings—the "Protestant ethic" and the "Puritan temper"—emphasized the values of work, sobriety, sexual restraint, and a forbidding attitude toward life. Such values were rooted in small-town American life, nourished by the Protestant church, and transmitted through the schools. This culture began its demise in the early part of the twentieth century with the transformation of the American social structure and the end of small town domination of American life, demographic changes which saw the growth of urban centers and, more broadly, the emergence of a consumption-oriented society with its emphasis on spending and material possessions. It is this last phenomenon that Bell designates as the most crucial. Mass consumption, made possible by the revolution in technology, began in the 1920s. The introduction of movies ("a window on the world, a set of ready made daydreams, fantasy and projection, escapism and omnipotence"), installment selling (the acceptance of living beyond one's means), and, of course, advertising and planned obsolescence all contributed towards the transformation of a culture that "was no longer concerned with how to work and achieve, but how to spend and enjoy."[31] All of this, argues Bell, leaves capitalism with an extraordinary contradiction:

> On the one hand the business corporation wants an individual to work hard, pursue a career, accept delayed gratification—to be, in the crude sense, an organization man. And yet, in its products and advertisements, the corporation promotes pleasure, instant joy, relaxation and letting go. One is to be "straight" by day and a "swinger" by night.[32]

What, says Bell, the "new capitalism" (the consumption-oriented capitalism) continued to demand was a Protestant ethic in the area of production, coupled with pleasure and play in the area of consumption.

It is precisely the value of this consumption-oriented capitalism that has been the focus of "moral-majoritarians" and conservative cultural critics. Their protests have demanded a renunciation of the culture of pleasure, gratification, and the emphasis on the immediate and a reinstatement of traditional (bourgeois) values. While I have posed the cultural conflict as issuing from the heart of the capitalist system (with its contradictory aims of duty vs. pleasure, gratification vs. restraint), this is not reflected in the concerns of these critics (for whom liberals, an extravagant government, and "humanistic" educators are the chief villains). For this reason, the conservative campaign to control cultural symbols and meanings is frequently mystifying and reactionary. At the same time there is significance to the claim that meanings and symbols ought to be subject to popular consideration or control. Given the overwhelming power of corporate interests to manufacture and manipulate culture, such a claim cannot be dismissed as merely a violation of liberal rights or freedoms. Such freedoms, more often than not, support the totalitarian power of big business. The cultural contradictions of capitalism confront the modern consciousness with a bewildering set of conflicts and moral dilemmas: authority vs. freedom, restraint vs. indulgence, satisfaction vs. denial. Given what I have argued is the origin of such conflicts (the contradictory ideologies associated with the system of production and distribution), the extent to which they are felt to be out of popular control makes a good deal of sense. Attempts to restrict or regulate the production and dissemination of culture may be seen as a democratic intervention into the autonomy of the capitalist market, an attempt to subject to popular scrutiny the cultural power of largely unregulated corporate interests.

Once again struggles for cultural control have been fundamentally centered around education or education-related concerns; widespread demands for "accountability" and challenges to curriculum materials and texts do represent an important assertion of popular rights around the dissemination of values, meanings, and symbols. In all of its illiberal judgments and intolerant authoritarianism such a challenge must, at the same time, be seen as an attempt to control the culture of "a world turned upside down."[33] It is a reflection of a growing unwillingness to leave decisions about the allocation of cultural resources to bureaucratic prerogative or the invisible, though far from benign, hand of advertising executives. The struggle for the "hearts and minds" of young people, whether in school or in the increasingly important wider circles of informal socialization (TV, movies) must inevitably politicize (that is, subject to popular accountability) social and economic structures previously immune from popular scrutiny. The conflict between private interests and public influence (especially over the moral and intellectual development of the young) cannot but increasingly call into question the self-serving autonomy of capitalist institutions. It is the possibilities and limits in this conflict between private interests and public influence—between capitalism and democracy—that we turn to in our final chapter.

8
Crisis and Hope: The Dialectic of the Welfare-Educational State, II

IN WAYS THAT HAVE been typical of right-wing movements, the conservative politics of the 1980s in America may be seen as the alliance of two distinct social forces: On the one hand are the concerns of economically threatened corporate interests and, on the other hand, the concerns of a beleaguered middle class.[1] While the former has sought to alleviate its position through government policies aimed at enhancing profitability and the income of upper-level social groups, the latter has sought to right a world that appeared to be turning upside-down, by the pursuit of legislation that would restore traditional values and a prior social order. Against the cultural anxieties (catalyzed as they are by economic concerns) of the middle class, the goals of the corporate element in the conservative movement have been far more direct and explicit. Its aims, put simply, have been to raise the profitability of big business in America. Arguing that a capital shortage was the cause of declining productivity in American industry, businessmen and their political and intellectual allies have sought to hold down or cut back social and educational programs, restrain wages and, hence, increase the return to capital. Such policies have amounted to a redistribution of the social product in favor of business and away from the welfare state and the New Frontier and Great Society programs of the 1960s. Whatever else might be said of such policies, it is clear that the profitability of United States business has declined as it has met stiffer competition from capitalist rivals in Japan, West Germany and elsewhere in Europe, and as small Third World nations have begun to resist United States political and economic domination. In addition, the problem has been compounded by the extended period of "stagflation" that has followed the domestic boom of the late '60s, during which time the American economic pie began to shrink and the real incomes of both working people and capitalists stagnated or declined.

There can be little doubt that in terms of the government measures proposed to meet this situation corporate interests had remarkable success.[2] There was, indeed, a significant redistribution of wealth to upper-income groups (who, it was argued, would use the increased income to fund the national economy). The sharp decline in the relative weight of the taxation in the national economy carried by big business is vividly illustrated by the fact that corporate taxes now represent just 7 percent of the total taxes levied (in 1948 it stood at 23 percent). Since corporate wealth is distributed disproportionately among a very small group of individuals at the top of the income ladder, this only confirms the sharply redistributive effects of recent tax policies in favor of the rich. The Congressional Budget Office estimated that the 1981 Reagan tax plan gave 162,000 people who made over $200,000 a year $22,000 in tax cuts per capita, while 32 million people earning $15,000 or less got just $92.00. The net effect on annual family income of the 1981 tax and benefit cuts ranged from an additional income of $15,000 for those earning $80,000 and above, to an added $810 for those receiving between $20,000 and $40,000, down to a low of $240 for those earning less than $10,000. The Reagan tax plan of 1985, despite its lowering of the tax rate for low-income earners, continued the trend towards a less progressive income tax. The real beneficiaries of Reagan's second tax reform were those with the highest incomes whose tax rates fell to 35 percent (from 70 percent in 1979) and whose capital gains taxes were reduced from 20 percent to 17.5 percent.

In effecting such a redistribution of income the impact on social and educational programs can be little doubted. In North Carolina, for example, reductions in federal aid included the following results: the major education block grant lost 33 percent of its funding; child nutrition programs lost 96 percent of the Special Milk Program, 15.3 percent of the School Breakfast Program, and 9.4 percent of the Child Care Food Program; infant aid was cut by 47.6 percent; and Appalachian regional education aid by 86 percent. In other areas, the Primary Health Care Block grant was cut by 13 percent, the Health Prevention and Health Service block grant by 29 percent, Maternal and Child Health grants by 17 percent, and immunization of infants and preschool children by 48 percent. The Alcohol, Drug Abuse and Mental Health Services block grant lost 30 percent, and the Social Services (Title XX) block grant was reduced by 18.5 percent.[3]

At the ideological core of these very significant cutbacks was the attempt to restrain, curtail, and even revoke the expansion of social rights, economic expectations, and entitlement that have accompanied the enlargement of the state (in which the notion of educational rights has played an important role). Thus in the pursuit of raised profitability for the corporate sector, the attack on social and educational rights (as those are embodied in the programs and outlays of the state) was a central policy concern. While there can be little doubt as to unparalleled influence of corporate interests in the policies of the Reagan administration, it is also important to note the limitations that emerged around such policies. The dominant role of the big business in the formation of government policies—whatever its obvious and massive influence—must also be viewed in terms of the countervailing power that such policies evoked. Despite its wide and clear successes, capital does indeed face barriers to the implementation of its programs. For those concerned with education, for example, any review of the policies of the Reagan administration will reveal two outstanding features. First were the massive and unparalleled attacks on the programs that constitute the federal role in education in this country. The second, paradoxically, has been the emergence of countervailing pressures on the pursuit or implementation of such policies. Whatever the extent of the butchery committed by the Reagan administration in the field of education, its goals fell significantly short of what was anticipated. Despite the ferocity of the attack on the social-educational state, it is now clear that the expansion of social rights and economic entitlements represent an expansion of the political rights of citizenship that will not easily be revoked. The expansion of political rights into an increasing number of social, economic and cultural rights forms a formidable barrier to the pursuit of corporate goals.

These barriers represent, according to Richard Cloward and Frances Fox Piven, a profound change, especially during the last fifty years, in the perceptions that ordinary people have of the relationship between politics and economics.[4] There has been a fundamental erosion, they argue, of the idea that democratic rights do not enable ordinary people to act upon the most urgent economic problems of their lives. There has been an erosion of the doctrine of *laissez-faire* which holds that economic relationships are determined by "natural" laws in which neither the state, nor the majorities that come to participate in the state, should interfere. In the nineteenth century:

> Political rights were thus separated from economic rights, and the economic experiences of ordinary people were made to have little bearing on their ideas about politics. . . .The world of the market was in effect shielded from the world of politics to which common people had gained some access.[5]

During the course of the twentieth century, however, the doctrine of separation has weakened. Grievances against property and the effects of the market increasingly took the form of protests directed against the state:

The broad movement by common people to exercise political rights in behalf of economic rights culminated in the great popular struggles of the 1930s and 1960s—in mass protests by the unemployed, industrial workers, the aged, blacks and women. Politics and economics fused in the granting of federal emergency relief to the masses of unemployed, in collective bargaining legislation, in wage-and-hour laws, in unemployment insurance, in pensions for the aged and disabled, in the enactment of public welfare subsidies for unemployable, in occupational health and safety standards, in medical and housing programs, in civil rights legislation and affirmative action programs, and in a spate of general environmental protection.[6]

The process by which the doctrine of separation collapsed and political rights expanded to a place where they could be used by ordinary people to act on the most pressing issues of their lives, meant that the state became the major area of class conflict. More and more, the poor, working-class and middle-income Americans have expected or demanded that the state protect them against the vicissitudes of the market, the inequities of a class society, the injustices of racism and sexism, and the effects of uncontrolled industrial growth. Increasingly, unemployment, inflation, the availability of credit, the questions of adequate health care or nutrition, the effects of disability or retirement, the quality of consumer products and the environment, and access to schooling have become the subject of popular demands and democratic expectations.

As Cloward and Piven point out, the rising tide of expectations and entitlements that have accompanied the emergence of the welfare state is part of the wider process of the politicization of our economic system. While the distinctive American political institutions of the nineteenth century shielded the various ways in which the state served capital from public view (and thus gave the ideology of *laissez-faire* a certain credibility), by the twentieth century the penetration of the economy by the state on behalf of business had so expanded that the hypocrisy of *laissez-faire* became more transparently evident. It was no longer possible, they assert, to sustain a doctrine prescribing the separation of economy and polity because it was so at odds with the reality.

All of this has contributed to the demystification of *laissez-faire* ideas and made clear the way in which the interests of capital depend on the state. Such developments have, in turn, led to pressures for new kinds of state interventions into the economy—ones which have involved demands that arise from the bottom end of the social structure rather than from the top. The movements which embodied these demands wrought fundamental changes in both the perceptions of social reality, and in the reality itself. The movements of the 1930s and of the 1960s, though they have subsided, left in their wake a profound transformation:

> The new programs of the 1930s and 1960s produced pervasive new linkages between the state and democratic publics that paralleled older

linkages between the state and business. . . . The agencies established to administer new benefit programs, services, and regulations represent another set of linkages, not with business but with the unemployed and the poor, women and blacks, the elderly and the disabled, and unions and environmental groups. By incorporating so wide a range of an enfranchised population, the state itself has become partially democratized.[7]

The process of democratization has meant an expanding array of laws and regulations which have embodied the popular ideology of the twentieth century—the notion that political rights are also social and economic rights. It has meant accelerating popular demands for political interventions that ameliorate the effects of industrial change, redress inequities caused by the market, and protect the casualties of the economic cycle and the process of capital accumulation. Not surprisingly, such a democratization of the state has had deleterious consequences for big business. The politicization of economic life—the notion that more and more aspects of the lives of ordinary people become matters of public policy and areas of popular entitlement—has weakened the bargaining power of capital, and has placed increasing restrictions around the operation and effects of the market in capitalist society. It is precisely this that corporate support of the campaign against "big government" has sought to address. Cloward and Piven argue that the concern with big government is really a concern with the expansion of the welfare state. It is an issue of resisting and disassembling the interventions of the state around matters of equity or social and occupational responsibility. They note:

> The Reagan administration may rail against interference in the economy by "big business," but what it actually means to condemn and eliminate is government interference on behalf of ordinary people, not government interference on behalf of business.[8]

Indeed far from a reduction in the costs or obligations of government, the policies of the Reagan administration involved a massive expansion of support for corporate interests and their high income beneficiaries. The campaign against big government meant a *shifting* of government support, far more than any contraction. The reduction in support of social and educational programs, the restructuring of tax policies, the curtailment of regulative activity, and the huge enlargement of defense outlays, made government policies enormously favorable to the interest of capital. The unprecedented levels of unemployment coupled with reductions in the levels of subsistence benefits have been important forces weakening the bargaining power of working people. The result has been a lowering of the rate of inflation through a reduction in the incomes of working and middle class Americans.

The campaign against government was an attempt to revitalize *laissez-faire* ideology so that the economic process would be disconnected from popular pressures and political rights. Whether around the question of jobs, educational opportunities, clean air, the provisions of health care, nutrition, or safe working conditions, the campaign has sought to convince Americans that their interests are best served if the state is required to respond less to the "clamor of popular demands." It has sought to reassert the idea that the market, not the government, ought to be the mechanism that regulates the conditions of our social and economic lives.

Despite the apparently contradictory election results of the 1980s, there is now mounting evidence that there has been no real abandonment of the notion that the state must intervene to ameliorate or redress the effects of the market and that the state is compelled to protect the livelihoods and opportunities of ordinary people. Certainly the election of Ronald Reagan and the emergence of the policies of "supply-side" economics did not signify a massive embrace of *laissez-faire* ideology or an abandonment of the idea that political rights are also economic rights.[9] The present government, no less than any other since 1932, was directed by a popular mandate to resolve the problems facing working people, especially inflation and unemployment. Indeed, as Cloward and Piven note, unless these problems are resolved, worsening economic conditions will likely once again bring to power national administrations committed to resolve popular economic grievances by rebuilding the welfare state, and even adding to its power.

The Politics of Resistance in the 1980s

Despite some profound changes that have occurred in recent years, there are limits to the implementation of conservative policies in education and in other areas connected to the welfare or social state in the United States. Such limits on reform are not simply consequences of the particular acumen, skill, or statecraft of politicians on the Right (of which there certainly is no lack) but, more substantially, reflect deepening structural restraints in the alignments and dynamics typically associated with conservative social and educational policy making.

From the earliest days of its ascent to power the Reagan administration showed itself to be, both in its choice of functionaries and in its programmatic emphases, aligned far more closely with the concerns and goals of capital, rather than with the social agenda of the New Right which had not a single successful act of substantial legislation pass in the 97th Congress. In the field of education the New Right was unable to pass legislation that would allow prayer in public schools, or amendments limiting the jurisdiction of the court in matters of school busing, or legislation supporting tax credits for private school attendance.

While failure at the congressional level represents an important political phenomenon, this does not reflect the sum total of New Right achievements. Activities at the local and state levels—censorship of school materials, reinstatement of more severe (traditional) behavioral standards, and exclusion of unwanted teachers—represent a shift in the politics and ideology of schooling in the United States that predate the Reagan presidency but are certainly buoyed by the events of the 1980s. Our concern, however, is with the relationship of such grassroots influences on the priorities of those wielding national power. The last few years reveal a pattern in which middle-class interests have achieved little significant power. While these grassroots groups have played an indispensable role in mobilizing public opinion and electoral support for right wing politicians, their influence in the formation of national policies has been more illusory than real. Capital, through its alliance with reactionary groups that express the fears and anxieties of the middle class, has been able to construct a political battering ram for the achievement of its own profit-oriented ends.

Still, the economic reforms of the Right have been considerably more radical in their effects. At the same time, there has indeed been significant, at times aggressive, resistance to policies that have attempted to reduce the scope of social and economic rights. In struggles around environmental issues, social security, and questions of educational opportunity, there have been widespread mobilizations to stop attempts to reduce the protections, safeguards, and opportunities hitherto guaranteed by the state. While clearly not forestalling the Reagan budget axe, popular pressures over educational issues significantly impacted proposed cuts. Popular resistance to such cuts has, at least in some areas, stayed the hand of the executioner. Evidence of this is found in a recent report of the Congressional Research Service. The report notes that the 97th Congress generally supported education assistance programs in the face of the Administration's efforts to reduce sharply federal funding and influence in education. It continued:

> The Congress reduced the funding for some programs in FY 1982, but the total amount was increased over FY 1980 funding levels. Additional reductions were made to some elementary and secondary education programs in FY 1982 but large increases in some of the higher education student assistance programs nearly maintained the overall funding levels. Efforts by the Administration to make further reduction in FY 1982 funding by means of rescissions to enacted appropriations have been rejected.[10]

We may assume that such action was motivated, at least in part, by popular and democratic pressures unleashed by the harshness of the administration's proposals.[11]

The area of student loans provides probably the most dramatic evidence of the connection between political rights and economic rights (mediated through the opportunity for higher education). Cuts in student loans were opposed by a broad coalition of groups that stretched from the minority poor to sections of the white middle class. (Far larger cuts in many other areas were implemented in programs that touched smaller and more vulnerable segments of the population.) The breadth of the mobilization in this case makes clear the extent to which the state in America has politicized the hopes and aspirations of a larger and larger proportion of the population. It is precisely the size of this population that stands as a barrier to any simple return to the ideology of an unhindered economic marketplace. Nor, despite the ballyhoo about electoral realignments, is there much evidence that the majority of the electorate wants such a return. Neither in electoral results nor opinion surveys is there evidence of a fundamental shift in ideology. The latter, for example, continually underline the salience of the kind of complex consciousness suggested by Antonio Gramsci. Whatever support there is at the level of "formal" beliefs for smaller government, unrestricted free enterprise, and leaving it to the market, at the level of "practical" consciousness a majority of the people want continued interventions into the market and social interventions, to ensure a cleaner environment, access to schooling, protection as a result of age, disability, and unemployment, safe working conditions, regulation of consumer quality standards, and more. Indeed, there is reason to believe that there are sizable majorities in favor of an expanded social state (concerned, for example, with universal health care or affordable day care). Electoral results in 1980, 1982, and 1984 show more than anything else the class-skewed nature of voter-turnout.[12] The slightly more than half of the eligible electorate that turned out in the presidential elections was disproportionately represented by more affluent voters who know well how their class interests are best served. While more than a third of all Democratic support comes now from low-income voters, the remaining working-class and middle-class voters showed a frequent disposition toward split voting—supporting a popular president who was, at the same time, clearly identified with the interests of the wealthy, as well as electing Democratic congressional candidates who are perceived as more likely to protect social security, student loans, medicare, and the environment. As Thomas Edsall makes so clear in his study, the real problems for the Democratic Party among middle-class and working-class voters is the tendency to see the party as beneficent to the poor (and especially minorities) without responding adequately to these voters' interest—indeed to perceive the Democratic Party as siding with those groups against the middle class.[13] There is a political vacuum which cannot, ultimately, be filled by a Republican Party that is so strongly the representative of the wealthy and the powerful.

These prevarications at the electoral level are certainly reflected in subsequent budget discussions and decisions. The limits of economic conservatism were made very clear when, even with the nearly unprecedented scale of the 1984 presidential victory, the president's budget-cutting proposals could not safely be accepted by politicians.

While Reagan's extraordinary success in the passage of the 1982 budget was not unrelated to the fact that about 40 percent of the Federal savings resulted from changes in benefit programs affecting households with incomes of less than $10,000, and another 30 percent from those with incomes between $10,000 and $20,000—certainly the most vulnerable strata of the population—larger budget proposals attempted to undermine or dismantle the social state of the middle class.[14] It is at this point that we see the extent to which the social state in America has politicized the expectations and aspirations of an increasingly larger proportion of the population. They are now strongly invested in the expansion of social rights and antipathetic to, in anything but the most abstract sense, reductions in those rights.

Notwithstanding the rootedness among broad sections of the population of social and economic rights that have politicized so many of the areas of our lives that were previously left to the market, this is, in no sense, meant to diminish what have been the accomplishments of the Reagan years. While the politicization of our access to schooling, environmental quality, work conditions, the inability to work for a living, means the emergence of a powerful ideological and political bulwark against too much budget-cutting, the damage to the social state has, nonetheless, been extensive. Measured in human suffering—poverty, hunger, infant mortality, joblessness—the effects are incalculable. The results are only just beginning to be seen and felt. Most importantly, this "golden age" of conservatism has been able to alter the boundaries of political debate. It has upset the political consensus surrounding the welfare state, reconstructing the political agenda so that a series of hitherto long-fought for civil rights or entitlements can no longer be assumed or taken for granted. To whatever extend these entitlements were diminished as a result of the Reagan budgetary initiatives, the more serious consequence is that their fundamental assuredness as a result of previous social and political struggles can no longer be relied upon. The balance of ideological and political power that has constituted the particular form of hegemonic domination until this time has reformed on terms that are distinctively less advantageous to those in the middle and lower end of the social order.

Yet the social and political agenda of this era has its ideological limits. Such limits are reinforced by a number of effects noted by Alan Wolfe. He says that conservative economic programs are based on an explosive combination of pain and hope:

> Accept pain now, the right wing suggests, and with faith your life will improve. Cutbacks in social services, higher tax burdens for those least able to afford them and increasing rates of unemployment are, it is claimed, the necessary price to pay for reindustrialization and eventual prosperity.[15]

Yet, says Wolfe, such behavior runs directly counter to the taste for immediate gratification so powerfully nurtured by modern capitalism:

Right-wing governments ask for patience, but capitalism finds patience intolerable. It expects quick results, immediate consumption, instant pleasure. The political time needed for conservative programs to work is negated by every television commercial and money market fund. Conservatives are done in by the very rhetoric that brings them to power.[16]

The austerity and deprivation imposed on unprecedented numbers during this time stand in ever sharper relief against the accentuated privileges available to the rich. These developments have given rise to one of the most startling and hopeful phenomena in American politics—the Jackson candidacy and the Rainbow Coalition—the first significant popularly based social democratic movement in fifty years. In addition to the resulting heightening of class awareness and class antagonism, the transfer of wealth into a massive build-up of America's nuclear arsenal generated, within a relatively short space of time, a mass movement in favor of a weapons freeze and arms limitation agreements. The moral dimensions of a politics that deprive individuals of basic human resources, like housing, while funding, at unprecedented levels, the programs of the military-industrial complex, become increasingly unpalatable to a significant segment of the American population.

Interestingly, however, the limits on economic conservatism that could prove most decisive in the long run may not be the ones that "surge from the bottom up." Within the corporate sector itself and among a growing band of economists there is an accelerating recognition that modern organized bureaucratic capitalism demands policies quite different from those conservative remedies that emphasize a nostalgic return to the free, unregulated market. For those opposing such policies, the critical issues facing America in the area of industrial investment and productivity can be met only through enhanced levels of state planning and coordinated interventions into the economic market. One of the most prominent spokesmen for this renewed role of the national state is Lester C. Thurow, professor of economics at M.I.T. He writes:

> If current policies do not restore economic growth, then it will be obviously true that salvation does not lie in the direction of "getting the government off the backs of the people." Debates about less government will die out and be replaced with debates not about more government but about what government should do to promote economic growth.[17]

Thurow and others favor government interventions in the market to enhance the competitiveness of American industry *vis-à-vis* other industrial nations.[18] Through the development of a formal industrial-planning policy (as in France or Japan) it would be possible to "develop an integrated strategy that treats public investment, private investment and investment in human capital as part of one policy."[19] Its purpose would be to encourage the fast-growth sector of the economy (the so-called sunrise industries), administer re-industrialization of America's basic industries, and renovate the disintegrating economic infrastructure (roads, bridges, and tunnels).

In all such alternatives for enhancing the competitiveness of the corporate sector, policies concerned with "investments in human capital" are strongly emphasized. Such policies speak to the need for a renewed funding of America's educational system as the means to ensure a workforce equipped with an adequate level of technical or other skills. Indeed, as I have argued previously, it is precisely those concerns that are the cornerstone of the most influential of the recent reports on the crisis in our system of education.[20] As the antigovernment politics of Reagan's conservatism runs its course without really enhancing the productivity of American industry, a new politics is likely to emerge—one that will emphasize a renewed role for the state in the revitalization of the corporate sector. While the renewed federal commitment to the educational system that is likely to follow will certainly proclaim an end to the policies of neglect, inequity, and the unfulfilled opportunities of the Reagan era, those concerned about education may, however, find renewed cause for concern. In the brave new world of corporate-state-school cooperation, education becomes ever more widely defined as technical training, the means to ensure industrial harmony, and the mechanism for assuring individuals well-adjusted to the demands of the bureaucratic world. In this "human capital" view of education, the ideals of a critically intelligent, liberally educated, and humane citizenry is likely to be a subordinate goal. Transcending the limits of conservative policy in education may spell more money and more resources for the hard-pressed domain of schooling. It is unlikely, however, to mean any fundamental reorientation in the nature of the school experience itself. Such an experience is likely to become ever more suffused with the positivist and hierarchical values of bureaucratic capitalism.

Conclusion: The Dialectic of the Welfare-Educational State

Above all else, this chapter and the ones preceding it have attempted to refute interpretations of schooling in which it is perceived only in terms of its social control functions. Education, and especially public education, does far more than ensure a passive, compliant, or submissive population. While studies of the hidden curriculum and other critically oriented work have made clear the relationship of schooling to the socialization of a workforce differentiated and adapted to the values, norms, and beliefs of a bureaucratically organized capitalist economy, this is only a partial description of the effects of education in the United States. Such partiality has drawn our attention away from the total process—the dialectic of schooling in this country. In ways that are analogous to the effects of the welfare state as a whole, education must be seen as both regulating and invigorating popular concerns. Education not only cools out social and economic demands, it also infuses them with greater energy and assertiveness.[21] The important expansion of social and economic rights over the last fifty years has been buttressed by the expansion of educational opportunities and educational rights. There has been an enlargement of the realm in which democratic rights, rather than the criteria of the marketplace, have become the arbiter of the distribution of services, benefits, and resources; in which jobs and the economy need to be responsive to the popular will; and the dissemination of cultural meanings need to be submitted to public scrutiny. Education has been a leading force in reducing the autonomy of the market and the unresponsiveness of capital; it has been an important catalyst in the increasing politicization of social and economic life. Even Reaganomics, which purported to stand for an end to government "interference" in the economy, and a return to *laissez-faire* economics, was not so much predicated on the natural right of capital to pursue its goals unhindered by collective concerns, but as an alternative means to ensure fulfillment of popular economic demands. The 1980 and 1984 elections were little different from any other since 1932 which have 'featured claims and counter-claims, promises and counterpromises, intended to appease popular economic discontent."[22]

By placing education within the broader structures of the welfare state, which has caused increasing areas of our social and economic lives to be subjected to democratic demands arising from citizenship rather than the marketplace, the nature of recent administrations' policies towards education are most clearly understood. The unprecedented cuts in student loans, for example, can be seen as part of the wider strategy by which popular expectations of the economy and wider demands for economic opportunity are lowered; changes in the regulations concerning the education of the handicapped reduce the scope and extent of citizens' social rights; and support of vouchers for private schooling expands the field in which market criteria are utilized to decide the distribution of resources, opportunity and experience. In all of these ways (and many more) the attack on public education becomes an assault on the realm of social and economic rights won in the struggles of the past fifty years.

Education, paradoxically, is also uniquely placed in attempts to reinvigorate the ideology of the marketplace in American society. It clearly expresses in its practices the individualistic and competitive values which are at the center of the ideology. Attempts to legitimate policies that weaken the social-educational state are able to exploit precisely this ideology in order to support such goals. In particular, through reductions in federal educational interventions, it appears that middle-class anxieties concerning the oversupply of educated manpower can be assuaged. Such interventions, it is suggested, have weakened educational standards, opening up the possibilities of educational success to a far greater (and, it is argued, far less qualified) population. Changes in curriculum and teaching methods have weakened the competitive structure of American education, contributing, so conservatives charge, to reduce standards of ability or achievement. Whatever the truth in these assertions, changes in education, especially in the late 1960s and early '70s, did indeed open up the possibilities of educational success to a far broader population of students. The elimination of liberal educational reforms and the interventions of the federal government are desired so far as to return education to the pre-existing forms of competition and selectivity in which the cultural inheritance of the middle and upper middle classes imbues their offspring with overwhelming educational advantages. Typical of such forms of political mobilization, middle-class support rests on the fears and anxiety that are the product of declining economic circumstances—the increasing competition with other groups for the shrinking number of middle-class jobs. While improving educational standards is the ostensible claim of conservative rhetoric, its real effect is to reinforce the selective and competitive nature of schooling, by pitting the middle class against the poor, blacks against whites, men against women.

The complex and contradictory nature of education presented here facilitates both challenges and adaptation to the structures of power and opportunity in American society. It mirrors the fluid and unresolved nature of the struggle to achieve social and political change in the United States. Thus, as Cloward and Piven argue, despite the powerful assault on the welfare state there is no assuredness that it will, in the long run, be successful. The popular ideology of the twentieth century (the view that citizenship includes not only political rights but also economic rights) is deeply rooted in, and continually confirmed by, twentieth-century experience, they argue. Such experience is rooted in the structural changes that have transformed American society over the past century:

> Neither the decentralization of a few popularly oriented programs nor the restructuring of the regulatory agencies will suffice to obscure the change of interdependencies between state and economy. . . . the scale and obviousness of the state's penetration of the economy will continue to nourish popular convictions that government has a great deal to do with the economic circumstances of people . . . [and] the democratic right to participate is likely to continue to produce demands that government enact policies of economic reform.[23]

It will require, they argue, more than propaganda and the still relatively minor structural changes to restore the nineteenth-century doctrine that economic activities are regulated by the law of the market rather than the law of the state, and to persuade people that the government is not the proper arbiter from which to seek solutions to their social and economic troubles.

Such belief must be a tempered one. In the present and continuing economic crisis more fundamental change can, in no way, be discounted. The lessons of history in this century must alert us to the catastrophic possibilities that may emerge in moments of such crisis. What must be affirmed here, both in connection to the study of education and in terms of the wider society, is the relatively open and undetermined nature of change. While the structural situation rules out certain possibilities and makes others more likely, this is the most that can be said. Such situations represent no more than the parameters of the terrain on which the struggle for change is able to occur. It is finally the situation itself that must be acted upon—and for this, the conscious intentionality of human involvement is indispensable. The institutions of the welfare-education state offer a terrain on which the interest and ideology of those who are most powerful in society may be contested, defined in alternative ways, and, sometimes, transformed. The history of public institutions must be understood as testimony to such possibilities.

Notes

1.

1. Christopher Lasch, *The Agony of the American Left* (New York: Knopf, 1969).
2. James Weinstein, *The Decline of Socialism in America, 1912–1925* (New York: Monthly Review, 1967).
3. *New York Times,* March 25, 1984.
4. Speech to the Democratic National Convention, *New York Times,* July 19, 1984.
5. "A National Program for Elementary and Secondary Education." Senator John Glenn, June 29, 1983.
6. Walter Mondale press release, May 9, 1983.
7. "The Candidate's 'Basic' Campaign Speech." *New York Times,* February 22, 1984.
8. Mondale press release, May 9, 1983.
9. Mike Davis, *Prisoners of the American Dream* (London: Verso, 1986), p. 292.
10. *Ibid.*
11. *Ibid.* p. 294.
12. "Education for Economic Renewal," summary of proposals to the Arizona Legislature, Governor Bruce Babbitt, January, 1983, p. 1.
13. *Ibid.*
14. "Bruce Babbitt on Education," 1987 Campaign Issue Brief.
15. U.S. Senator Joseph R. Biden, Jr., "Making the Grade in Education," speech at Clark College, Dubuque, Iowa, April 12, 1987, p. 2.
16. *Ibid.*, p. 3.
17. *Ibid.*, p. 4.

18. *Ibid.*, p. 6.
19. "Education," Senator Joseph R. Biden, Jr. 1987 Campaign Statement.
20. "Making the Grade in Education," p. 6.
21. Speech to the Democratic National Convention, July 18, 1984.
22. *New York Times,* May 7, 1984.
23. *New York Times,* February 27, 1984.
24. *New York Times,* April 6, 1984.
25. "Iowa Democratic Candidates' Debate," *New York Times,* February 13, 1984.
26. "Education: A Community Project," speech by the Reverend Jesse Jackson, Newark, New Jersey, May 25, 1984.
27. *Ibid.*
28. *Ibid.*
29. *Ibid.*
30. *Ibid.*
31. *Ibid.*
32. *Ibid.*
33. See, for example, John I. Goodlad, *A Place Called School* (New York: McGraw–Hill, 1984).
34. Bertell Ollman and Howard Vernoff, eds., *The Left Academy* (New York: McGraw–Hill, 1982).
35. Jürgen Habermas, *Legitimation Crisis* (Boston: Beacon, 1975).
36. See, for example, Stuart Hall and Tony Jefferson, eds., *Resistance Through Rituals* (London: Hutchinson, 1976).
37. Henry Giroux, "The Crisis of Reproduction and Resistance in the New Sociology of Education: A Critical Analysis," *Harvard Education Review* 53 (Aug. 1983): 262.
38. *Ibid.*, p. 267.
39. Harvey Cox, *Religion in the Secular City* (New York: Simon & Schuster, 1984); see also Kevin Phillips, *Post-Conservative America* (New York: Vintage, 1983).
40. Karl Marx, *Selected Works* (Moscow: 1935), Vol. 1:208–9.

2.

1. For a good summary of the arguments concerning the functional aspects of neo-Marxist educational theory, see "Introduction," in Jerome Karabel and A. H. Halsey, eds., *Power and Ideology in Education* (New York: Oxford University Press, 1977).
2. Paul Willis, *Learning to Labour: How Working Class Kids Get Working Class Jobs* (Farnborough, England: Saxon House, 1977), pp. 175–76.
3. *Ibid.*, p. 160.
4. A number of writers have made similar observations about the functional nature of Althusser's version of ideology. See, for

example, Tony Bennett, *Formalism and Marxism* (London and New York: Methuen, 1979), pp. 112–26.
5. See, for example, Daniel Bell, *The Cultural Contradictions of Capitalism* (New York: Basic Books, 1976).
6. "Recasting Marxism: Hegemony and New Political Movements," interview with Ernesto Laclau and Chantal Mouffe, in *Socialist Review* 12 (Nov.–Dec. 1982): 91–113.
7. *Ibid.*, p. 94.
8. *Ibid.*, p. 108.
9. *Ibid.*
10. *Ibid.*, p. 100.
11. For a good discussion of issues connected to socialization, gender, and schooling, see the special issue of *Journal of Education* 166 (March 1984).
12. Christopher Lasch, *The Culture of Narcissism* (New York: Norton, 1978), pp. 125–53.
13. Habermas, *Legitimation Crisis*.
14. Thomas McCarthy, *The Critical Theory of Jürgen Habermas* (Cambridge, Mass.: MIT Press, 1978), p. 371.
15. Habermas, quoted in McCarthy, *The Critical Theory of Jürgen Habermas*, p. 371.
16. Habermas, *Legitimation Crisis*, p. 81.
17. *Ibid.*, p. 83.
18. *Ibid.*, p. 86.
19. *Ibid.*, p. 85.
20. *Ibid.*
21. *Ibid.*
22. *Ibid.*, p. 91.
23. *Ibid.*, p. 81.
24. *Ibid.*
25. Michael Harrington, *Decade of Decision* (New York: Simon & Schuster, 1980), p. 270.
26. Habermas, *Legitimation Crisis*, p. 82.
27. See Stanley Aronowitz, *False Promises* (New York: McGraw-Hill, 1973), Chapter 6.
28. Bell, *The Cultural Contradictions of Capitalism*, p. 70.
29. *Ibid.*, pp. 71–72.
30. *Ibid.*, p. 66.
31. *Ibid.*, p. 67.
32. *Ibid.*, p. 69.
33. *Ibid.*
34. *Ibid.*, p. 70.
35. Eli Zaretsky, *Capitalism, The Family and Personal Life* (New York: Harper Colophon, 1976).
36. *Ibid.*, p. 66.
37. *Ibid.*, p. 68.
38. *Ibid.*, p. 71.

39. *Ibid.*, p. 34.
40. *Ibid.*, p. 76.
41. Arthur Brittan, *The Privatized World* (London: Routledge & Kegan Paul, 1977).
42. *Ibid.*, p. 64.
43. Alain Touraine, *The Post-Industrial Society* (New York: Random House, 1971).
44. *Ibid.*, pp. 196–97.
45. Herbert Marcuse, *One Dimensional Man* (Boston: Beacon, 1964), Chapter 1.
46. Lasch, *The Culture of Narcissism.*
47. *Ibid.*, p. 53.
48. *Ibid.*, p. 72.
49. Theodore Roszak, *Person/Planet* (Garden City, N.Y.: Anchor Press/Doubleday, 1978). A somewhat similar thesis is found in Peter Clecak, *America's Quest for the Ideal Self* (New York: Oxford University Press, 1983). Clecak's thesis, with its reduction of all social movements of the Left and Right to the quest for "salvation and social justice," is especially simplistic.
50. *Ibid.*, p. 4.
51. *Ibid.*
52. Hans Peter Dreitzel, "On the Political Meaning of Culture," in Norman Birnbaum, ed., *Beyond the Crisis* (Oxford: Oxford University Press, 1977), pp. 83–129.
53. *Ibid.*, p. 99.
54. *Ibid.*, pp. 99–100.
55. *Ibid.*, p. 100.
56. *Ibid.*
57. *Ibid.*
58. *Ibid.*
59. Daniel Yankelovitch, *New Rules* (New York: Random House, 1981). For an especially sensitive description of the role of radical individualism in American life, see Robert N. Bellah et al., *Habits of the Heart* (Berkeley: University of California Press, 1985), Chapter 6.
60. *Ibid.*, p. 5.
61. *Ibid.*, p. 4.
62. For further discussion, chapter 4 in this volume; see also H. Svi Shapiro, "Functionalism, the State and Education: Towards a New Analysis," *Social Praxis* 8 (1981): 5–24.
63. Lasch, *The Culture of Narcissism*, pp. 131–32.
64. *Ibid.*, p. 23.
65. *Ibid.*, p. 21.
66. *Ibid.*, p. 245.
67. See, for example, Aronowitz, *False Promises,* chapter 2, "Colonized Leisure, Trivialized Work"; William Pinar, "Sanity, Madness and the School," in William Pinar, ed., *Curriculum Theoriz-*

ing: *The Reconceptualists* (Berkeley: McCutchen 1974), pp. 359–383.
68. See H. Svi Shapiro, "Radical Movements, Ideology, and the Sociology of Educational Ideas," in *Social Praxis* 6 (1979): 193–215; H. Svi Shapiro, "Education and Ideology: A Sociological Study of Educational Thought in the American Radical Movement, 1900–1925" (Ed.D. diss., Boston University, 1978).
69. Lasch, *The Culture of Narcissism*, p. 249.
70. Some of the more noted accounts include Jonathan Kozol, *Death at an Early Age* (Boston: Houghton Mifflin, 1967); James Herndon, *The Way It Spozed To Be* (New York: Simon & Schuster, 1968); Herbert Kohl, *36 Children* (New York: New American Library, 1967); Edgar Friedenberg, *Coming of Age in America* (New York: Vintage, 1963).
71. See, for example, H. Svi Shapiro, "Society, Ideology and the Reform of Special Education," *Educational Theory* 30 (Summer 1980): 211–23.
72. For an interesting discussion of this, see Zvi Lamm, "The Status of Knowledge in the Radical Concept of Education," in David E. Purpel and Maurice Belanger, eds., *Curriculum and the Cultural Revolution* (Berkeley: McCutchen, 1972), pp. 124–42.
73. Horkheimer, in a letter to Lowenthal, quoted in Martin Jay, *The Dialectical Imagination* (London: Heinemann, 1974), p. 213.
74. Herbert Marcuse, *Negations: Essays in Critical Theory*, quoted in Jay, *The Dialectical Imagination*, p. 180.
75. Aronowitz, *False Promises*, chapter 2.
76. *Ibid.*, p. 130.
77. *Ibid.*, p. 123.

3.

1. Raymond Williams, "Base and Superstructure in Marxist Cultural Theory," *New Left Review* 82 (December 1973): 3–16.
2. See, for example, Raymond Williams, *Marxism and Literature* (Oxford: Oxford University Press, 1977).
3. Raymond Williams, *The Long Revolution* (Middlesex, England: Penguin, 1965), pp. 125–55.
4. See, for example, Nicos Poulantzas, *Political Power & Social Classes* (London: New Left Books and Sheed & Ward, 1973).
5. Williams, "Base and Superstructure," p. 5.
6. *Ibid.*
7. *Ibid.*
8. *Ibid.*
9. This formulation of the organizing principles of academic knowledge is drawn from Michael F. D. Young, ed., *Knowledge and Control* (London: Collier–Macmillan, 1971), p. 38.

10. "School is not as 'real' as work, which means that one can be less responsible and adult-like in school because 'school is not the point of life'—work is." Quoted in Dennis Schapiro, "The Crisis in Minnesota Classrooms," *Mpls, St. Paul Magazine,* September 1980.
11. Caleb Gattegno, *Towards a Visual Culture* (New York: Avon Books, 1969).
12. This is a theme that has formed a key element in the Frankfurt School of Social Research's critical theory view of culture. See, for example, Theodor W. Adorno and Max Horkheimer, *Aspects of Sociology* (Boston: Beacon, 1972), especially chapter 6.
13. Such ideas were originally formulated by Marcuse in a number of papers published between 1934 and 1938 in the *Zeitschrift für Sozial Forschung*—the journal of the Institute of Social Research. The ideas constituted a first statement of the thesis which informs the whole of his later work.
14. Alasdair MacIntyre, *Marcuse* (London: Fontana/Collins, 1970), pp. 14–15.
15. Raymond Williams, *Culture and Society 1780–1950* (Middlesex, England: Penguin Books, 1968), p. 273.
16. Michael F. D. Young, quoted in Geoff Whitty, "Sociology and the Problem of Radical Educational Change," in Michael Young and Geoff Whitty, eds., *Society, State, and Schooling* (Sussex: The Falmer Press, 1977), p. 33.
17. Norman Birnbaum, *The Crisis of Industrial Society* (New York: Oxford University Press, 1969), p. 136.
18. *Ibid.*
19. Joel Spring, *Education and the Rise of the Corporate State* (Boston: Beacon, 1972), chapter 5.
20. The limited (and I believe inadequate) response to the nature of the curriculum is expressed in the statement of Bowles and Gintis that "one is struck more by the irrelevance of the material than by its utilitarian value." *Schooling in Capitalist America* (New York: Basic Books, 1976), p. 168.
21. Nicos Poulantzas, *Classes in Contemporary Capitalism,* p. 266.
22. *Ibid.,* p. 266.
23. *Ibid.,* p. 268.
24. Goran Therborn, *What Does the Ruling Class Do When It Rules?* (London: New Left Books, 1978), pp. 43–44.
25. For a good review of the basis of P. L. 94–142 see A. Abeson and J. Zettel, "The End of the Quiet Revolution: The Education for All Handicapped Children Act of 1975," *Exceptional Children:* 44 (October 1977): 114–28.
26. See, for example, Schlomo Avineri, *The Social and Political Thought of Karl Marx* (London: Cambridge University Press, 1968).
27. For a critical examination of the process, see Julienne Ford,

Social Class and the Comprehensive School (London: Routledge & Kegan Paul, 1969).
28. Daniel Bell, *The Cultural Contradictions of Capitalism*, p. 42.
29. *Ibid.*, p. 130.
30. H. Svi Shapiro, "Radical Movements," pp. 193–215.
31. See, for example, Stephen Castles and Wiebke Wustenberg, *The Education of the Future* (London: Pluto, 1979); Shapiro, "Education and Ideology: A Sociological Study of Educational Thought in the American Radical Movement, 1900–25."
32. May Wood Simons, "Education and Socialism," *International Socialist Review* (April 1901): 600–607.

4.

1. Schlomo Avineri, *The Social and Political Thought of Karl Marx* (Cambridge: Cambridge University Press, 1970), chapter 1.
2. Bertell Ollman, *Alienation: Marx's Conception of Man in Capitalist Society,* (New York: Cambridge University Press, 1976), p. 221.
3. A. Abeson and J. Zettel, "The End of the Quiet Revolution," p. 115.
4. Quoted in Abeson and Zettel, "The End of the Quiet Revolution," p. 117.
5. See, for example, J. R. Mercer, *Labelling the Mentally Retarded* (Berkeley: University of California Press, 1973).
6. For a discussion of these, see Ray C. Rist, "On Understanding the Process of Schooling: The Contributions of Labelling Theory," in Karabel and Halsey, eds., *Power and Ideology in Education,* pp. 292–305.
7. See, for example, Donald Hammil and J. Lee Weiderholt, *The Resource Room: Rationale and Implementation* (Philadelphia: Buttonwood Farms, 1972).
8. Ford, *Social Class and the Comprehensive School.*
9. Boston, *Documents of the School Committee,* No. 7 (1908), p. 53.
10. John Dewey, *Democracy and Education* (New York: Macmillan, 1961), pp. 260–61.
11. Especially good examples of this literature include Friedenberg, *Coming of Age in America,* and Henry, *Culture Against Man* (New York: Vintage, 1963).
12. See, for example, James A. Tucker, "Ethnic Proportions in Classes for the Learning Disabled: Issues in Non-Biased Assessment," paper presented to Council for Exceptional Children, Kansas City, Missouri, 1978.
13. "Double Jeopardy," Report of the Massachusetts Advocacy Center, 1978.
14. Gerald S. Coles, "The Learning Disabilities Test Battery: Empirical and Social Issues," *Harvard Educational Review* 48 (August 1978), reviews validation studies of the ten most frequently

recommended procedures used for diagnosing learning disabilities and finds them lacking in any sound empirical base. Coles argues that specialists in the field have resorted to biological explanations for institutional failures; they focus attention and attempts at remediation on the child rather than on the social context in which the child must perform.

15. In an unpublished study, Ewa Pytowska and N. J. Pesci have shown that the assessment of special needs students as requiring a "substantially separate" educational program undergoes a significant rise between elementary and secondary education. The trend towards a more "restrictive" setting for students at higher levels of the educational structure would seem to suggest the differential effects of institutional settings and environment on a student's "ability" or "handicap."
16. Williams, "Base and Superstructure," pp. 3–16.
17. Lamm, "The Status of Knowledge," p. 178.
18. It is precisely this phenomenon that is described by William Ryan in his concept of blaming the victim. See William Ryan, *Blaming the Victim* (New York: Vintage, 1976). Of course, on the question of "normality" and "deviance" the explorations of Michel Foucault are unparalleled. See, for example, his *Discipline and Punish: The Birth of the Prison* (London: Allen Lane, Penguin, 1977).
19. For an excellent elaboration of this thesis see Jean Anyon, "Social Class and the Hidden Curriculum of Work," *Journal of Education* 162 (Winter 1980): 67–92.
20. See, for example, Anthony Green and Rachael Sharp, *Education and Social Control: A Study in Progressive Primary Education* (London: Routledge & Kegan Paul, 1979).
21. One of the most interesting collections exemplifying this alternative approach is John Beck et al., eds., *Towards a Sociology of Education* (New Brunswick, N.J.: Transaction Books, 1976).
22. Poulantzas, *Classes in Contemporary Capitalism*, Part 3, pp. 191–327.
23. Erik Olin Wright, *Class, Crisis, and the State* (London: New Left Books, 1978), p. 59.
24. See the discussion of classes and social imagery in John H. Goldthorpe, *The Affluent Worker in the Class Structure* (London: Cambridge University Press, 1969), pp. 116–56.

5.

1. See, for example, Jürgen Habermas, *Knowledge and Human Interests* (Boston: Beacon, 1971).
2. For an excellent discussion of this, see Ian Connell, "Monopoly Capitalism and the Media," in Sally Hibbin, ed., *Politics, Ideology, and the State* (London: Lawrence & Wishart, 1978), pp. 69–98.

3. Poulantzas, *Political Power and Social Classes*, p. 192.
4. For a useful discussion of Gramsci, the state, and ideology, see Chantal Mouffe, *Gramsci and Marxist Theory* (Boston: Routledge & Kegan–Paul, 1979).
5. Goran Therborn, *What Does the Ruling Class Do*, p. 181.
6. Antonio Gramsci, quoted in Mouffe, *Gramsci*, p. 181.
7. Poulantzas, *Political Power and Social Classes*, p. 192.
8. *Ibid.*, p. 194.
9. James O'Connor, *The Fiscal Crisis of the State* (New York: St. Martin's Press, 1973).
10. My references to Jürgen Habermas in this chapter are from his *Legitimation Crisis*. I have also drawn heavily on McCarthy, *The Critical Theory of Jürgen Habermas*.
11. McCarthy, *The Critical Theory of Jürgen Habermas*, p. 368.
12. Habermas, *Legitimation*, p. 52.
13. *Ibid.*, p. 66.
14. McCarthy, *The Critical Theory of Jürgen Habermas*, pp. 369–70.
15. Habermas, *Legitimation*, p. 70.
16. *Ibid.*, p. 93.
17. Alan Wolfe, *The Limits of Legitimacy* (New York: Free Press, 1977).
18. *Ibid.*, pp. 262–63.
19. *Ibid.*, p. 263.
20. *Ibid.*, p. 268.
21. O'Connor, *Fiscal Crisis of the State*, p. 1.
22. O'Connor notes the distinction between the "monopoly sector" and the "competitive sector" of industry. While the former concerns production and marketing that is, typically, large scale (national or international in scope) where wages are relatively high and the demand for labor (that includes a high ratio of bureaucratic-administrative and scientific-technical jobs) is available on a full-time, year-round basis, the latter involved production that is typically small-scale, where wages are relatively low, and employment casual, temporary, or seasonal. O'Connor adds that workers who want and are unable to find full-time, year-round, well-paid work in the monopoly or state sectors, will accept employment in the competitive sector on almost any terms. In the United States, he says, the chief examples are black and other minority workers who are cut off from "mainstream" opportunities by racism and discrimination, women who are excluded from good jobs and good pay, and older workers who are retired involuntarily from high-wage industries.
23. *Ibid.*, p. 138.
24. *Ibid.*, pp. 162–63.
25. *Ibid.*, pp. 9–10.
26. "Public and Private Schools," *Harvard Educational Review* 51 (November 1981).

27. Most recently displayed in Secretary of Education William Bennett's 1985 voucher proposals. Similar proposals have already been made by the Thatcher government in Great Britain.
28. James W. Guthrie and Ami Zusman, "Unasked Questions," *Harvard Educational Review* 51 (November 1981): 517.
29. *NEA Reporter* 21 (June 1982): 3.
30. *NEA Advocate* 16 (May 1982): 4.
31. Habermas, *Legitimation Crisis*, p. 81.

6.

1. Sam Zuckerman, "Reagan's Domestic Policy a Disaster," *Guardian* (Fall 1981): 3.
2. Harrington, *Decade of Decision*, p. 120.
3. Bell, *Cultural Contradictions*, p. 74.
4. See, for example, Zaretsky, *Capitalism*, chapter 4.
5. For a good account of such distinctions see Richard Sennett and Jonathan Cobb, *The Hidden Injuries of Class* (New York: Alfred E. Knopf, 1972), p. 185.
6. Poulantzas, *Classes in Contemporary Capitalism*, p. 258.
7. *Ibid.*, p. 266.
8. Aronowitz, *False Promises*, chapter 6.
9. Colin Greer, *The Great School Legend* (New York: Basic Books, 1972).
10. Thurow, quoted in Harrington, *Decade of Decision*, p. 267.
11. Harrington, *Decade of Decision*, p. 269.
12. Dresch, quoted in Harrington, *Decade of Decision*, p. 270.
13. "An Imperiled Generation," the Report of the Trustees of the Carnegie Foundation for the Advancement of Teaching (1988).
14. See, for example, Frances Fox Piven and Richard A. Cloward, *The New Class War* (New York: Pantheon, 1982).
15. Felix G. Rohatyn, "New York and the Nation," *The New York Review of Books* 23 (Jan. 21, 1982): 88.
16. Erik Olin Wright, *Class, Crisis, and the State* (London: New Left Books, 1978), chapter 3.
17. "Action for Excellence: A Comprehensive Plan to Improve Our Nation's Schools," report of the Task Force on Education for Economic Growth (Denver: Education Commission of the States, 1983).
18. "A Nation at Risk," the final report of the National Commission on Excellence in Education, *Education Week*, April 27, 1983, pp. 12–16.
19. Poulantzas, *Classes in Contemporary Capitalism*.
20. Bob Jessup, "Capitalism and Democracy: The Best Possible Political Shell?" in Gary Littlejohn, Barry Smart, John Wakeford, and Nira Yuval-Davis, *Power and the State* (New York: St. Martin's Press, 1978), p. 42.

21. Manuel Castells, *The Economic Crisis of American Society* (Princeton, N.J.: Princeton University Press, 1980), p. 122.
22. G. William Domhoff, "Book Reviews," *Social Policy* (Winter 1983): 58.
23. Castells, *Economic Crisis*, pp. 57–58.
24. Report of the National Task Force on Education for Economic Growth. Quoted in *Education Week*, Vol. II, No. 33 (May 11, 1983): 1.
25. Quoted in *Education Week*, Vol. II, No. 33 (May 11, 1983): 14.
26. Report of the National Commission on Excellence in Education. Quoted in *Education Week*, Vol. II, No. 31 (April 27, 1983): 14.
27. NCEE report quoted in *Education Week*, Vol. II, No. 31 (April 27, 1983): 15.
28. Quoted in *Education Week*, Vol. II, No. 33 (May 11, 1983): 15.
29. See, for example, Thomas P. Rohlen, *Japan's High Schools* (Berkeley: University of California Press, 1983).
30. Martin Carnoy and Derek Shearer, *Economic Democracy* (New York: M. E. Sharpe, 1980); Samuel Bowles, David Gordon, and Thomas E. Weiskopf, *Beyond the Wasteland: A Democratic Alternative to Economic Decline* (New York: Anchor Press/Doubleday, 1983).

7.

1. Piven and Cloward, *The New Class War*, p. 1. Surprisingly, virtually no attention is given by these authors to the role of education in the development of the welfare state. Also on the theme of the expansion of social rights, see the important article by Samuel Bowles and Herbert Gintis, "The Crisis of Liberal Democratic Capitalism: The Case of the United States," *Politics and Society* 2 (1982): 51–93.
2. College Press Service report, October 1981.
3. *NEA Reporter* 21 (June 1982): 3.
4. The justification of such redistributive policies has to do with the whole notion of supply-side economics. It has been questioned whether the problem of reinvestment in the United States has to do with a genuine shortage of capital or a consequence of unproductive forms of capital expenditure (corporate mergers, speculation, exports of capital). Piven and Cloward cite a 1978 *Business Week* report that "the nation's biggest corporations are sitting atop a record $80 billion pile of cash that could finance a grand boom in capital spending."
5. Piven and Cloward, *The New Class War*, pp. 26–28.
6. *Ibid.*, p. 122.
7. *Ibid.*, p. 123.
8. *Ibid.*

9. MacIntyre, *Marcuse*, p. 69.
10. Ralph Miliband, "The Capitalist State: Reply to Nicos Poulantzas," *New Left Review* 59 (1970): 57.
11. Poulantzas, *Political Power and Social Classes*, p. 192.
12. Ollman, *Alienation*, chapter 30.
13. Paradoxically, a good example of the viewpoint is found in Frances Fox Piven and Richard A. Cloward's own book, *Regulating the Poor* (New York: Pantheon, 1971). For further illustrations of this perspective, see Shapiro, "Functionalism, The State and Education," *Social Praxis* 8(1981): 5–24.
14. Piven and Cloward, *The New Class War*, p. 29.
15. For a fuller discussion of this problem see H. Svi Shapiro, "Towards a Reconsideration of the State in Educational Policy," *Teachers College Record* 83 (Summer 1982): 515–27.
16. It is precisely these conclusions that have been refuted in the work of authors such as Henry Giroux in the United States and Paul Willis in Britain. Their work insists on the need to see the individual as actively engaged in the construction of his own social reality. They have alerted us to the dangers of the overdetermined view of human behavior.
17. *Digest for Educational Statistics*, 1981 (Washington, D.C.: United States Department of Education).
18. *What Head Start Means to Families* (Washington, D.C.: United States Department of Health, Education, and Welfare, 1979).
19. See, for example, Avineri, *The Social and Political Thought of Karl Marx*, p. 44.
20. Sennett and Cobb, *The Hidden Injuries of Class*.
21. *Ibid.*, p. 186.
22. Habermas, *Legitimation Crisis*, p. 47.
23. *Ibid.*, p. 72.
24. *Ibid.*
25. *Ibid.*, p. 71.
26. *Ibid.*
27. *Ibid.*, p. 36.
28. *Ibid.*
29. *Ibid.*, pp. 70–71.
30. Bell, *The Cultural Contradictions of Capitalism*.
31. *Ibid.*, p. 70.
32. *Ibid.*, pp. 71–72.
33. Not all of cultural politics is organized by the Right. We must also note the work of liberal groups such as the Massachusetts-based Action for Children's Television and feminists concerned about advertising and the media.

8.

1. For a fuller discussion, see H. Svi Shapiro, "The Making of Conservative Educational Policy," *Urban Education* 17 (July 1982): 233–52.
2. See, for example, Judis, "To the Wealthy," p. 3.
3. *Federal Budget Cuts in North Carolina, Part II* (Raleigh, N. C.: The North Carolina Center for Public Policy Research, 1982).
4. Piven and Cloward, *The New Class War*.
5. *Ibid.*, p. 42.
6. *Ibid.*, p. 43.
7. *Ibid.*, pp. 118–19.
8. *Ibid.*, p. 44.
9. While opinion surveys have certainly noted the public's desire for smaller, less expensive government, they also paradoxically emphasize strong and continued support for the specified categories of social spending—whether in environmental protection, social security, medical care, educational aid, or housing.
10. *Impact of Budget Changes in Major Education Programs, Both Enacted and Proposed, During the 97th Congress* (Washington, D.C.: Congressional Research Service, The Library of Congress, IP199E, September 25, 1982).
11. Dramatic, if surprising, testimony to this is provided by arch-conservative David Stockman, who described Reagan's "failed revolution" in his book, *The Triumph of Politics* (New York: Harper and Row, 1986).
12. See Thomas B. Edsall, *The New Politics of Inequality* (New York: Norton, 1984), chapter 5.
13. *Ibid.*
14. See, for example, *Major Legislative Changes in Human Resources Programs since January 1981*. Staff Memorandum from the Congressional Budget Office (August 1983).
15. Alan Wolfe, "The Retreat of the Right," *Nation*, October 23, 1982, p. 400.
16. *Ibid.*
17. Lester C. Thurow, "How to Rescue a Drowning Economy," *The New York Review of Books* 29 (April 1, 1982).
18. Prominent among these are Felix Rohatyn, Barry Bosworth, James Galbraith, Barry Bluestone, Bennett Harrison, and David A. Smith.
19. Quoted in "The New Liberal Economists," *Newsweek*, November 8, 1982.
20. H. Svi Shapiro, "Capitalism at Risk: The Political Economy of the Education Reports of 1982," *Educational Theory* 35 (Winter 1985): 57–72.
21. Piven and Cloward, *The New Class War*, p. 125.
22. More recent critical education theory has begun to orient us

towards the democratic and citizenship traditions in American schooling as a springboard for transforming schools into public spaces where forms of self and social empowerment might be fostered. See for example, Henry A. Giroux and Peter McLaren, "Teacher Education and the Politics of Engagement: The Case for Democratic Schooling," *Harvard Educational Review*, 56 (August 1986); also Martin Carnoy and Henry M. Levin, *Schooling and Work in the Democratic State* (Stanford, Calif.: Stanford University Press, 1985). See also the work of the Public Education Information Network.
23. Piven and Cloward, *The New Class War*, p. 135.

Selected Bibliography

Apple, Michael W. *Education and Power*. London: Routledge & Kegan Paul, 1983.

———. *Teachers and Texts*. New York: Routledge & Kegan Paul, 1986.

Aronowitz, Stanley, and Henry Giroux. *Education Under Seige*. S. Hadley, Mass.: Bergin & Garvey, 1985.

———. *False Promises*. New York: McGraw-Hill, 1973.

Avineri, Schlomo. *The Social and Political Thought of Karl Marx*. Cambridge: Cambridge University Press, 1970.

Bell, Daniel. *The Cultural Contradictions of Capitalism*. New York: Basic Books, 1976.

Bellah, Robert N., et. al. *Habits of the Heart*. New York: Harper & Row, 1985.

Birnbaum, Norman. *The Crisis of Industrial Society*. New York: Oxford University Press, 1969.

———, ed. *Beyond the Crisis*. Oxford: Oxford University Press, 1977.

Bloom, Alan. *The Closing of the American Mind*. New York: Simon & Schuster, 1987.

Bowers, C. A. *Elements of a Post-Liberal Theory of Education*. New York: Teachers College Press, 1987.

Bowles, Samuel, and Herbert Gintis. *Schooling in Capitalist America*. New York: Basic Books, 1976.

Bowles, Samuel, David Gordon, and Thomas E. Weiskopf. *Beyond the Wasteland: A Democratic Alternative to Economic Decline*. New York: Anchor Press/Doubleday, 1983.

Bowman, Zygmunt. *Towards a Critical Sociology*. London: Routledge & Kegan Paul, 1976.

Boyte, Harry C. *The Backyard Revolution*. Philadelphia, Pa.: Temple University Press, 1980.

Brittan, Arthur. *The Privatized World*. London: Routledge & Kegan Paul, 1977.

Carnoy, Martin, and Henry M. Levin. *Schooling and Work in the Democratic State*. Stanford, Calif.: Stanford University Press, 1985.
Carnoy, Martin, and Derek Shearer. *Economic Democracy*. New York: M.E. Sharpe, 1980.
Castells, Manuel. *The Economic Crisis of American Society*. Princeton, N.J.: Princeton University Press, 1980.
Castles, Stephen, and Wiebke Wustenberg. *The Education of the Future*. London: Pluto, 1979.
Center for Contemporary Cultural Studies. *Unpopular Education*. London: Hutchinson, 1981.
Clecak, Peter. *America's Quest for the Ideal Self*. New York: Oxford University Press, 1983.
Cohen, Joshua, and Joel Rogers. *On Democracy*. Middlesex, England: Penguin, 1983.
Connell, Ian. "Monopoly, Capitalism and the Media." In *Politics, Ideology, and the State*, edited by Sally Hibben. London: Lawrence & Wishart, 1978.
Cox, Harvey. *Religion in the Secular City*. New York: Simon & Schuster, 1984.
Davis, Mike. *Prisoners of the American Dream*. London: Verso, 1986.
Edsall, Thomas B. *The New Politics of Inequality*. New York: Norton, 1984.
Foucault, Michel. *Discipline and Punishment: The Birth of the Prison*. London: Allen Lane, Penguin, 1977.
Freire, Paulo. *Pedagogy of the Oppressed*. New York: Continuum, 1970.
Giroux, Henry A. *Theory and Resistance in Education*. S. Hadley, Mass.: Bergin & Garvey, 1983.
Goldthorpe, John H. *The Affluent Worker in the Class Structure*. London: Cambridge University Press, 1969.
Goodlad, John I. *A Place Called School*. New York: McGraw-Hill, 1984.
Gorz, Andre. *Socialism and Revolution*. Garden City, N.Y.: Anchor, 1973.
Green, Anthony, and Rachel Sharp. *Education and Social Control: A Study in Progressive Primary Education*. London: Routledge & Kegan Paul, 1979.
Habermas, Jürgen. *Legitimation Crisis*. Boston: Beacon, 1975.
Hall, Stuart, and M. Jacques. *The Politics of Thatcherism*. London: Lawrence & Wishart, 1983.
Hall, Stuart, and Tony Jefferson, eds. *Resistance Through Rituals*. London: Hutchinson, 1976.
Harrington, Michael. *Decade of Decision*. New York: Simon & Schuster, 1980.
Harrison, Beverly. *Making the Connections*. Boston: Beacon, 1985.
Hirsch, E.D., Jr. *Cultural Literacy*. Boston: Houghton Mifflin, 1987.
Jacoby, Russell. *The Last Intellectuals: American Culture in the Age of Academe*. New York: Rosie, 1987.

Jay, Martin. *The Dialectical Imagination*. London: Heinemann, 1974.
Jessup, Bob. "Capitalism and Democracy: The Best Possible Political Shell?" In *Power and the State*, edited by Gary Littlejohn, Barry Smart, John Wakeford, and Nira Yuval-Davis. New York: St. Martin's Press, 1978.
Jones, Ken. *Beyond Progressive Education*. London: MacMillan, 1983.
Karabel, Jerome, and A.H. Halsey, eds. *Power and Ideology in Education*. New York: Oxford University Press, 1977.
Katznelson, Ira, and Margaret Weir. *Schooling for All*. New York: Basic, 1985.
Kozol, Jonathan. *Illiterate America*. Garden City, N.Y.: Anchor Press/Doubleday, 1985.
Laclau, Ernesto, and Chantal Mouffe. *Hegemony and Socialist Strategy*. London: Verso, 1985.
Lasch, Christopher. *The Culture of Narcissism*. New York: Norton, 1978.
_____. *The Minimal Self*. New York: Norton, 1984.
McCarthy, Thomas. *The Critical Theory of Jürgen Habermas*. Cambridge, Mass.: MIT Press, 1978.
Marcuse, Herbert. *One Dimensional Man*. Boston: Beacon, 1964.
Mouffe, Chantal. *Gramsci and Marxist Theory*. Boston: Routledge & Kegan Paul, 1979.
O'Connor, James. *The Fiscal Crisis of the State*. New York: St. Martin's Press, 1973.
Ollman, Bertell. *Alienation: Marx's Conception of Man in Capitalist Society*. New York: Cambridge University Press, 1976.
Ollman, Bertell, and Howard Vernoff, eds. *The Left Academy*. New York: McGraw-Hill, 1982.
Omi, Michael, and Howard Winant. *Racial Formation in the United States*. New York: Routledge & Kegan Paul, 1986.
Phillips, Kevin. *Post-Conservative America*. New York: Vintage, 1983.
Piven, Frances Fox, and Richard A. Cloward. *The New Class War*. New York: Pantheon, 1982.
_____. *Regulating the Poor*. New York: Pantheon, 1971.
Poulantzas, Nicos. *Political Power and Social Classes*. London: Verso, 1978.
Purpel, David E. *The Moral and Spiritual Crisis in Education*. S. Hadley, Mass.: Bergin & Garvey, 1988.
Ravitch, Diane, and Chester E. Finn, Jr. *What Do Our 17-Year-Olds Know?* New York: Harper & Row, 1987.
Roszak, Theodore. *Person/Planet*. Garden City, N.Y.: Anchor Press/Doubleday, 1978.
Ryan, William. *Blaming the Victim*. New York: Vintage, 1976.
Shor, Ira. *Culture Wars*. Boston: Routledge & Kegan Paul, 1986.
Stockman, David. *The Triumph of Politics*. New York: Harper & Row, 1986.
Therborn, Goran. *What Does the Ruling Class Do When It Rules?*

London: New Left Books, 1978.
Welch, Sharon. *Communities of Resistance and Solidarity*. New York: Orbis, 1985.
West, Cornel. *Prophetic Deliverance: Towards a Revolutionary Afro-American Christianity*. Philadelphia: Westminster, 1982.
Whitty, Geoff. *Sociology and School Knowledge*. London: Methuen, 1985.
Williams, Raymond. *The Long Revolution*. England: Penguin Books, 1965.
_____. *Marxism and Literature*. Oxford: Oxford University Press, 1977.
Willis, Paul. *Learning to Labour: How Working Class Kids Get Working Class Jobs*. Farnborough, England: Saxon House, 1977.
Wolfe, Alan. *The Limits of Legitimacy*. New York: Free Press, 1977.
Wright, Erik Olin. *Class, Crisis, and the State*. London: New Left Books, 1978.
Yankelovitch, Daniel. *New Rules*. New York: Random House, 1981.
Young, Michael F.D., ed. *Knowledge and Control: New Directions for the Sociology of Education*. London: Collier-MacMillan, 1985.
Zaretsky, Eli. *Capitalism, the Family and Personal Life*. New York: Harper Colophon, 1976.

Index

Accumulation of capital, state responsibility for, 109–11
Achievement ideology: consumption and, 37–46; dissonance between realities of reward and failure and, 19; erosion of, 35, 108
Administrative crisis of state, 109–11, 116–17
Adolescence, 36–37
Advertising: appetite for consumption and, 42, 43; privatization sold by, 41
Affirmation, period of, 61–62
Alienation: from instruments of political democracy, 15; school, 16–17; of the young, 95
Alternative schools, 74, 88–89
American dream, education's link to, 147
Antistate sentiment, mobilization of, 128–29
Aristocratic influence, 60–64
Aronowitz, Stanley, 37–38, 51, 55–56
Authority, erosion of, 19
Avineri, Shlomo, 79

Babbitt, Bruce, 6
Basics movement, 50, 53, 77–78, 124; positivist emphasis on basic skills, 14
Beliefs. *See* Values
Bell, Daniel, 38–39, 43, 51, 71, 121, 151–52
Biden, Joseph, 6–7, 14
Big business: democratization of state and, 158; growth of state sector as basis for growth of, 132–33. *See also* Corporate business interests and needs
Big government, campaign against, 158–59. *See also* State
Birmingham, University of, Center for Contemporary Cultural Studies at, 21
Birnbaum, Norman, 64
Black view of public education, 15–16. *See also* Jackson, Jesse
Blaming the victim, 89
Block grants, reduction of federal, 155
Bourdieu, Pierre, 22
Bourgeois culture and ideology, 33; bifurcation of, 65, 66; complex duality of, 145; consumption and erosion of achievement ideology in, 37–46; delayed gratification and, 48; education as embodiment of, 48–

49; education for life and culture as compromise of, 64–68; hegemonic structure of, 75–77; motivation crisis and, 34–37; replacement of production values by consumption-oriented values, 46–47; segregation in values of, 55–56
Bourgeois "economic man," decline of, 44
Bourgeois role of individual, 79–80, 145–46
Bowles, Samuel, 22, 138
British Labour Party, 70
British youth, subcultures of resistance found among, 21
Brittan, Arthur, 41
Brown v. Board of Education, 82
Bureaucracy: bureaucratic nature of schooling, 52; control systems in, struggle against, 26; problems of, 109–11; success in, individualism expressed through, 65

Calculative–instrumentalist rationality, 65
California State Department of Education, 82
Capital: accumulation of, state responsibility for, 109–11; cultural, 98, 124; formation, conservative educational policy and promotion of, 120–21; reallocation of wealth to, 119–21, 154–56
Capitalism: functions of family and historical development of, 39–41; need to reconcile demand for accumulation and for legitimacy, 109–11; state-directed, need for, 129–35
Capitalism, cultural contradictions of, 29–56, 151–52; consumption and decline of achievement ideology, 37–46; cultural crisis and the schools, 51–54; education and culture of narcissism, 42, 46–51; motivation crisis, origins of, 34–37; toward a radical negativity, 54–56
Career education movement, 65
Carnegie Report, 126
Carnoy, Martin, 138
Carter campaign, antistate sentiment of, 129
Castells, Manuel, 132, 133–34, 138
Catholic schools' "Infusion" project, 26
Center for Contemporary Cultural Studies at University of Birmingham, England, 21
Citizen role of individual, 79–80, 145–46
Citizenship preparation, reinvigoration of notion of, 25
Civilization and culture, separation between, 67, 68; aristocratic influence and, 60–64; movement to eliminate, 71, 72; radical negativity and, 54–56
Civil privatism, 150
Class, social. *See* Middle class; Social class; Working class
Class conflicts, 21; state in capitalist society as site of, 141–42, 143
Class reductionist theories of ideology, 31, 32
Cloward, Richard, 140, 156–59, 166
Cobb, Jonathan, 147
Cohen, David V., 86
Coleman, James, 114
Communicative ethics, 36–37
Community power, 16
Community responsibility, education as, 11–13
Comprehensive high school, 80–81, 85–89; in England, 70, 85
Congress, 97th, failure of New

Right educational policy in, 159, 160
Congressional Budget Office, 155
Congressional Research Service, 160
Consciousness and conscience, synthesis of, 27
Conservative educational policy, making of, 119–38; educational change and demise of middle-class expectations, 121–27; educational reform and need for state-directed capitalism, 129–35; educational reports of 1983, 127–29, 134; harnessing concerns of middle class, 119–20, 165–66; intensification of social conflict and effort to preserve hegemony, 135–38; limits to implementation after, 159–64; mobilization of antistate sentiment, 128–29; political divergences in ruling class, 127–29; reallocation of wealth and, 119–21
Conservative movement in education, 53
Conservative politics: alliance of corporate and middle class interest in, 154–56; assault on welfare state, 165–67; crises of state and, 114–18; results of, 162
Consumption and consumption-oriented culture: contradictions between production culture and, 39–41; crisis of values and meanings due to, 24–25, 38; emergence of, 151–52; erosion of achievement ideology and, 37–46; erosion of authority and, 19; Lasch on, 46–47; liberating or humanizing effects of, 43–46; social inventions facilitating, 38–39; trivialization of work and self-

realization through, 55–56; values, 46–47
Corporate business interests and needs: conservative politics of 1980s and, 154–56; individualization in education defined for, 95–96; National Commission on Excellence in Education's report on need to harmonize education with, 131
Corporate-integrative educational activities, 65, 66–67
Corporate taxes as percentage of total taxes levied, 155
Correspondence theory, 95
Counterculture, 36, 44–45, 99
Counter school culture, 30
Cox, Harvey, 24
Crisis of effort in schools, Jackson on, 16–17
Crisis of state: administrative, 109–11, 116–17; conservative politics and resolution of, 114–18; educational policy in 1980s and, 103–18; fiscal, 20, 111–16; legitimation, 107–8, 117–18; origins of politics of retrenchment, 106–9; rationality, 107
Croly, Herbert, 65
Cultural capital, 98, 124
Cultural contradictions of capitalism. *See* Capitalism, cultural contradictions of
"Cultural Contradictions of Capitalism" (Bell), 121
Cultural crisis, schools and, 51–54
Cultural power, socialization and emerging struggle for, 151–53
Cultural reinvigoration, concerns about, 24
Cultural-reproductive theories of schooling, 22–23
Culture: counter school, 30; democratization of, 71; emergent, 59, 60, 94, 95; politicization of cultural traditions, 149–50; re-

sidual, 59, 60; youth, 19, 44–45, 94–95. See also Bourgeois culture and ideology; Consumption and consumption-oriented culture; Hegemonic culture; Production culture
Culture and civilization, separation between, 67, 68; aristocratic influence and, 60–64; movement to eliminate, 71, 72; radical negativity and, 54–56
Culture of narcissism, education and, 42, 46–51
Culture of Narcissism, The (Lasch), 34, 42
Cuomo, Mario, 9
Curriculum: changes reflecting issues of personal and social relevance, 73–74; discourse on, 14; hidden, 66, 80, 84, 95, 164; language of positivism and, 14

Dahrendorf, Ralf, 42
Davis, Mike, 5–6
Decentralization, proposals for, 111
Deficiency, psychologizing of educational, 97–99
Delayed gratification, education as embodiment of, 48–49
Demands, politicization of social, 139–43
Democracy: absence of economic, 15; alienation from instruments of political, 15; Jackson's campaign and issue of, 14, 15–17; relationship between schooling and values of, 14–15. See also Liberal democracy
Democratic National Convention (1984), 4
Democratic Party: educational agenda in 1980s, 3–8; Jackson's 1983–1984 primary campaign, 9–13; middle class and working class perceptions of, 161; 1984 and 1988 primary campaigns for presidential nomination, 3–8
Democratic pluralism, myth of, 88–89
Democratization: of culture, 71; of state, 158
"De-schooled" notions of educational experience, 77
Dewey, John, 66, 86–87
Differentiation of education experiences, mainstreaming and, 83–85
Discontinuity of experience in school, 61
Disempowerment, sense of, 25–26
Division of labor: ideological struggle between social classes centered around, 67–68, 78, 122–23, 146–48; mental–manual, 67–68, 122–23, 146–48; middle-class perceptions of, 122–23; schooling and, 67–68
Domhoff, William, 133
Dreitzel, Hans, 44–45
Dresch, Steven, 125
Drug Abuse Act of 1970, 144
Dukakis, Michael, 6
Durkheim, Emile, 84

Economic aspirations, expansion of, 148–51
Economic crisis, state absorption of, 148–49, 156–59
Economic-reproduction theories of schooling, 22
Economics, perceptions of relationship between politics and, 156–61
Edsall, Thomas, 161
Education: black view of public,

15–16; as "complex unity," 57–58; declining value as investment, 51–52, 117–18, 125; Democratic Party agenda in 1980s for, 3–8; human capital view of, 3–5, 164; social purpose to, 16
Education, Department of, 128
Educational justice, 37
Educational policy: conservative, making of, 119–38; from melding of diverse class imperatives and viewpoints, 104–5; in 1980s, crisis of state and, 103–18
Educational reform. See Reforms, educational
Educational reports of 1983, 127–29, 134
Education for All Handicapped Children Act (Public Law 94–142), 68–71, 81–83, 101, 102, 144. See also Special education
Emergent culture, 59, 60, 94, 95
England, comprehensivisation in, 70, 85
Entitlements, 140, 141; reallocation of wealth and revocation of, 155–56. See also Rights
Ethic(s): communicative, 36–37; formalistic, 36; Protestant, 38–39, 121, 136, 151, 152; of rationalizations, 35
Ethnic concerns, relating educational purposes to, 9–10
European education, specialization found in, 64
Expectations: associated with lengthy schooling, contradictions in, 66; for job opportunities, 146–48; middle class, educational change and demise of, 121–27; reallocation of wealth and revocation of, 155–56

Family: assistance, 145; development of capitalism and functions in personal life of, 39–41; as focus of mass consumption market, 40
Feminist studies of socialization, 33
Fiscal crisis of state, 20, 111–16
Formalistic ethics, 36
France, student-led uprising in (1968), 51
Frankfurt Institute of Social Research, 50, 54, 55
Freire, Paulo, 26, 27

Galbraith, Kenneth, 42
Gary School Plan, 72
Gattegno, Caleb, 61
Gender socialization, 33
Gender struggle, 22
Gephardt, Richard, 5–6
Gifted and talented students, individualized instruction for, 93, 94–96
Gintis, Herbert, 22
Giroux, Henry, 22
Glenn, John, 4
Gramsci, Antonio, 23, 27, 57–58, 104, 105, 127, 161
Grassroots influences, 160. See also Populist influences
"Great School Legend, The," 125
Greene, T. H., 65
Greer, Colin, 125
Guthries, James W., 116

Habermas, Jürgen, 19, 34–38, 106–9, 117, 141, 148–50
Handicapped, the: labeling of, reduction of, 68–69, 83, 89; mainstreaming, 68–71. See also Special education
Harrington, Michael, 37, 120
Hart, Gary, 3–4, 6, 14

Harvard Educational Review, 114
Head Start Program, 144–45
Health and Human Services, Department of, 144
Hegemonic culture, 75–77; educational legitimacy and, 57–60; Gramsci's notion of hegemonic domination, 104–5; hegemony in politics of educational discourse, 8–13; incorporation of individualized instruction in, 93–100; intensification of social conflict and effort to preserve, 135–38
Hidden curriculum, 66, 80, 84, 95, 164
High technology, focus on, 6
Horkheimer, Max, 54–55
Human capital view of education, 3–5, 163

Ideology: assumption of uniformity of dominant, 31, 32–34; class reductionist theories of, 31, 32; as correlate of human practices and social relationships, 31–32; incorporational process in schools and transmission of, 91–94; liberal, in 1980s, 3–8; New Right, 34; socialization and, 30–31. *See also* Achievement ideology, erosion of; Bourgeois culture and ideology
Income-maintenance programs, 140
Incorporational process, 91–94, 100
Individual, bourgeois vs. citizen role of, 79–80, 145–46
Individual-development educational activities, 65, 66–67
Individualism: expressed through success in climbing bureaucratic occupational ladder, 65; of new vs. old petit-bourgeoisie, 99; possessive, 35, 108–9
Individualized Education Plan (IEP), 52, 54, 83, 84, 96–97, 144
Individualizing instruction, 91–101; differentiation of meaning of, 94–97; for gifted and talented students, 93, 94–96; incorporational process, 91–94, 100; psychologizing of educational deficiency, 97–99
Industrial education, 72–74
Industrial-planning policy, 163–64
Industrial strategy, educational policy as part of, 3–4
"Infusion" project of Catholic schools, 26
Installment buying, spread of, 38, 39
"Instrumental rationality," crisis of, 44–45
Investment, declining value of education as, 51–52, 117–18, 125

Jackson, Jesse, 9–17, 163
Jay, Martin, 55
Jessup, Bob, 132
Justice: educational, 37; social, 26
Juvenile Justice and Delinquency Prevention Act (P.L. 93–145), 144

Keynes, John Maynard, 1

Labeling of the handicapped, reduction of, 68–69, 83, 89
Labor. *See* Work
Laclau, Ernesto, 32–33
Laissez-faire, erosion of doctrine of, 156–59
Lamm, Zvi, 92
Lasch, Christopher, 1, 34, 42–43, 46–51
Lazerson, Marvin, 86

Least restrictive setting, 69, 83
Left, the: agony of educational, in 1980s, 1–3; toward educational agenda of political, 23–28; failure to reorient education debate or politics of educational agenda, 3–8; socialist movement, 1–2, 72–73; social upsurge of 1960s, 2; in U.S., history of, 1–2
Left academy, 17–18
Legitimation: educational, occurring through hegemony, 57–60; of social order, state responsibility for, 109–11
Legitimation crisis: of schooling, 77, 149–50; of state, 107–8, 117–18
Legitimation Crisis (Habermas), 34
Leisure, trivialization of work and self-realization through, 55–56. *See also* Consumption and consumption-oriented culture
Liberal democracy: educational reform and, 79–102; Jackson's departure from mainstream of discourse of, 16–17
Liberal ideology in 1980s, 3–8
Liberation, pedagogy of, 17
Loans, student, 160–61, 165

McCarthy, Thomas, 34, 109
MacIntyre, Alasdair, 141
Mainstreaming, 68–71; contradictions of schooling demonstrated in, 83–85
Manual-mental division of labor, 67–68, 122–23, 146–48
Marcuse, Herbert, 42, 55, 56, 61–62
Marketing, facilitation of consumption-oriented culture and, 38–39
Marx, Karl, 24, 27, 79, 80, 106, 140

Massachusetts, special education programming in, 90–91
Mass media: consumption-oriented values disseminated by, 53; effect of, 11, 15
Mathematics, focus on, 6
Mental-manual division of labor, 67–68, 122–23, 147–48
Middle class: conservative educational policy harnessing concerns of, 119–20, 165–66; conservative politics of 1980s and, 154–56; expectations, educational change and demise of, 121–27; influence of, 160; perceived distinctions emanating from division of labor, 122–23; perception of Democratic Party, 161
Mills, C. Wright, 114
Minorities, special education and segregation of, 82, 90–91
Mondale, Walter, 4–5
Moral-majoritarians, 152
Moral renewal, concerns about, 24
"Motivation crisis," origins of, 34–37. *See also* Achievement ideology, erosion of
Mouffe, Chantal, 32, 105

Narcissism, education and culture of, 42, 46–51
National Commission on Excellence in Education (NCEE) report, 7, 130, 131, 136–37
National Task Force on Education for Economics Growth (NTFEEG), 131, 134
Negativity, radical, 54–56
Neoliberals, 5–6, 7
New Class War, The (Cloward and Piven), 140
New petit-bourgeoisie, ideology of, 99–100
New Right, 50; ideology, 34; lim-

its on conservative educational policies of, 159–60
"New working class" thesis in western society, 42
Nixon, Richard, 111
North Carolina, impact of reallocation of wealth in, 155
Nuclear arsenal, reaction to transfer of wealth into, 163

Occupational success, formal schooling and, 37. See also Work
O'Connor, James, 105, 106, 111–14, 116, 132
Offe, Claus, 110
Ollman, Bertel, 17, 80, 142
One Dimensional Man (Marcuse), 55

Parent involvement, 12
Pedagogy of liberation, 17
Personalist sensibility, 44, 53
Personal life, development of capitalism and creation of sphere of, 39–41
Petit-bourgeoisie: ideology, selective incorporation into conservative educational policy, 119, 121; new vs. old, 99–100
Phillips Curve, 140
Piven, Frances Fox, 140, 156–59, 166
Play and work, socialization and distinction between, 48
Pluralism, democratic, myth of, 88–89
"Political Meaning of Culture" (Dreitzel), 44
Politicization of cultural traditions, 149–50
Politicization of social demands, 139–43
Politics: economics and, perceptions of relationship between, 156–61; of educational discourse, opposition and hegemony in, 8–13; Jackson's 1983–1984 primary campaign, 9–13; 1984 and 1988 Democratic party primary campaigns for presidential nomination, 3–13; of resistance in 1980s, 159–64; of retrenchment, 106–9, 128; of schooling, educational agenda of the political Left, 23–28; themes of the Right in, 24. See also Conservative politics
Populist influences, 71–74, 77–78, 147
Positivism, educational reform and language of, 13–17
Possessive individualism, 35, 108–9
Post-auratic art, incompatibility with traditional beliefs or values, 36
Poulantzas, Nicos, 20, 57, 58, 67, 99, 103, 105, 122, 142
Power, struggle for: cultural power, socialization and emerging, 151–53; education and, 15–16; sense of disempowerment and, 25–26
Power bloc, Gramsci's notion of, 127
President's Commission on Technology, Automation and Economic Progress, 125
Privatism, civil, 150
Privatistic syndrome, 108–9
Privatization, 41–42
Production: as purely instrumental activity, 56; separation of family from, 39–41
Production culture: contradictions between consumption-oriented culture and, 39–41; school characteristics connected with, 51–54; values, replacement by consumption-oriented values, 46–47
Productivity increases: agenda

for, 138; with support of state intervention, 133–35
Profitability of U.S. business, decline of, 154–55; reallocation of wealth to stop, 154–56
Proletarianization of white-collar labor, 37–38, 123
Protestant ethic, 38–39, 121, 136, 151, 152
Psychologizing of educational deficiency, 97–99
Public education, duality in ideological meaning of, 146
Public Law 93–145, 144
Public Law 94–142, 68–71, 81–83, 101, 102, 144
Puritan temper, 38–39, 121, 136, 151

Quantity of education, 7

Race struggle, 22
Radical educational mode, 71–73
Radical educational theory, sociology of, 17–23
Radical negativity, 54–56
Rainbow Coalition, 163
Rationality: calculative-instrumentalist, 65; crisis of instrumental, 44–45
Rationality crisis of state, 107
Rationalizations, ethic of, 35
Reagan, Ronald, 137, 159, 162, 164
Reagan administration policies, 1, 7–8, 117, 127, 128, 129–30, 139, 156, 158, 159
Reaganomics, 142, 148, 165
Reagan tax plans, 155
Reallocation of wealth, 139–40; to capital, 119–21, 154–56; conservative educational policies and, 119–21; revocation of rights, expectations and entitlements and, 155–56
Reforms, educational: comprehensive high school, vocationalism, and myth of democratic pluralism, 85–89; expansion of economic aspirations and, 148–51; individualized instruction, 91–101; language of positivism and, 13–17; Lasch on, 47–51; liberal democracy and, 79–102; need for state-directed capitalism and, 129–35; social democratic, working-class and populist influences, 68–74, 77–78, 147; special education, 68–71, 81–83, 91–101
Reich, Robert, 131
Relative autonomy of state, 20
Relevance, notion of, 73–74
Religion in Secular City (Cox), 24
Report of the Task Force on Federal Elementary and Secondary Education Policy, 130, 134, 136
Reproduction, theories of, 21–23
Republican Party, 8, 161. *See also* Reagan administration policies; Right, the
Residual culture, influence on education of, 59, 60
Resistance: politics of, in 1980s, 159–64; theories of, 21
Resource room, 84, 89–90
Responsibility: community, education as, 11–13; social, education to generate, 10–11
Retrenchment, politics of, 106–9, 128
Revisionist educational historians, 19, 64–65, 137
Right, the: concerns of, 54; mobilization of antistate sentiment, 128–29; New Right, 34, 50, 159–60; themes of politics, 24
Rights: educational, emergence of welfare-educational state and, 143–48; educational policy to reduce, 165; political and

economic, weakening of separation of, 156–61; reallocation of wealth and revocation of, 155–56
Rohatyn, Felix, 130–31
Romantic critics of schooling, 18–19
Roszak, Theodore, 43–44
Ruling class, political divergences of, 127–29
Ryan, William, 89

School: alternative, 74, 88–89; characteristics connected with production culture, 51–54; comprehensive high schools, 70, 80–81, 85–89
School alienation, 16–17
"School without walls," 74
Science, focus on, 6, 134
Scientism, incompatibility with traditional beliefs or values, 35–36
Segregation of minorities, special education and, 82, 90–91
Self-fulfillment, search for, 46
Sennett, Richard, 42, 147
Separation of polity and economy, weakening of doctrine of, 156–59
Social class: heightening of awareness of, 163; ideological struggle centered around social division of labor between, 67–68, 78, 122–23, 146–48; voter turnout in 1980s and, 161. *See also* Middle class; Working class
Social conflict, intensification of, 135–38
Social demands, politicization of, 139–43
Social democratic movement: influence of ideology, 68–71; Rainbow Coalition, 163
Socialist movement, 1–2, 72–73
Socialist Party, 2

Socialization: communicative ethics and countercultures determining, 36–37; contradictions in process of, 80; cultural crisis and the schools, 51–54; distinction between play and work and, 48; education as agent of moral, 69, 84; emerging struggle for cultural power and, 151–53; feminist studies of gender, 33; ideology and, 30–31; revision of theory of, 20–21; schooling as part of contradictory process of, 34
Social justice, issue of, 26
Social responsibility and social concern, education to generate, 10–11
Sociology of radical educational theory, 17–23
Special education: use of alternative schools in context of, 88–89; assessment of students for, 90–91; Individualized Education Plan, 52, 54, 83, 84, 96–97, 144; individualizing instruction, 91–101; mainstreaming, 68–71, 83–85; 1978 reform (P.L. 94–142) of, 68–71, 81–83, 101, 102, 144; resource room, 84, 89–90; segregation of minorities and, 82, 90–91; vocational training, 86–89
Spring, Joel, 65
Stagflation, 155
"Star Schools," 7
State: absorption of economic crisis, 148–49, 156–59; antistate sentiment, mobilization of, 128–29; bifurcated role of, 20, 132; campaign against big government, 158–59; democratization of, 158; in hegemonic culture, 58; in liberal–capitalist society, nature of, 105–6; productivity increases with support of, 133–35; relative auton-

omy of, 20; sector growth as basis for growth of big business, 132–33; as site of class conflict and domain of conflicting social demands, 141–42, 143. *See also* Crisis of state; Welfare-educational state, dialectic of

State-directed capitalism, 129–35

Stockman, David, 117

Stratification of educational programs, mainstreaming and, 83–85

Student loans, cuts in, 160–61, 165

Superstructure as reflection of economic base, 57

Supreme Court, 82, 144

Tax plans, Reagan, 155

Technical training, focus on, 134

Television, influence of, 15

Therborn, Goran, 68, 105–6

Thurow, Lester, 125, 131, 163

Touraine, Alain, 42

Tracking of students, 67, 83, 84. *See also* Division of labor

Twentieth Century Fund report, 134, 136–37

Universalistic value system, 36–37

Values: complex dialectic contained within contemporary culture, 55–56; consumption-oriented society and crisis of, 24–25, 38; incompatibility of scientism and post-auratic art with traditional, 35–36; mainstreaming to facilitate shared, 70; production culture, replacement by consumption-oriented values, 46–47; universalistic, 36–37

Victim, blaming the, 89

Vocationalism, 67, 86–89

Wealth, reallocation of, 139–40; to capital, 119–21, 154–56; conservative educational policies and, 119–21; revocation of rights, expectations and entitlements and, 155–56

Weinstein, James, 1

Welfare-educational state, dialectic of, 139–53; crisis and hope, 154–67; educational reforms and expansion of economic aspirations, 148–51; educational rights and, 143–48; politics of resistance in 1980s, 159–64; socialization and emerging struggle for cultural power, 151–53

Welfare state: assault of conservative policies on, 165–67; campaign against big government as concern about expanding, 158–59; politicization of social demands and, 139–43

White-collar labor, proletarianization of, 37–38, 123

Williams, Raymond, 57–59, 62, 91

Willis, Paul, 30

Withdrawal and protest, syndrome of, 36

Wolfe, Alan, 106, 109–12, 116, 162–63

Women, privatization and isolation of, 41–42

Work: distinction between play and socialization and, 48; expectations for job opportunities, 146–48; proletarianization of white-collar labor, 37–38, 123; relationship between schooling and, 22, 37; trivialization of, in conditions of modern capitalism, 55–56

Working class: influence of, 70;

new, 42; perception of Democratic Party, 161
Work schools in Soviet Republic, 72
Wright, Erik Olin, 99, 131

Yankelovitch, Daniel, 45–46
Young, Michael, 62–63
Youth culture, 19, 44–45, 94–95

Zaretsky, Eli, 39–41
Zusman, Ami, 116

ABOUT THE AUTHOR

SVI SHAPIRO teaches the social foundations of education at the University of North Carolina at Greensboro. He has published widely on questions of education, ideology, and the state in capitalist society. With David Purpel he edited *Schools and Meaning: Essays on the Moral Nature of Schooling* (1985).

www.ingramcontent.com/pod-product-compliance
Lightning Source LLC
Chambersburg PA
CBHW070322230426
43663CB00011B/2194